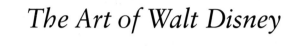

The Art of Walt Disney

from Mickey Mouse to the Magic Kingdoms

The Art of Disney

Christopher Finch

Harry N. Abrams, Inc., Publishers

For my daughter Chloe

Editor: Eric Himmel
Designer: Judith Hudson

Library of Congress Cataloging-in-Publication Data

Finch, Christopher.
The art of Walt Disney : from Mickey Mouse to the Magic Kingdoms /
Christopher Finch. — Newly rev. and updated ed.
p. cm.
ISBN 0–8109–1962–1
1. Disney, Walt, 1901–1966. 2. Walt Disney Productions.
1. Title.
NC1766.U52D533 1995
741.5'8'0979493—dc20 95–1746

Published in 1995 by Harry N. Abrams, Incorporated, New York
A Times Mirror Company

Printed and bound in Japan

Contents

Introduction

The Walt Disney Company occupies a unique place in the history of American popular culture. Among all major entertainment corporations, none is so marked by the imagination and persona of its founder.

More than seventy years ago, Walt Disney came to Los Angeles and with his brother launched a tiny animation studio. Assisted by a sympathetic mouse, a dyspeptic duck, and many talented artists, he built that studio into a production center that made his name world famous. He single-handedly developed the animated feature film – creating classics of the genre – then branched out into live-action films, television, and other fields of entertainment. He rethought the amusement park – inventing the theme park – and dreamed of building a prototype city of the future.

Walt Disney achieved all this while, for much of his career, fending off financial disaster that was just a flop away. For all the precariousness of his position, Disney never wavered in his vision, and time and again he was vindicated by the success of enterprises that observers – including some of his closest advisers – had seen as follies.

So attuned was this vision to public taste that, almost thirty years after his death, Walt Disney is still a powerful presence in the world of popular culture.

In the meantime, the entertainment empire he built has expanded and become more diversified. In the past dozen years in particular, since Michael Eisner and the late Frank Wells took charge of the corporation (with the crucial support of Walt's nephew Roy E. Disney), The Walt Disney Company has enjoyed glittering successes, becoming one of Hollywood's most prosperous organizations. The revamped company is now a major player in every aspect of entertainment, from the Broadway stage to cable television, but, significantly, much of its strength still derives from the areas with which Walt Disney's name is most keenly associated: animated films and theme parks.

The story of Walt Disney's rise to fame and of the recent renaissance of the company he created are the twin subjects of this fully revised and updated version of *The Art of Walt Disney*.

When I completed the first version of *The Art of Walt Disney*, toward the end of 1972, I believed that the Disney Studio would continue to thrive in one form or another, and I had no doubt that the theme parks had a healthy future. The *raison d'être* for the book, however, was Disney's achievement in the field of animation. Everything else – no matter how remarkable in and of itself – grew out of that achievement, and it seemed, in the early seventies, that the Studio's great string of animated features was playing itself out.

The fate of Disney animation seemed to lie in the hands of a few veteran character animators and story artists who had been with Disney since the thirties and were, in the seventies, on the verge of retirement. True, there were gifted younger artists in the animation department, and the veterans had helped implement an ambitious training program (which has paid off handsomely), but it was hard to imagine then that the future held a full-fledged resurgence of Disney feature animation.

Yet that is exactly what we have seen during the past decade. Since the mid-eighties, Disney's feature animation department has produced several movies that deserve to be counted among the finest animated films ever made.

This is an extraordinary achievement, and much of the credit for it must go to the management team that has been in place since Michael Eisner became chairman, in 1984, of what was later renamed The Walt Disney Company. The Eisner team made sweeping changes where they were necessary, so that the Studio could become fully competitive with industry giants like Warner Brothers and Paramount. The feature animation department, however, was a special case, left largely to its own devices and to the care of Roy Disney, the one man in the management team who fully understood animation.

Feature animation, therefore, was given an opportunity to make a place for itself in the new Disney firmament. Guided by department head Peter Schneider, a brilliant team of young veterans began to produce films that Walt Disney would have been proud of. They received solid support from Eisner, from Roy Disney, and from Studio chief Jeffrey Katzenberg, who, prior to his departure from the company in 1994, came to play an important role in shaping the future of Disney animation, involving himself in the creative process and encouraging the artists to set their sights high.

Unlike feature animation, the Disney theme parks were thriving when the new management team took over. EPCOT® Center in particular was a success that should be credited to the interim management team, led by Card Walker, which guided the company for more than a decade after the deaths of first Walt Disney and then his brother Roy.

Michael Eisner and Frank Wells brought fresh energy to this already flourishing situation. Making use of the established corps of "imagineers," many of whom had worked with Walt Disney, they set out to revivify the existing parks while at the same time developing new theme parks in Florida, Europe, and Japan (where Tokyo Disneyland had already opened in 1983).

Like the recent animated feature films, the Disney theme parks have been modernized in response to the taste of a new generation brought up in a world that has changed greatly since Disneyland® Park opened its gates in 1955. The remarkable thing is that this has been achieved without in any way diluting the special character that has been drawing visitors to the theme parks for more than four decades.

Which brings me full circle to the assertion that today's Walt Disney Company is still powerfully stamped by its founder's vision and persona.

Who was the man behind the persona and what was he like?

Walt Disney was a celebrity before he was out of his twenties, and he stayed in the public eye for the remainder of his life, notably as the on-camera host of his own television show. Yet he remains an enigma. Even with his closest associates, he always held some aspects of his personality just out of reach.

Certain things are indisputable. He was a man who believed absolutely in his own instincts and abilities, an artist who would go to any lengths to ensure that a project was carried out exactly as he had conceived it. He surrounded himself with many talented men and women but always remained completely in control. Consider Walt Disney at any point in his career and it is difficult to avoid the feeling that a master plan was unfolding. That plan existed only in his head and remained unknowable until, piece by piece, it was given concrete form and grafted onto the mythology of our century.

Some reviewers of the first edition of this book objected to the assertion that Walt Disney was a great artist. A great entrepreneur, perhaps, they conceded, but how could he be considered an artist when he was dependent on the very evident talents of such immensely gifted animators as Ub Iwerks, Fred Moore, Art Babbitt, Bill Tytla, and the legendary nine old men?

Iwerks, Moore, Babbitt, Tytla, and the rest deserve enormous credit for their brilliant contributions to the Disney oeuvre, but ultimately Walt Disney himself was the architect of all that was achieved in his name from 1923 until his death in 1966. He was not an outstanding draftsman and had given up animating by the time Mickey Mouse was created. (It was relevant to the expression of his genius, however, that he could turn his hand to every aspect of the making of an animated film, from drawing to operating a camera.) But he was the ultimate *auteur*. He had an astonishing command of the language of filmmaking, and beyond that he had an uncanny sense of how to shape a movie, and of how to squeeze the maximum emotional impact from a story.

Walt Disney's grasp of cinema was both intuitive and learned. He would have made an outstanding live-action director, but since he worked in the field of animation – where anything is possible, at least in theory – he developed an even broader vision than might otherwise have been the case. At the same time, his early experience as a producer of eight-minute cartoon comedies refined his sense of dramatic economy. In a Mickey Mouse cartoon or a Silly Symphony, not a single frame could be wasted. When he graduated to producing feature-length films, Disney remained as parsimonious as ever in terms of story-telling technique. In films like *Snow White and the Seven Dwarfs* and *Pinocchio,* nothing that was not essential to advancing the story or the delineation of character was allowed to slow the screen narrative.

Beyond that, Disney dared to do things that no one else had done. He was a visionary – but a visionary who had the common touch that enabled him to take the mass audience along with him into uncharted territory.

At the outset of his career, Walt Disney was often underestimated by his rivals and by unscrupulous impresarios. They recognized the caliber of the talents he surrounded himself with and assumed that if these talents could be lured away, the Disney Studio would collapse. In reality, the one man who made Walt Disney Productions so successful was Walt Disney himself.

Later, Disney was underestimated for other reasons. Since the values expressed in his movies and other enterprises are the deceptively simple values of the cartoon and the fairy tale, some observers have been fooled into presenting simplistic pictures of Walt Disney the man, and of what he stood for. Some have portrayed him as a naive genius – a natural rather than a cultivated talent – a notion that might help explain his popular appeal but that totally overlooks the subtlety, complexity, and refinement of vision in his best work.

Other commentators have ignored Walt Disney's gifts altogether and have presented him as an exploiter of talent with political views that verged on the despotic. It should be acknowledged that his record in the area of labor relations was far from unblemished, but it has never been convincingly demonstrated that he was an advocate of political authoritarianism, as has been suggested. (In one recent book that espoused this point of view, I counted more than thirty factual errors in a single chapter, which did little to encourage my trust in the author's more outrageous assertions.) It can accurately be said, I believe, that Walt Disney was sometimes guilty of high-handed paternalism toward his employees. Some artists thrived in this paternalistic atmosphere. Others – among them a handful of major talents – eventually became disenchanted and left the Studio.

So far as Disney's personal politics are concerned, they remain as mysterious as the man himself and would probably make a worthwhile – and possibly frustrating – subject of study for someone who was prepared to do some painstaking research. Doubtless Disney was subject to some of the misconceptions and prejudices that were common to most Americans of his generation. Having the common touch – the intuitive understanding of what the masses want – inevitably involves the popular artist with some of the questionable dogmas espoused by those same masses.

In any case, it must be emphasized again that Walt Disney was a complex man, not easily pinned down. To attempt to define him in terms of political cliché does a disservice to the intelligence of the reader. This is especially the case since Disney's sphere of influence was not the Republic that is governed from Washington; it was the Magic Kingdom that he ruled from Burbank.

There, Walt Disney's imagination was sovereign.

The sequence of recent animated films that began with *The Little Mermaid*, along with parallel developments in the Disney theme parks, is proof of the fact that the creative achievements of one man of genius can be sustained and built upon by a team of gifted individuals who have thoroughly immersed themselves in the master's imagination without surrendering their own sense of adventure and enterprise.

The word "team" is important here, because films like *Beauty and the Beast* and *Pocahontas* are brought into being by groups of artists who have learned how to interact creatively with their peers without sacrificing their own individuality. In certain respects, the way a Disney animated feature is created today is the *opposite* of the way *Snow White* was created. Although character suggestions were solicited from the outset, and concept art helped determine the look of the film, to all intents and purposes, *Snow White* took shape in one man's brain. It was then carried out by virtuoso artists, the way a well-rehearsed orchestra performs a composer's score. *Beauty and the Beast,* though it evolved with considerable guidance from Jeffrey Katzenberg, Roy Disney, Howard Ashman, Don Hahn, Kirk Wise, and Gary Trousdale – a leadership team within the greater creative team – was rooted in the contributions of scores of artists who helped shape the film at every stage. The musical analogy evoked is that of a very large jazz band with many soloists and group improvisers responding to the challenge presented by a handful of skilled arrangers and by a great precursor – Walt Disney.

The system evolves and responds to changed times. New technology comes into play. But still the end product remains consistent with Disney's original vision. The sense of continuity is apparent in the films and in the theme parks.

I hope it is equally evident in this book, which attempts to remain faithful to the spirit of the original edition while bringing the story up to date. So far as the text is concerned, chapters 1 to 7 – dealing with Disney animation up to *Dumbo* – have been subjected to minor revisions and updating but appear largely as they did in 1973. Chapter 8 uses material from the old edition but has been substantially revised. Chapter 9 borrows a few paragraphs from the old edition but is mostly new. Chapters 10, 11, and 12 are entirely new. Chapter 13 draws upon the old edition but has been completely rewritten. Chapter 14 is new. Chapter 15 is adapted from the old edition but has been considerably revised. Chapters 16, 17, and 18 are new.

Approximately half of the text, then, is completely new to this edition, which also includes more than 200 new illustrations, many of them never published before.

I A New Art Form

1 Early Enterprises

Walter Elias Disney was born into a modest Chicago household on December 5, 1901. His birthplace, 1249 Tripp Avenue, was a small wood-frame structure of the type that can be found in the inner suburbs of any Midwestern city. His father, Elias Disney, was Canadian born and of Anglo-Irish descent. At this time Elias was a building contractor, and we may judge the success of that operation by the fact that Walt later described how his mother sometimes went out to the building site with the men, sawing and hammering planks. Mrs. Disney was the former Flora Call, an Ohio girl whose family had moved to Kansas in 1879. There the Call and Disney families became friends. When the Calls moved to Florida in 1884, Elias followed and bought a citrus plantation. Four years later he married Flora, who was by then teaching school. At the time of Walt's birth, there were already three children in the family – Herbert, Raymond, and Roy. Walt was to develop an especially close relationship with Roy, who was nearest to him in age, a relationship that was to be of great importance to both of them. Later a daughter – Ruth – was added to the family.

In 1906, Elias Disney decided to pull up his roots once again and moved his family to a forty-eight-acre farm outside Marceline, Missouri. Then as now, small farms did not offer an easy route to prosperity. Herbert and Raymond, both in their teens, had developed a taste for city life and soon returned to Chicago. Walt and Roy were, of course, expect-

Walt Disney's birthplace at 1249 Tripp Avenue, Chicago, built by his father, Elias Disney.

Below, from left: Walt Disney at the age of nine months; Roy Disney in 1913; Elias and Flora Disney in 1913; Walt Disney at the age of twelve

ed to help their parents with the farm chores. It was an extremely hard life, but one which Walt later remembered with considerable affection.

It was on the farm that he began to draw. We may be sure that this was not encouraged by his parents, but he did make the first tentative steps toward his eventual career. Meanwhile, the farm operation was in trouble. In 1910, Elias sold the property with all its livestock and moved the family once again – this time to Kansas City, ninety-five miles southwest. There Elias bought a newspaper delivery business. Naturally, Walt and Roy were co-opted into contributing their services and found themselves getting up at 3:30 in the morning to meet the trucks of the *Kansas City Star*. Walt, then just nine years old, made his rounds every day, even in the depths of the Kansas City winter, which often brought several feet of snow. Roy, eight years his senior, would soon be in a position to escape this drudgery, but he maintained his close relationship with Walt, giving him good advice and finding ways for him to earn a little money (the work for their father was unpaid). The good advice included telling Walt that he need no longer stand for the beatings Elias was in the habit of administering.

The hard work continued, but Walt's interest in drawing persisted, as did a growing taste for theatrical expression. In a rare gesture of indulgence, Elias allowed Walt to enroll for Saturday morning classes at the Kansas City Art Institute (the elder Disney justified this on the grounds that the classes would be "educational"). Thus, at the age of fourteen, Walt acquired a smattering of formal art training. Just as important, in view of later developments, was Disney's relationship with one of his schoolmates, Walt Pfeiffer. Pfeiffer (in later years a Disney staffer, holding for a while the position of Studio manager) shared Disney's budding interest in the performing arts. They evolved a kind of juvenile vaudeville act – "The Two Walts" – and made occasional appearances at amateur nights in local theaters, even managing to win a few prizes.

Pfeiffer remembers that getting to these performances was not easy because of the strictness of Disney's parents. "Walt's dad always hated anything that had to do with entertainment. A lot of times, when we were fooling around, getting on amateur nights and things like that, I'd go down and sneak Walt out the window. We'd be real quiet and I don't think his dad ever missed him not being in the room. When we'd get through, we'd shove him back in the window and I'd go home. I'd always tell my folks where I was going because my dad encouraged me. He encouraged Walt too."

Pfeiffer recalls another incident that occurred when Disney was about twelve. "We went to Benton School, where J. M. Cottingham, the principal, ran the place like a king. One Lincoln's birthday, Walt came to school all dressed up like Lincoln. He had a shawl that I guess he got from his dad, he made a stovepipe hat out of cardboard, and he got a beard from some place downtown that had theatrical things to sell. He did this all on his own. When Cottingham saw him, he said, 'Walter, you look just like Lincoln. Why are you dressed this way?' Walt said, 'Well, it's his birthday and I want to give the Gettysburg Address.' He had

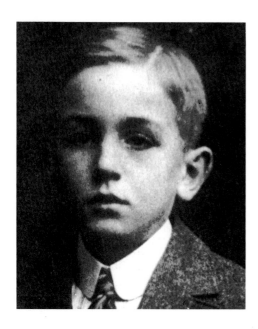

memorized it. So he got up in front of his class and the kids thought this was terrific. Then Cottingham took him to each of the other classes and he repeated the performance."

We know too that Disney was fascinated by Charlie Chaplin and the other great silent comedians, so he must have managed to visit the movies from time to time. This first Kansas City period seems, for all its stringencies, to have provided the young Disney with ample opportunities for learning and entertainment.

In 1917, Elias decided upon another move. This time he returned to Chicago, where he purchased a part share in a small factory. Walt remained in Kansas City to finish out his school year (Roy was still there, working as a bank teller); then he spent the summer as a news butcher on the Santa Fe Railroad (news butchers hawked newspapers, fruit, candy, and soft drinks), a job which enabled him to see a little more of the country while feeding his enthusiasm for trains – an enthusiasm which would provide him with an important outlet later in life. In the fall, he joined the family in Chicago and enrolled at McKinley High School. Here he contributed drawings to the school paper and managed to get some further art instruction from a newspaper cartoonist named Leroy Gossett. World War I was in progress, and on June 22, 1917, Roy Disney enlisted in the Navy. Walt had dreams of enlisting too, but he was underage. He discovered that one could become a Red Cross ambulance driver at seventeen and, though still sixteen, managed to join up. (His

Left: "The Two Walts": Walt Pfeiffer, left, and Walt Disney pose in costumes they devised for one of their amateur night performances, c. 1915. Right: Walt Disney, center right, on an outing of Benton School students

Left: Walt Disney with the cartoon-decorated ambulance he drove in France in 1919. Center: in his barracks in Neufchâtel, Disney set up a drawing board and continued cartooning. Right: back to civilian life, Disney soon found work in a Kansas City commercial art studio

mother, probably relieved that he would be driving an ambulance rather than handling a rifle, allowed him to falsify his birth date on the application.) He was sent to a staging post at Sound Beach, Connecticut, but the armistice was signed before he got any further. There was still a need for drivers in Europe, however, and he eventually found himself in France, assigned to a military canteen in Neufchâtel, where he soon established himself as the unit's unofficial artist, earning a few extra francs with such enterprises as painting fake medals onto leather jackets and camouflaging captured German helmets so that they could be passed off as snipers' helmets.

Disney returned to the United States in 1919. His father had a job waiting for him, but Walt was determined to make a career in commercial art. He headed for Kansas City and found work at a local studio where he made friends with another employee, Ubbe "Ub" Iwerks, a young man of Dutch descent who was to become the most important associate of his early career. Iwerks was a talented draftsman, and it soon occurred to them to go into business for themselves. They acquired desk space at the offices of a publication called *Restaurant News* and immediately achieved some modest success. But then Disney saw a newspaper advertisement for a job with an organization called Kansas City Slide Company (soon changed to Kansas City Film Ad). This company made what we would now call commercials for display in local movie theaters. They were, in fact, producing crude animated films. This new medium and the salary

The staff of Kansas City Film Ad Service, with Disney seated on the right-hand brick post. Ub Iwerks is standing seventh from the right

offered – forty dollars a week – appealed to Disney. He applied for the job and got it. Iwerks took over the business they had started, but within a few months he, too, joined Kansas City Film Ad.

Throughout the nineteenth century, scientists and inventors had intrigued the general public with a whole series of devices which could take a sequence of drawings and make them seem to move. Most of these were variants upon a simple machine which had been conceived almost simultaneously by Dr. Joseph Antoine Plateau of the University of Ghent and Dr. Simon Ritter von Stampfer of Vienna. (The inspiration for their experiments was a paper entitled "The Persistence of Vision with Regard to Moving Objects," which Peter Mark Roget presented to the British Royal Society in 1824.)

    The Plateau–Stampfer device consisted of two disks mounted on a single shaft. The images to be viewed – they might portray a man running or a horse jumping – were attached in chronological sequence to the rim of the inner disk. When this disk was rotated, an observer looking through one of the slits cut into the rim of the outer disk would perceive an illusion of movement. This system was developed into the zoetrope, which remained a popular toy for many years.

    Photography had meanwhile come to the public's attention in 1839, and its own more spectacular development paralleled that of these "wheel of life" novelties. In 1872, Eadweard Muybridge began his

While at McKinley High School in Chicago, Disney contributed numerous drawings to the school paper and, during his service in France, sent an illustrated letter to his former schoolmates

eyes hold disregard for others? The door opened noisily—Marie stood in the bright glare of the hall lamp.

"I beg your pardon," she murmured, backing into the hall, "my friend used to rent this studio. I did not know she had moved."

The door was closing—in a moment she would be gone—

"Marie!"

The door reopened.

"Won't you please come in?"

Marie came in and upon his invitation demurely seated herself on the edge of the chair before the painting.

"Oh! You are drawing my picture, aren't you?"

Kenneth was one vast monument of suppressed emotion. Marie knew this very well, but her gaze was as innocent as a baby's when she turned. Her smile brought out dimples—two of them.

Was she playing with him? He did not care. She was at least worth another trial.

"I—I didn't wait to hear your reason for not marrying—that is not caring to marry me."

He was a very embarrassed young man.

Again she smiled.

"I haven't any reason now. You see I was afraid people would say that I married you for your money. I thought I couldn't stand that. But, do you know, I've been thinking it over and I can't see that it matters what people think. *You'll* know that it isn't so—so I think I will marry—Kenneth—Kenneth you're mussing my hair—Kenneth really—now—please—I haven't any powder with me and my nose—"

A very flushed young woman made her appearance.

"Kenneth," a pause, "by the way—I—I—haven't any friend who ever lived here. I looked you up and came on purpose to make you ask me again. Now—Ken—"

The End.

"Oh! You are drawing my picture, aren't you?"

famous photographic studies of animals and humans in motion. In 1887, aware of Muybridge's work, Thomas Edison began to experiment with the idea of motion pictures, which he thought of as a logical extension of and accompaniment to his phonograph. By 1889 he had built the first kinetoscope, a kind of peep-show viewer which held fifty feet of film, enough to run for about thirteen seconds. The machine made its commercial debut on April 14, 1894, at a kinetoscope parlor in New York City. Several of these machines were exported to Europe, leading a number of pioneers there to explore the possibilities opened up by this invention. In 1895, the brothers Louis and Auguste Lumière took out a patent on a device which successfully combined the principles of the kinetoscope with those of the magic lantern – which is to say that it was able to project moving pictures onto a screen. They called their machine the *cinematographe*. By the following year, Edison films were being shown on a more sophisticated projector built by Thomas Armat of Washington. The Armat machine, known as the vitascope, was the direct ancestor of the modern movie projector.

These sudden advances, from the kinetoscope onward, were made possible by the fact that, in 1889, George Eastman of Rochester, New York, had begun to manufacture flexible strips of photographic film using a nitrocellulose base. This film – far more convenient than anything available until that time – was designed specifically to meet the mechanical requirements of "roller photography" in the Eastman Kodak camera. It was also ideally suited to the needs of the men who sired the motion picture industry, and it followed naturally that movies evolved primarily in terms of the photographic image.

Eadweard Muybridge, *Figure Hopping,* 1887

It was not until 1906 that the first animated film was attempted. In that year J. Stuart Blackton, a commercial artist who later produced movies for Edison, conceived a little entertainment which he called *Humorous Phases of Funny Faces*. The level of animation achieved in this first effort was rudimentary. It did not capitalize so much on drawings seeming to move as on drawings seeming to complete themselves (though there was some primitive use of movement – a man might, for example, appear to wiggle his ears). The notion that it was possible to photograph drawings and make them appear to move did, however, spark the imaginations of one or two other innovators. In 1908, Winsor McCay put his comic-strip character Little Nemo into an animated film. Later he toured the vaudeville circuit with a cartoon titled *Gertie the Trained Dinosaur*. McCay appeared on stage as the film was projected, and the gimmick was that Gertie seemed to obey his commands, concluding her performance by "catching" an apple which he pretended to throw to her. McCay was a gifted draftsman and, viewed today, the animation in this movie seems surprisingly accomplished. (He had selected a dinosaur as his subject so that nobody could accuse him of tracing photographs.) Gertie was devised to fit in with a stage act, which may account for the fact that the story line, crude as it is, is well enough shaped so that the film can still be watched with pleasure.

McCay's success prompted several other producers to experiment with animation. In 1913, two series were launched – *Colonel Heeza Liar,* devised by J. R. Bray, and *Old Doc Yak,* created by Sidney Smith. Bray's series was the more popular of the two, in part because he made it more comfortable to watch by using a range of grays, rather than just black and white, thus reducing screen glare. Within a couple of years he had three major competitors: Paul Terry launched *Farmer Al Falfa,* Wallace Carlson entered the market with *Dreamy Dubb,* and Earl Hurd introduced *Bobby Bump.* Hurd is a key figure in the history of animation, for he invented the idea of painting the animated figures onto celluloid. Previous to this, everything – including the static background – had to be drawn anew for each frame of the picture. Now, only the moving characters required this attention. A single background could be placed under the sequence of celluloid sheets – "cels," as they came to be known – and remain there until the scene was changed. This system offered an enormous saving in time and money, and, although other methods persisted for a while, it was the one that became generally adopted throughout the industry.

By 1917, the International Feature Syndicate was releasing animated versions of popular newspaper cartoon strips, including *Bringing Up Father, The Katzenjammer Kids, Krazy Kat,* and *Silk Hat Harry.* That same year, Max Fleischer introduced his *Out of the Inkwell* series, in which live action was combined with animation.

At that time the industry was centered in New York City. One of several studios there was that of Raoul Barre, best known for his early work on the *Mutt and Jeff* series. Dick Huemer, later a Disney animator and story man, was, in 1916, a student at the Art Students League and

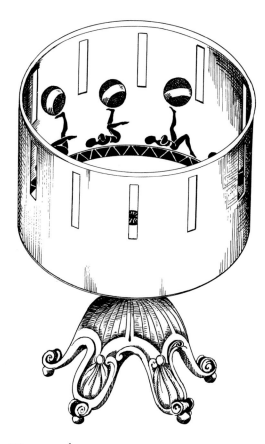

Diagram of a zoetrope

The photograph at left, taken in 1922, was probably intended to promote the young Disney's image as a filmmaker (the man with the gun is Walt himself). At right, we see him in another role, behind the camera

Disney, left, and an assistant filming on location

Disney at work in the Laugh-o-Grams office, 1922

living in the Bronx, where the Barre studio was located. He recalls seeing Barre's business sign on a door at the corner of Fordham Road and Webster Avenue.

"I had done a lot of illustrating, in yearbooks and things like that. One day, out of curiosity, I just walked upstairs and there was this plump little guy sitting there – a very genial character with a French accent. I told him I'd seen his sign and would like to be a cartoonist. He said, 'All right – go into the next room, they'll put you to work.' And that's how I got into the business. Because in those days, who knew about animated cartoons? I don't believe the name had even been coined yet."

The picture Huemer paints of the industry in those days is not one that suggests that *Snow White and the Seven Dwarfs* was barely two decades away.

"I'm afraid that we only did our cartoons to please ourselves. There was no story – we'd say 'Let's have a picture about building, it'll add up in the end.' Each guy sat at his desk with a pile of paper and did his animation, and when it was finished he handed it over and they would put it together. Enter left, exit right – that's what it amounted to. No definite plot line. Never. We were having fun. We'd laugh at each other's stuff, but when it ran in the theater – plop! Nothing. . . . Because we hadn't considered what the impact of what we were drawing would be. What were these old cartoons, anyway? There was no reality or life in them."

In these comments, Huemer is a little too hard on himself and his fellow pioneers. The movies they made possess, if nothing else, a certain period charm. It is undeniable, however, that they were very crude in terms of both animation and plot construction. As for character development, it didn't exist since characters were established in the most schematic of ways. They were recognizable because one had a big nose and another flat feet. Rough exaggeration of physical characteristics served as a substitute for personality.

This, then, was the state of the art when Disney joined the staff of Kansas City Film Ad.

The animation done at Kansas City Film Ad was, in fact, even cruder than that which was coming out of New York. It consisted mainly of stop-action photography of jointed cardboard figures – a technique that precluded any serious effort toward naturalism. Nonetheless, it provided Disney, still just eighteen years old, and Iwerks with the basic training they needed. Before long, Disney borrowed a camera and tried some animation on his own. The result was a little reel of topical gags – reminiscent in character of newspaper cartoons – which he managed to sell to the Newman Theater, a local movie house. A number of short "commercials" and illustrated jokes – known collectively as the Newman Laugh-O-Grams – were made for the theater. They dealt with such topics as shorter skirts and police corruption. Technically, they were very competent by the standards of the day, and, encouraged by this initial success, Disney managed to raise enough capital to leave Kansas City Film Ad and set up on his own, retaining Laugh-O-Grams as the company's name. It might be assumed that a young man just emerging from his teens would have been content to stick with familiar material, at least for a while, but Disney was ambitious and immediately started work on a series of updated fairy tales. Six of these were made: *Cinderella, The Four Musicians of Bremen, Goldie Locks and the Three Bears, Jack and the Beanstalk, Little Red Riding Hood,* and *Puss in Boots.* The Disney archives have prints of *The Four Musicians of Bremen* and *Puss in Boots,* and they provide clear evidence that Disney was not overestimating his ability when he entered production at this tender age. *Puss in Boots,* for example, is rather well animated, and the story displays a nice sense of humor (the fairy-tale atmosphere is updated so that, for instance, the King rides around in a chauffeur-driven convertible).

In the course of producing these short cartoons, Disney began to build up an able staff, which soon included, besides Iwerks, Rudolf Ising, Hugh and Walker Harman, Carmen "Max" Maxwell, and Red Lyon. Unfortunately, the Laugh-O-Grams were not selling (one sale was made but the purchaser went bankrupt after making a hundred dollar deposit), and the Disney production team was always having to look for alternate sources of income. They worked on a live-action short called *Martha* and, sponsored by a local dentist, even made a film on dental hygiene which combined live action and animation to get its didactic message across. Max Fleischer had been using this same combination in his *Out of the Inkwell* series. Since the live-action sections of the movies were relatively inexpensive to produce, the overall cost was reduced. At some time in 1923, Disney decided to try to save his Laugh-O-Grams venture by making just such a movie, in which a human heroine could cavort with cartoon characters. The film that resulted was *Alice's Wonderland.*

For his Alice, Disney chose a little girl named Virginia Davis, who had had some modeling experience with Kansas City Film Ad. The story begins as Alice explores the Laugh-O-Grams offices. She discovers Disney seated at his drawing board, on which a dog kennel has been sketched. Suddenly, a dog emerges from the kennel and, before she knows what has happened, Alice has become a part of the cartoon and finds herself involved with a variety of animals, including a quartet of lions who eventually chase her over a cliff (the surviving print is incomplete).

The effect of blending the real Alice with the cartoon characters was achieved by photographing Virginia Davis against a white background and then combining this film, in the printing process, with another strip on which the animation was shot. The technique worked well, but *Alice's Wonderland* exhausted Disney's remaining credit, and he was forced to close the studio.

Top: the Laugh-O-Grams office, 1922; center: filming *Martha,* with Disney in the director's chair; bottom: Disney, at right, with friends at an artists' ball in Kansas City, 1922

He was not the type to be put off by a setback of this kind, however, and immediately planned to restart his career. Evidently he could not do this in Kansas City, and so, with very little hesitation, he made his move. We can assume that he considered the possibility of trying New York, which was still the center of the animation industry, but he chose Hollywood. There is reason to suppose that he considered abandoning animation and trying his luck with one of the major studios, most of

The title frame from a Laugh-O-Grams cartoon, c. 1922

Walt Disney's letterhead, c. 1922

which were by now established in the pleasant foothills of the Santa Monica Mountains. Another important influence was the fact that his brother Roy was already in the West, recuperating in a veterans' hospital from a bout with tuberculosis. In the summer of 1923 Walt Disney, aged twenty-one, took a train to California, carrying *Alice's Wonderland* with him as a sample.

On arriving in Los Angeles, Disney moved in with his uncle Robert Disney at 4406 Kingswell Avenue. Walt began to look for a job and, in his spare time, used his uncle's garage to build a stand for the animation camera he had purchased (this would have been a conventional movie camera converted to shoot stop-action).

Two months after his arrival, Margaret J. Winkler, a New York distributor, commissioned a series of Alice Comedies which Disney would produce. With Roy, Walt rented space in the rear of a small office occupied by Holly-Vermont Realty at 4651 Kingswell. They paid a rent of ten dollars per month. On October 16, 1923, they signed their first contract and were in business. The following January they increased their overhead by another ten dollars a month, renting a vacant lot on Hollywood Boulevard, about three blocks from the Studio (this lot was needed for outdoor shooting on the Alice films). By February they had outgrown their original studio space (the staff had grown to seven) and moved into the adjoining store, at 4649 Kingswell, which they rented for thirty-five dollars a month. A separate garage was rented for seven dollars a month.

The initial contract called for one Alice Comedy a month. Virginia Davis's parents had visions of her achieving Hollywood stardom, and they brought her out to California so that she could continue to play the lead. The first half dozen or so of the Alice Comedies featured a great deal of live action which involved Virginia with other children in fairly conventional comedy situations. Animation sequences were kept to a bare minimum, since they cost more and took longer to produce. It seems that Miss Winkler was not entirely satisfied with the results and wanted to cancel the contract. The Disneys were not prepared to loosen their tenuous grip on the future and persuaded Ub Iwerks to join them in California. He arrived in July (Hugh Harman and Rudolf Ising followed in June of 1925). Iwerks was just the man to streamline their productions. Soon they were able to increase the amount of animation included in each film, and the series began to enjoy a modest success. Virginia Davis was replaced, briefly, by a young lady named Dawn O'Day and then by Margie Gay, who held the role for the remainder of the series. Virginia Davis had had something of a post-Victorian image – her appeal was that of a juvenile Mary Pickford – whereas Margie Gay was more the flapper type, and this updating of Alice's image may have contributed something to the increasing popularity of the series.

Further additions to the staff had to be made to accommodate Alice's success, and one new employee was an Idaho girl named Lillian Bounds. She often worked nights, and Walt would sometimes drive her home in his car. A romance blossomed and, in July 1925, the pair was married.

Margie Gay poses with, left to right, Ham Hamilton, Roy Disney, Hugh Harman, Walt Disney, Rudy Ising, Ub Iwerks, and Walker Harman

Margie Gay as Alice with animated friends and, at top, with director Walt Disney

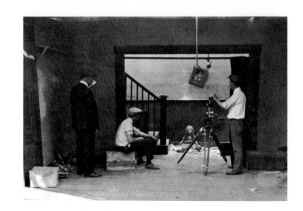

Clowning on the Alice set: Rudy Ising holding the hose; under the umbrella are Hugh Harman, Ub Iwerks, and Walt Disney

Early Alice Comedies involved a good deal of live-action filming. The original Alice, featured on this page, was Virginia Davis, whom Disney brought out from Kansas City to star in the series

Roy Disney had meanwhile married Edna Francis, his Kansas City sweetheart.

Another consequence of expansion was that the Studio was once again outgrowing its accommodations. On July 6, 1925, four hundred dollars was deposited to secure a lot at 2719 Hyperion Avenue, quite close to their existing premises (Hyperion lies just to the south of Griffith Park, not far from the present-day site of Dodger Stadium). A single-story building was erected there and this formed the nucleus of the plant which was to serve as the company's base for the next fifteen years (it was almost constantly being expanded). By 1927, it became evident that Disney had to find a replacement for the Alice movies if the Studio was to remain viable. By then the filmmakers were approaching the sixtieth episode, and the series was running out of steam. Apart from anything else, the use of live action placed severe restrictions on the artists' sense of fantasy, and Walt was anxious to get back to full animation. As the last of the Alice films were completed, work began on a new series which was to feature the adventures of Oswald the Lucky Rabbit.

By now Disney had completely abandoned his career as an animator to concentrate all his energies on the production side of the business. Animation could be left in the capable hands of Iwerks, Ising, and the Harman brothers, along with other newly signed draftsmen, such as Ham Hamilton and Friz Freleng. Disney was also recruiting apprentice animators, young men who showed some enthusiasm for the business. One of these was Les Clark.

Excuse these Blushes—
—but they're naming
things after me now !

The latest tribute to Oswald's popularity is the new OSWALD
MILK CHOCOLATE FRAPPE CANDY BAR.

A great little tie-up and a fine publicity stunt.

The Vogan Candy Company of Portland, Ore., put them out.
The advertising and wrapper bear a cartoon of "The Lucky
Rabbit" as he appears in the comedies and his face as well as his
name is fast becoming a bye-word for FUN to film fans everywhere.

**Get him—he's a great
asset for any
theatre.**

Oswald is a Winkler Pro-
duction created by Walt
Disney and released thru
UNIVERSAL. 26 of them,
1 reel each.

Sketch for an Oswald poster

The series of cartoons (opposite) that Disney built around Oswald the Lucky Rabbit was successful enough to attract merchandising tie-ins. The model sheet on the opposite page, top right, shows that Oswald anticipated some of the physical characteristics of Mickey Mouse. The page of story continuity sketches, bottom right, illustrates how cartoon stories were worked out in this period

Overleaf: Poster for an Alice Comedy, left, and original art by Hugh Harman and Carmen Maxwell for an Oswald poster, right

"I was working a part-time summer job at a lunch counter and confectionery store on Vermont and Kingswell," Clark recalled in 1972. "Walt and Roy used to come over there for lunch. While I was still in high school, I asked Walt for a job. He said, 'Bring some of your drawings in and let me see what they look like.' Well, I copied some cartoons out of *College Humor* and showed them to him. I told him I had copied them but he said I had a good line and invited me to start work the following Monday. So I graduated from high school on a Thursday and I went to work on Monday and I haven't been out of his employ since."

That was in 1927. What Clark did not know at the time was that the Studio was on the brink of a major crisis.

Most business crises are brought on by incompetence. The near catastrophe that the Disneys faced in 1927 resulted from the very opposite. The new cartoon series turned out to be very successful, making Oswald the Lucky Rabbit a desirable property.

Oswald was a likable little creature, all soft curves and energy. He had no voice, of course – this was still the silent era – but the adventures he found himself caught up in were, to judge by surviving examples, inventive and well constructed for the time. The Disney animators were becoming very skilled, and they took full advantage of the fact that they no longer had to compete with a live Alice. With Oswald, Disney equaled – and perhaps surpassed – the best products of his competitors. *The Mechanical Cow,* for instance, is chock-full of zany invention and surrealistic humor.

There was just one snag. Disney had signed a one-year contract with Charles Mintz, who had married Margaret Winkler in 1924 (their distribution outlet now tied in with Universal Pictures). The advertising announced "Oswald the Lucky Rabbit, created by Walt Disney," but – and this proved to be the fatal flaw in the contract – Oswald's name belonged to Mintz (who had, apparently, picked it out of a hat). As the first year moved to a successful conclusion, Walt Disney and his wife embarked for New York, where he expected to renegotiate the contract with provisions for a modest increase of income. He had kept in close contact with his distributor through George Winkler, Margaret's brother, who had made several visits to California, and there was no reason to suspect that anything was amiss. When Disney arrived in New York, however, the true reasons for Winkler's visits became painfully obvious.

Instead of offering an improved contract, Mintz actually proposed one which would entail a *reduction* of income for the Studio. This was clearly absurd, since Oswald had been very profitable. Obviously, Disney could not accept such a deal, and the reality of the situation became apparent. Mintz had decided to repossess Oswald. The character's name belonged to him, and his brother-in-law had persuaded several of Disney's best animators to take over production of the Oswald series. The motive was, of course, reduction of costs to the distributor. Mintz was the first of many people to underestimate Disney. He figured that if

Standing in front of their storefront studio, Walt and Roy Disney with, left to right, Walt's wife Lillian, Ruth Disney, and Roy's wife Edna

he could hire away Disney's best men, he would be getting the same product for a reduced outlay.

Disney was shocked and hurt. He had trusted Mintz, and he had trusted his employees. It is not hard to imagine the kinds of thoughts that must have run through his head as he and Lillian waited out the long, slow train ride back to California. He was disgusted but not, as the next few months would prove, discouraged. His team was depleted but it still included his two most important associates – his brother Roy and Ub Iwerks (who was, by then, a partner in the business). More important still, Walt Disney had faith in his own abilities. He had reached the age of twenty-six after touching many of the bases of hardship that had come to seem archetypal of America in the first quarter of this century. His personal creed must have included the notion that success does not come easily.

2 Mickey Mouse and Silly Symphonies

It seems appropriate that the birth of Mickey Mouse – a creature of mythic stature – should be shrouded in legend. Walt Disney is said to have conceived Mickey on the train, returning to Hollywood from his angry encounter with Mintz. There is no reason to suppose that this is not essentially true, but over the years this story became so polished by repetition that it began to lose its sense of reality and to take on the character of an official myth. A further dimension was added to the legend by the fact that Disney had managed to tame a mouse in his old Kansas City studio, a mouse that he had nicknamed Mortimer. The name Mortimer now became the first choice for his new character, but before the Mouse cartoons were released, the name was changed to Mickey (it seems that Mrs. Disney thought the name Mortimer was a little pompous for a cartoon animal, but pressure from potential distributors may also have had something to do with the switch).

What we can be reasonably sure of is that the Mickey Mouse who made his debut in New York City in 1928 resulted from a collaborative effort between Disney and Ub Iwerks. It seems probable that Iwerks, easily the best animator of the day, was largely responsible for defining Mickey's physical characteristics. Mickey did bear a family resemblance to Oswald, but Iwerks – presumably in close consultation with Disney – made the figure more compact. He was constructed from two large circles, one for the trunk and one for the head, to which were appended

two smaller circles, representing ears, and rubber-hose arms and legs
which terminated in plump hands (ungloved at this early stage) and large
feet which gave him stability. He was also equipped with a long, skinny
tail and short pants decorated with buttons fore and aft. The circular
head was made expressive by the addition of a mischievous snout, a
plum-shaped nose, and button eyes. He was designed for maximum ease
of animation (it had been discovered that circular forms were simpler to
animate effectively), but beyond that, Mickey's identity had a dimension
which was quite new in cartoons. Certainly a character such as Felix the
Cat was immediately recognizable, but he did not have a real personality.
Mickey did have one, and an audience could identify with him in much
the same way it would with a human performer.

The gift of personality was probably Disney's own contribution to
Mickey. Iwerks made the whole thing possible through his skill as a
draftsman, but it was Disney's control over the situations in which the
Mouse found himself that allowed this personality to develop. Even at
this early date, Disney had grasped the notion that cartoon characters
should seem to think for themselves. In some ways he may even have
viewed Mickey as his alter ego. He always maintained a special affection
for the Mouse, a fact which suggests that he was intimately involved in
every stage of its creation.

The Disney brothers had managed to save enough money to go ahead
with the first Mickey Mouse cartoons even without a distributor, and
work began almost at once. This was carried out in secret at first, since
the Oswald contract had not yet completely expired. On October 23, 1927,
a bombshell had hit the motion picture industry. Warner Brothers released *The Jazz Singer,* and the sound era became a reality. Lee DeForest
had developed a practical sound system at least four years earlier, but the
Hollywood production chiefs had fought shy of this new development.
Now they had to confront it.

As the first Mouse cartoons went into production, the industry was
still in chaos. One Disney cartoon, *Plane Crazy,* had been completed, and
another, *The Gallopin' Gaucho,* was on the drawing boards before the
decision was made – perhaps the most important decision that Disney
ever made. He wanted Mickey to have real impact, and he saw that the
future lay with sound. What he had in mind was a cartoon in which music,
effects, and action would all be synchronized. Max and Dave Fleischer had
already produced a cartoon which used a Lee DeForest sound track, but
the track had been unsynchronized and the experiment had had little
impact on the industry. Disney's plan was for something far more radical.

Wedding sound to animated drawings was not, he realized, something
that could be approached casually. Where live actors were concerned, it
might be enough for the audience to hear them speak – that seemed like
a miracle after the decades of silence (the fact that sound pictures were
quickly labeled "talkies" indicates just where the public's interest lay) –
but Disney did not have the ready-made stars to whom he could return
the gift of speech. He had to come up with a more imaginative solution.

When the great French director René Clair was first exposed to the

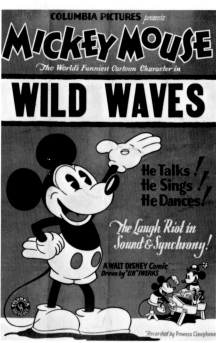

Mickey Mouse was originally drawn by Ub
Iwerks, top, who was given credit in early
publicity; center: an early poster. At bottom,
Mickey is inked onto a cel

-Main Title-

Orchestra starts playing opening
verses of ' Steamboat Bill ',
as soon as title flashes on.

The orchestration can be so
arrainged that many variations
may be included before the title
fades out.

It would be best if the music
was arrainged so that the end of
a verse would end at the end of
the title...... and a new verse
start at beginning of the first
scene.

Scene # 1.
Opening effect of black foliage
passing by in front of camera
gradually getting thinner until
full scene is revealed

Action......Old side'wheel river
steamboat paddleing down stream.
The two smoke stacks work up
and down alternately.... shooting
black chunks of smoke out as they
shoot up....smoke makes stacks
bulge out as it goes up and out.
(16 drawing cycle) 12 Ft. from
opening, the Three whistles on top
of cabin squat down before they
whistle tune ' TA--DA-DE-DA-DA---
DA-DA-'....2 Ft. of action after
whistle and out.

Scene # 2.
Close up of Mickey in cabin of
wheel'house, keeping time to last
two measures of verse of ' steamboat Bill '. With gesture he starts
whistleing the chorus in perfect
time to music....his body keeping
time with every other beat while
his shoulders and foot keep time
with each beat. At the end of every
two measures he twirls wheel which
makes a ratchet sound as it spins.
He takes in breath at proper time
according to music. When he finishes
last measure he reaches up and pulls
on whistle cord above his head.
(Use FIFE to imitate his whistle)

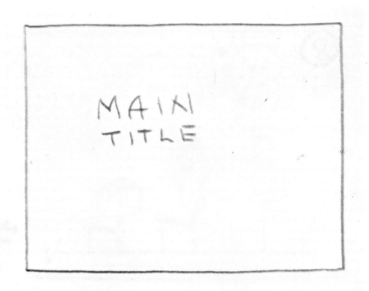

The first page of the *Steamboat Willie* continuity
script. Disney kept this souvenir of his first major
breakthrough in his office

In *Steamboat Willie*, 1928, the first cartoon to feature a fully synchronized sound track, Mickey and Minnie transform the cargo of a riverboat – including livestock – into an orchestra

Plane Crazy, 1928, was the first Mickey Mouse vehicle to go into production, but it was not released until after the success of *Steamboat Willie*

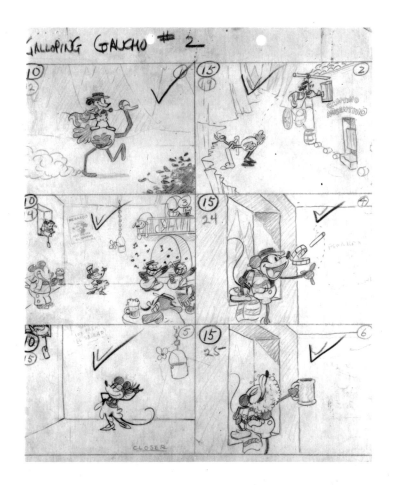

The Gallopin' Gaucho was the second Mickey Mouse cartoon to be made, but, like *Plane Crazy*, it was produced as a silent film and not released until a sound track had been added

The Karnival Kid, 1929, used gags derived directly from earlier situations devised for Oswald

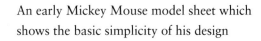
An early Mickey Mouse model sheet which shows the basic simplicity of his design

Scenes from *Mickey's Choo Choo*, 1929, and *The Fire Fighters*, 1930

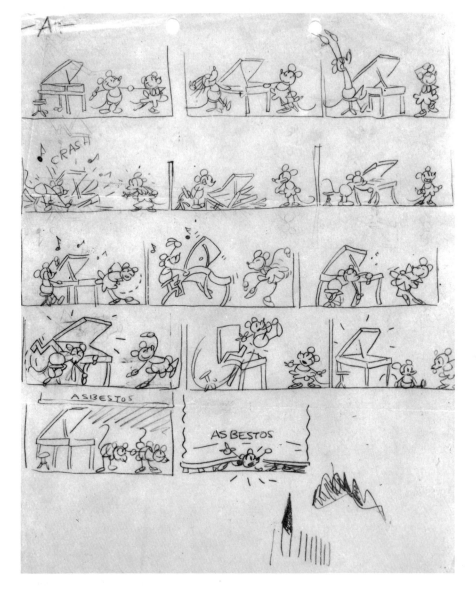

Rough story ideas were often worked out in thumbnail sketches, as in this example by Wilfred Jackson

talking pictures, he quickly realized that there would be an enormous difference between mere "talkies" and those that used sound creatively. Walt Disney, prompted by circumstance and predisposed by temperament, was to become the first producer to find a genuinely creative way of using sound. Cartoon animals making noises might have offered something in the way of novelty, but novelties have a tendency to become clichés all too quickly. Evidently Disney was quite conscious of this danger. Animated creatures synchronized to a carefully structured sound track, he realized, would have far more impact. He and his team began to develop a third Mickey Mouse story, this one conceived specially for sound. Cartoons had always depended on action rather than verbal jokes (in the silent era one could not afford to break up a short sequence of animated gags with title cards), so Disney decided to preserve this emphasis on action while underpinning it with carefully timed sound effects and a strongly rhythmic music track.

Not that this was the easiest of things to achieve. To start with, no one at the Studio had any real knowledge of music theory, and there were also important technical problems to be solved. The artists had to proceed by trial and error. In their favor was the fact that Iwerks was something of a wizard with machinery and that almost everyone at the Studio knew something about practically everything within the animation field (specialization was still in the future; Walt Disney himself had a firsthand knowledge of every aspect of the business, from cameras to inking). A young animator named Wilfred Jackson played the harmonica and, since his mother was a music teacher, was familiar with the metronome, which, he suggested, might provide a means of relating a musical beat to the frames of film.

Les Clark, who was party to these early experiments, describes the system that was devised as follows:

"We worked with an exposure sheet on which every line was a single frame of action. We could break down the sound effects so that every eight frames we'd have an accent, or every sixteen frames, or every twelve frames. [Sound film runs through the projector at twenty-four frames a second.] And on that twelfth drawing, say, we'd accent whatever was happening – a hit on the head or a footstep or whatever it would be, to synchronize to the sound effect of the music."

By setting a metronome to correspond with the accents thus established in the action, a rough sound accompaniment could be improvised to the animation. One legendary evening, Disney and his coworkers presented a short sequence from *Steamboat Willie* – such was the title of the new cartoon – to an audience of wives and girlfriends. Roy Disney projected the film from outside a window (to eliminate motor noise) while his brother, along with Iwerks, Jackson, Clark, and a few others, improvised their sound accompaniment, live, in another room – all of them working carefully to the beat of the metronome. Jackson played his harmonica (the tune was probably "Steamboat Bill") while the others provided sound effects with cowbells, slide whistles, tin pans, and the like. This accompaniment was transmitted to the audience by way of a

In his early films Mickey often appeared as an entertainer. The examples shown here are, top to bottom, from *The Jazz Fool,* 1929; *Just Mickey,* 1930; and *Blue Rhythm,* 1931

crude loudspeaker system set up by Iwerks. The wives and girlfriends were only mildly impressed, but the performers were convinced that they had now found the answer.

By September 1928, a complete score had been committed to paper and Disney set out for New York to have it recorded. At that time, most recording devices were controlled by patents belonging to RCA and Western Electric, so it was necessary, first of all, to locate someone with "outlaw" sound equipment. Eventually, Disney came to terms with a man named Pat Powers, who operated a renegade sound system that gloried in the name Powers Cinephone. Walt wrote to Roy and Ub that Powers was a very much respected personage in the film business. "He is very shrewd and capable. He is careful and cautious." He might have added, had he known, that Powers was also somewhat notorious for his efforts to outflank producers in the sometimes informal business atmosphere that had prevailed earlier in the history of the film industry.

Disney hired Carl Edouwarde, who had led the pit orchestra at the Broadway Strand and worked for the Roxy chain, to provide a band and conduct the recording session. On September 14, Walt wrote to Roy and Ub: "We are using a seventeen-piece orchestra and three of the best trap drummers and effect men in town. They get ten dollars an hour for this work. It will take three hours to do it, plus the time the effect men put in today." Later in the same letter he says that there would be about thirty-five men on the job, but this may have included technicians. At all events, the first recording session was a disaster. Disney's team had developed a system of indicating – probably by flashes on the screen – the tempo to which the orchestra should play. Thus, the film could be projected and serve the same function as a metronome. Unfortunately, this system was a little crude, and Edouwarde did not feel inclined to have his tempo determined by such a coarse mechanical device. Disney was forced to cable California for more money and try again. Roy sent out enough money to proceed with a second session but not, it would seem, without some qualms. Walt, convinced that he had the problem licked, wrote back suggesting that he try to borrow another five thousand dollars so that they could be ready to go into full production. "I am firmly convinced," he insisted, "that it will be far cheaper in the long run to go into it in the proper manner. . . . Let's do things in the proper way and not try to save a penny here and there."

In the same letter (like the others, it was addressed to both Roy and Ub) he says, "We have all been working like the devil on the picture. . . . The orchestra leader and myself completely revised the Score . . . I finally got him to see it my way (he thinks he thought of the idea). The fact is that he just saw what I have been telling him for the last two weeks. . . . They are very clever in their line – but want too much beauty and too many Symphonic effects. . . . They think comedy music is low brow. . . . Believe me, I have had a tough fight getting them to come down to our level. . . . I wish you knew the whole story and I know you would sympathize with me. . . . I feel positive we have everything worked out perfect now."

One improvement was that instead of sticking with the crude flashing device that had been used at the first session, Disney had had the film reprinted with the addition of a bouncing ball system to indicate the accents as well as the beat, making it much easier for Edouwarde to follow. Fewer musicians were used at the second session, and everything went off without a hitch. *Steamboat Willie* now had a sound track and Mickey Mouse was ready for his debut.

Finding a distributor was not easy, however. Still in New York, Disney took his sound cartoon from screening room to screening room, but the industry remained in a state of confusion and the response he met with was discouraging. Eventually, Harry Reichenbach, then managing Manhattan's Colony Theater, saw *Steamboat Willie* and offered Disney a two-week run for the film. After some hesitation – he was hoping for a national distributor – Disney agreed. Reichenbach had made his reputation as a stop-at-nothing press agent and, when *Steamboat Willie* opened at the Colony on November 18, 1928, he saw to it that it received excellent coverage in the news media. This, combined with the fact that audiences roared with laughter at Mickey's adventures, encouraged the prestigious Roxy to book the movie. Pat Powers reentered the picture and offered to distribute Disney's cartoons on a States Rights basis (this was an old system of distribution that allowed an independent producer to bypass the major studios, which controlled most of the theaters at that time). The deal that Powers offered was not perfect, but it was the best offer Disney had received. He signed up for one year. He then busied himself with adding sound to *Plane Crazy* and *The Gallopin' Gaucho*. A fourth Mouse cartoon, *The Barn Dance,* was already animated, and work began on still another, *The Opry House.*

The Mickey Mouse who hit the movie houses in the late twenties was not quite the well-behaved character most of us are familiar with today. He was mischievous, to say the least, and even displayed a streak of cruelty (which soon disappeared), but from the very beginning he had that little germ of real personality, and this prevented him from seeming to be just another callously cruel cartoon animal. At times – when confronted by Pegleg Pete (the perennial villain who co-starred in both *Steamboat Willie* and *The Gallopin' Gaucho*) or when forced to defend Minnie's honor – he was even capable of heroic behavior. His heroism, however, was usually the heroism of the little man; it resembled the intermittent nobility of Charlie Chaplin's tramp. Chaplin undoubtedly provided Disney with one of his most important models, and we may say that Mickey and his gang provided for the sound era the kind of entertainment that Chaplin and the Mack Sennett comedians had provided for an earlier generation.

Since this *was* the sound era, Mickey had to have a voice. Several people, mostly from the Studio, had a shot at immortality as the Mouse's voice, but Disney was not satisfied with any of them. He knew just the kind of squeaky falsetto Mickey should have. He was also concerned, after his experience with Oswald, that no one should be able to steal his new creation. To help make sure of this, Disney became Mickey's voice

SCENE #3:

       Horse and cow in bathing suits. Horse puts his
fingers in his mouth and whistles to attract the attention
of Mickey and Minnie. Pantos, "watch me!" Runs out to
left along a dock.

SCENE #5:

       Mickey uses Pluto for a pump to
inflate the inner tube. Gag of Pluto letting
go to bite at a flea, tube goes down, and
Mickey bawls him out. Pluto gets back to work
again, and when the tube is blown up, Mickey
takes it, puts it on over his head, and runs
down to the beach and into the water. The dog
stops on the beach.

Typical gags from 1931 Mickey Mouse shorts:
The Beach Party, left, and *Mickey Cuts Up*

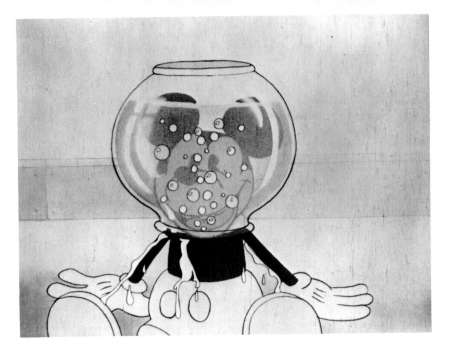

Scenes from *The Birthday Party,* 1931, top, and two 1932 cartoons, *Barnyard Olympics* and *The Grocery Boy*

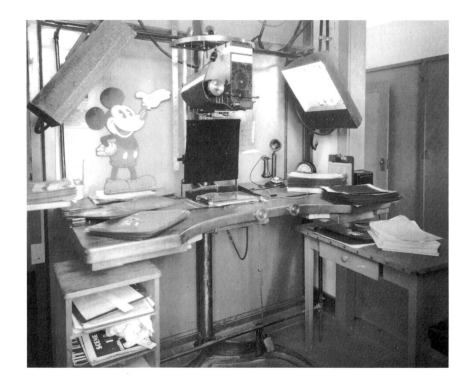

This camera – adapted in the late twenties to shoot animation – was used for many decades

Walt Disney at his desk, c. 1931

In 1930, Carl Stalling, seen here at the piano, composed "Minnie's Yoo Hoo" as a theme song for Mickey. Seated alongside Stalling are Jack King and Ben Sharpsteen, two of the animators Disney had imported from New York. Standing, left to right, are Johnny Cannon, Walt Disney, Bert Gillett, Ub Iwerks, Wilfred Jackson, and Les Clark

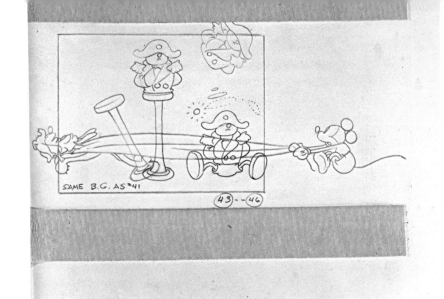

SAME B.G. AS #41

43 - 46

This story sketch for *The Grocery Boy* shows how the scene is to be laid out. Different stages of the action are indicated in a single drawing

SCENE #43:

Pluto drags Mickey into a pedestal holding a statue of Napoleon. The statue falls and lands over Mickey's head and shoulders. Pluto runs on out of scene with turkey.

Poster, 1932

and continued to fill this role for twenty years.

Minnie was with Mickey from the very first. In *Steamboat Willie*, after Pete has chased Mickey from the bridge of the riverboat on which he is employed as a deckhand, Minnie is discovered on shore, about to miss the boat. The ship is already moving downstream when Mickey manages to snag Minnie's patched panties with a boat hook and haul her aboard. Later, on the deck, they cavort with the cargo of livestock, using the various animals as musical instruments on which to improvise "Turkey in the Straw."

This sequence is by far the most interesting in the movie in that it contains the seeds of much that was to come. It is also marked by a kind of humor Disney was later to abandon on grounds of taste. Mickey, for example, stretches a cat's tail so that it becomes a stringed instrument; the cat gives vocal expression to its displeasure at this misuse of its anatomy. A good deal of music and laughter is milked out of a cow's udder (later, the Hays Office was to insist that Disney cows be udderless and, indeed, it was actively suggested that they find some suitable form of apparel). Minnie cranks a goat's tail, transforming the unfortunate beast into a hurdy-gurdy, while Mickey plays xylophone riffs on a cow's teeth. (The xylophone was a much-used instrument in the sound tracks of these early shorts, providing good opportunities for visual puns; almost any more or less regular group of solid objects – the rib cage of a skeleton, for example – could double as a xylophone.)

We might note that the callous attitude displayed by Mickey and Minnie toward other animals made it quite clear that, although not human, these were not ordinary mice. They were creatures invested with special powers. They wore clothing and acted out roles that parodied the habits of men and women. In this respect they belonged to a tradition that goes back to Aesop and Aristophanes. Audiences were fascinated to see this tradition come to life on the screen, and if the gags were a little rough-and-ready, they were certainly effective. The way the action was tied to music and sound effects was unlike anything anyone had ever experienced before. *Steamboat Willie* was both a success and a major breakthrough for the animation industry.

Since *Plane Crazy* and *The Gallopin' Gaucho* were made as silent films and then had sound added to them, they are not so interesting from the technical point of view. *The Gallopin' Gaucho* has a plot that parodies Douglas Fairbanks melodramas (Mickey, in the Argentine, rescues Minnie from the clutches of Pegleg Pete). The animation and most of the situations are strongly reminiscent of some of the things in the Oswald series. *Plane Crazy*, the first Mouse cartoon produced, has considerably more to recommend it. The plot is topical. Mickey fancies himself a second Lindbergh (studying a picture of the aviator, he musses his hair and adopts a boyish grin), and, after some mishaps set in a barnyard, an automobile is converted into an airplane. Mickey offers to take Minnie for a spin. She climbs aboard, but before he can join her, the motor starts and the plane takes off on a crazy trajectory across the countryside, narrowly avoiding disastrous collisions with various items of livestock and a passing car. Mickey catches up with the plane just as it is about to become airborne. Once clear of the ground, Mickey attempts to engage Minnie in a passionate kiss. She takes umbrage at his advances and bails out, using her panties as a parachute. Back on the ground, Mickey laughs at her disarray and Minnie floors him with a horseshoe. *Plane Crazy* was animated in its entirety by one man – Ub Iwerks – making it something of a tour de force. The whole thing moves along at a lively pace, and parts of it still seem funny today.

When *Steamboat Willie* was released, Walt Disney was twenty-six years old. His operation was still a very small one by Hollywood standards, but he had his foot on the first, and perhaps even the second, rung of the ladder. Jack Cutting, later head of the Disney foreign department and responsible for such matters as the dubbing of Disney films into other languages, joined the Studio the following year and still remembers the atmosphere vividly.

"I had to leave the Otis Art Institute and look for a job. I had heard about a small cartoon studio near Glendale, so I went around to 2719 Hyperion without an appointment, walked in off the street with a few samples, and was hired that same day in August 1929. I had just turned twenty-one and most of the nineteen fellows on the staff were very young, with the exception of one or two – Roy must have been about thirty-five and the oldest on the staff was an animator named Burt Gillett, who may have been thirty-eight. I soon found being part of what was going on in that little studio very exciting. Walt was determined to develop the art of animation far beyond the level at which it was practiced in those days. He did it by being persuasive, by convincing everyone that his ideas and dreams for the future were exciting and worth believing in.

"During the early Mickey days, Walt was only taking fifty dollars home a week and Roy thirty-five. Some of us, like myself, who were just out of art school, were making eighteen dollars a week. We worked eight hours a day, six days a week, and we'd often come back nights to help get the work out. We didn't get paid overtime but that didn't matter if you were under the spell of the animated cartoon business, as I was in those days. I came to the Studio without any experience in animation. A few of the older members of the staff, whom Walt had imported from the East, were experienced animators and, of course, Ub Iwerks was the Studio's top animator at that time. When you came in green, like I did, you learned to do a bit of everything. We began by inking cels, then we were taught in-betweening; we would come back at night and Ub would explain the principles of animation to us. The Studio was very small and the atmosphere informal. Most of us had a key to the front door.

"If you were an animator's assistant, after you did in-between drawings for a scene you had to shoot a pencil drawing test. [In-betweens are the drawings used to fill in the gaps between the key drawings made by the animator. There must be an image for every frame, and the animator supplies perhaps just one in three or four. Pencil testing, a way of check-

What appears to be clowning probably had a serious purpose. The two dancers are trying out a pose for the benefit of other animators. Those involved are, left to right, Bert Gillett, Norm Ferguson, Ted Sears, Fred Moore, Gilles "Frenchy" de Trémaudan, Tom Palmer, Ben Sharpsteen, Walt Disney, and Jack King

This photo of the production staff was taken in 1932, after Disney had won an Academy Award – his first – for the creation of Mickey Mouse

Recording the sound track for *The Beach Party* at the Hyperion Avenue studio, 1931. At the microphone is Marcellite Garner, the voice of Minnie Mouse

ing out the animation on a scene before it is inked and painted onto the cels, was a Disney innovation.] After hand developing the test and putting it in a revolving drum to dry, you went back to the drawing board. When it was dry, you spliced it into a loop and ran it for the animator. We all had a chance to try our hands at different phases of the work."

Cutting recalls that Disney and Wilfred Jackson were both directing at the time he joined the Studio. Two shorts would be in production at any given time (they cost an average of about five thousand dollars apiece to make), and, in addition to supervising Jackson's work, Disney would always be working on ideas for new cartoons. From the beginning, gag conferences were held. Everyone on the production staff was expected to attend and invited to contribute jokes or other ideas that would enable the animators to get the most out of each story. Disney was also passionately interested in audience response, convinced that everyone at the Studio could learn a great deal about humor by studying the reactions of a group of laymen.

"When a picture was finished," Cutting reports, "Walt would take the first print from the laboratory to the Alexander Theater in Glendale and tip the projectionist to run it between the first and second shows. We all paid our way to get in and, directly after the cartoon was run, we would meet outside in front of the theater and Walt would evaluate the audience reaction and we would discuss why certain gags didn't go over and why others got such a big laugh."

The Disney brothers were working hard for their first modest success. An account book, written in Roy's hand, survives and indicates that Cutting's estimate of their take-home pay is quite accurate. Accurate, that is, except for the weeks when there was not enough cash to go around

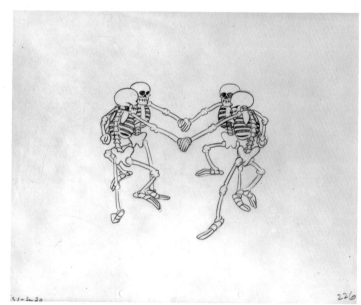

In 1929, Disney launched a new series of
cartoons which he called Silly Symphonies.
The first was *The Skeleton Dance,* which
featured some imaginative animation by
Ub Iwerks set to a macabre score devised
by Carl Stalling

Silly Symphony poster, 1932

MICKEY MOUSE
PRESENTS
A WALT DISNEY
SILLY SYMPHONY
FLOWERS
and TREES
UNITED
ARTISTS
PICTURE

and the brothers' pay shrank to less than that of the lowliest apprentice animator.

A number of new Mickey Mouse cartoons appeared in 1929, sporting titles such as *The Karnival Kid, Mickey's Choo Choo,* and *The Jazz Fool* (this last a takeoff on Al Jolson). Within the space of a few months, Mickey acquired gloves, shoes, and a more endearing manner. There were other developments too. The sound tracks became increasingly sophisticated, and in most cases they were now recorded before the animators began work. This is to say, once a story line was established, a score was prepared to fit the action; it was recorded and the animators worked to the rhythms and accents contained in the sound track. This system permitted greater flexibility.

To handle the music side of the business, Disney called in an old acquaintance from Kansas City, Carl Stalling. Stalling had had years of experience in the theater pit, providing music for silent movies – a background which left him well equipped for his new career. Already the Disney team was becoming extremely adept in synchronizing sound and action, and several of the earliest Mickey Mouse pictures – *The Opry House,* for instance, and *The Jazz Fool* – took music as the main substance of the plot. The director always had a piano in his office so that, at story conferences, the composer could illustrate the melodic and rhythmic lines the animators would have to follow (for this reason, the director's room became known as the music room, a designation it retained for many years). Most of the music used was – like "Turkey in the Straw" – in the public domain, meaning that no royalties would have to be paid. Stalling was quite capable of producing original material, however, and soon came up with "Minnie's Yoo Hoo," which served for some time as Mickey's theme song (in the 1970s, it was revived as the signature tune of television's *The Mouse Factory*).

This emphasis on music led in 1929 to quite a new kind of animated film – the Silly Symphony.

It seems likely that some of the credit for the concept of the Silly Symphonies should go to Carl Stalling. An account of how the series came about was given by Wilfred Jackson in the magazine *Funny World* dated spring 1971. Talking of the Mickey Mouse cartoons, he recalled that there were often arguments between Disney and Stalling when "Walt would want more or less time for the action than could fit the musical phrase." The rest of the staff would sit in the next room, enjoying the whole thing but glad they weren't involved ("Walt could be pretty stiff"). Eventually a solution was arrived at. Walt decided that, so far as Mickey was concerned, the music must be made to fit the action, but that another series would be launched in which the action would be keyed to the music.

Stalling, interviewed in the same issue of *Funny World,* claims he was responsible for the idea of a series of musical cartoons. These were to be not merely illustrated songs, but films in which music and animation were combined to provide a totally new experience. The name Silly Symphonies was selected for the series, and work began on the first of

them, *The Skeleton Dance*. (In the interview, Stalling indicates that the subject was his choice.)

The Skeleton Dance opens as cats, howling in a cemetery, are disturbed at midnight by four skeletons who emerge from their graves. The skeletons go through some fairly elaborate dance sequences and then, at dawn, scurry back to their resting places. The whole thing is set to suitably sepulchral music, a composition of Stalling's which utilized elements from Edvard Grieg's "March of the Dwarfs" (many film historians have erroneously reported that the music used is Camille Saint-Saëns's "Danse Macabre"). Despite the success of the Mickey Mouse shorts, theater owners were a little nervous of the reception that would be accorded this new kind of cartoon entertainment, and so *The Skeleton Dance* and its successors were released under the byline "Mickey Mouse Presents a Walt Disney Silly Symphony."

These first Symphonies were received well enough for the series to continue. Certainly they were very original in concept, but they now seem rather less interesting than the early Mouse shorts. Mickey gave his pictures a central core around which the action could develop. The Symphonies had no such core. Each of them was constructed around a rather generalized theme – *The Merry Dwarfs, Winter,* and *Spring* are typical early titles – which had to be stated before it could be explored; with the techniques available in 1929 and 1930, this was quite a challenge. In a Mouse cartoon, you had only to catch one glimpse of Mickey to know exactly what to expect, and this allowed the animators to take much more for granted.

For the first year or two of their existence, the Symphonies had little real focus. But we must emphasize just how significant it is that Disney instituted them and then persisted with them when it would have been far easier to exploit Mickey for all he was worth. Before long, the Symphonies would have an invaluable role to play in the development of the art of animation. We should lay to rest, too, the idea that the occasional classical music content of these cartoons showed Disney displaying pretensions toward high culture. All the evidence suggests that he saw himself as making motion picture entertainment for the masses. If he persisted with the Silly Symphonies, it was because he wanted to give his animators an opportunity to extend the range of subject matter they were dealing with. He was, as usual, looking to the future.

In 1930, another personnel crisis hit the Studio. Ub Iwerks and Carl Stalling quit the Disney operation.

The loss of Iwerks resulted directly from the fact that Disney's contract with Powers was due for renewal. It would seem that Powers had, at the beginning, thought of these cartoons as little more than a novelty that might help promote his Powers Cinephone system; but Mickey (and *The Skeleton Dance,* too, by dint of a successful run in New York) had proved that there was a real long-term potential for this kind of entertainment. Meanwhile, the Disneys had not been entirely happy in their relationship with Powers. For one thing, they had been unable to

From the very first, the Silly Symphonies touched a wide variety of subjects and moods. Examples illustrated here are, top to bottom, from *The Merry Dwarfs,* 1929; *Winter,* 1930; *The China Plate,* 1931; *Midnight in a Toy Shop,* 1930; and *Pioneer Days,* 1930

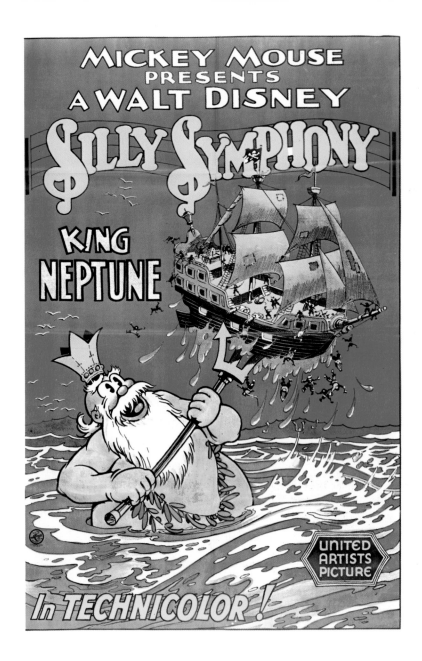

Silly Symphony posters, 1932

get detailed financial reports from him. His method of doing business consisted of sending sums of money from time to time – just enough to keep the Studio operating. Powers must have suspected that the Disneys might be disinclined to renew their contract, so behind their backs, he approached Ub Iwerks and offered him a series of his own. Iwerks accepted the offer. The distributor then confronted the Disneys with the *fait accompli* but promised to tear up the Iwerks contract if they would renegotiate. He made an offer of a guaranteed $2,500 a week, which must have sounded like a great deal of money, but the Disneys refused to sign and instead negotiated a distribution agreement with Columbia Pictures (Harry Cohn made the deal at the suggestion of director Frank Capra, who had been greatly impressed by the originality and vigor of Disney's cartoons). Iwerks found himself out on a limb. We can only guess at the acrimony that must have been stirred up by Powers's maneuverings, but the end result was that Iwerks sold out his partnership to the brothers for $2,920 and then, backed by Powers, set up his own studio. He produced, among other things, a series called Flip the Frog, which

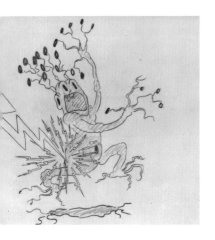

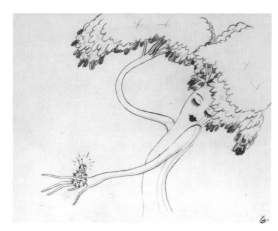

Flowers and Trees, 1932, has a special place in the history of animation as the first cartoon to be made in full color. From this point on, all Silly Symphonies were produced in the Technicolor® process

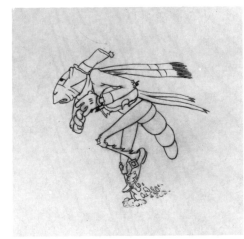

never attained any substantial success. Great as he was as an animator and technical innovator, Iwerks did not possess either the story sense or the business acumen of Walt Disney.

It should be acknowledged, however, that Iwerks had been an enormous asset to the Studio. His work on Mickey alone would have been enough to establish his importance, but he also contributed inventive work to practically all the early Disney cartoons. Not only were his drawings of absolute top quality, he also turned them out at a phenomenal rate – according to at least one source, as many as seven hundred a day. He had also been the resident technical genius, adapting most of the equipment used in the production of the early pictures. Next to Walt Disney himself, Ub Iwerks had been the most important single figure in the development of the Studio. Small wonder that Powers had figured he would not be an easy person to replace (like Charles Mintz before him, Powers was underestimating Disney's own importance).

Some ten years later, Iwerks returned to the Studio and reestablished himself there as a special-effects virtuoso, developing – among other things – the Xerox camera that was used in many Disney animated films and the traveling matte process that lent Mary Poppins some of her magic powers.

Stalling left at about the same time as Iwerks, mainly, it would seem, because he thought that without Iwerks the Studio had little future. He remained in the animation industry, eventually becoming musical director for Warner Brothers' Looney Tunes–Merry Melodies, an assignment that suited his talents perfectly.

Both these losses, then, were serious, but they do not seem to have caused Disney to so much as break his stride. He quickly replaced Stalling with Bert Lewis. Iwerks could not be replaced by any one man, so Disney coped with his loss by building up his stable of animators in two different ways: he brought in a number of apprentices and he imported experienced animators from New York. Certainly the Disney product did not seem to suffer. By the end of 1930, Mickey had become an international celebrity. Known in Italy as Topolino and as Miki Kuchi in Japan, the Mouse continued his adventures, saving Minnie

From 1932 to 1934 the Silly Symphonies evolved a new range of subtleties. Shown here are scenes from *Babes in the Woods, The Grasshopper and the Ants, Father Noah's Ark,* and *The Wise Little Hen*

from immolation by fire and worse, confronting Pete in various exotic situations, and performing to audiences of exuberant animals whose taste in music ranged from ragtime to violin concertos. A simple-minded bloodhound made an appearance in a 1930 picture called *The Chain Gang* and developed, before long, into Mickey's faithful companion Pluto. As Mickey's career unfolded in the thirties, other characters, such as Horace Horsecollar and Clarabelle Cow, began to enjoy the status of co-stars, but their personalities offered relatively little for the animators to work with, and, as the pictures became more sophisticated, their roles became less significant and eventually vanished entirely.

By 1931, Mickey was important enough for *Time* magazine to devote a feature article to him. Another feature, printed in *Motion Picture Daily* (July 20, 1931), tells us that the production staff, including assistants, had grown to more than forty. Several of the animators – Dave Hand, Ben Sharpsteen, Rudy Zamora, Tom Palmer, and Jack King, for instance – had experience in New York studios, as had story men like Ted Sears and Bert Gillett. Other animators – such as Les Clark, Jack Cutting, Dick Lundy, Gilles "Frenchy" de Trémaudan, and Johnny Cannon – had learned their craft with Disney. Emil Flohri, a former newspaper cartoonist and art director, was painting backgrounds, and Frank Churchill had joined Bert Lewis in the music department (both of them, like Stalling, had received their training in theater pit orchestras during the silent era). Floyd Gottfredson was drawing the daily Mickey Mouse comic strip (and continued to do so until the 1970s) while Hazel Sewell, Lillian Disney's sister, headed up the ink and paint department. Wilfred Jackson was directing and contributing to story. Still listed as assistants were Webb Smith, soon to be an important member of the story team; Roy Williams, who later attained fame on television's *Mickey Mouse Club*; and Fred Moore, who would become one of the very best animators of his generation.

The New York animators were employed, to a large extent, in a stop-gap capacity. Their experience was needed by the Studio at that point, but their approach to animation differed somewhat from that which had been established by the Disney artists under Iwerk's tutelage. Les Clark

In 1933, Walt Disney produced *Three Little Pigs* – a cartoon which had an extraordinary impact on the American public. Its hit tune, "Who's Afraid of the Big Bad Wolf?" swept the nation. Many people saw this film as Disney's comment in fable form on the Depression era. Whatever his motives for making it, it did display a marked advance in terms of story-telling and character development

explains that Disney-trained animators usually worked from key pose to key pose – that is to say, they picked out the signal poses in any action, established those first, then filled in the gaps afterward. The New York animators had been trained to animate "straight-ahead" – in other words, they started at point *a* of any action and worked their way through to point *z*. The New York animators were very good at this (Clark recalls his amazement as he watched Zamora animate the flight of a butterfly by the straight-ahead method), but in the long run the key-pose style of animation was much more efficient and flexible. Apart from anything else, it fitted in perfectly with the Disney system of animating to music (key poses being made to correspond with rhythmic accents). Gradually, Disney-trained animators took over, but the experience of the New York imports was not wasted. Dave Hand, Ben Sharpsteen, and Jack King all had important careers ahead of them at the Studio as animation directors.

It is interesting to note that there was, by 1931, a full-fledged story department. This was not like any other story department because everything was worked out in visual terms (all the story men were competent draftsmen). At about this time, or shortly after, the first "storyboards" made their appearance. The storyboard was an important innovation. It is difficult to attribute its invention with any certainty to one person, but Disney himself always credited it to Webb Smith. Until then, stories had been worked out comic-strip fashion in notebooks or on loose sheets of paper (generally there would be three or six drawings to a page, sometimes accompanied by a written description of the action and dialogue notes). Smith, on his own or in collaboration with other people, hit upon the idea of making each of his drawings on a separate sheet of paper and pinning them all, in sequence, to a bulletin board. The story for an entire short could be accommodated on a single board, and thus the director, or anyone else concerned with the production, could see the plot of an entire movie spread out in front of him. If changes had to be made, drawings could be moved or taken down and replaced by others. The ideal system for developing cartoon stories, it quickly came into general use throughout the Studio and eventually throughout the industry. Employed more than ever today, this invaluable tool has been adopted not only by other animation studios but also by producers of live-action films and commercials.

Disney himself must have been delighted by this innovation. The storyboard enabled him to participate even more closely in the development of his cartoons, allowing him to walk into a music room and see at a glance exactly what needed to be done.

Dick Huemer was working for Charles Mintz at this time and he recalls that everyone in the industry figured that Disney must have some trick – a gimmick or secret of some kind – that made his films so superior.

"Whenever we met a guy like Ted Sears or Ben Sharpsteen, we'd say, 'Oh, come on now – what is it that Walt does that we don't do?' and they would simply say something like, 'He analyzes.' Analyzes! So do we – we think! But we didn't and Walt did. He did chew everything over, did prepare beautifully, so the director could just take it and give it to the animator and then look at it and correct it."

By the end of 1931, Disney's demand for constant improvement had driven the cost of a single cartoon to more than $13,000. The Studio was barely breaking even, and in 1932 another innovation drove costs still higher. In that year, Disney released a Silly Symphony called *Flowers and Trees*. This cartoon caused something of a sensation in the industry. It was in full color.

Technicolor® had introduced a two-strip system – it required two strips of film running through the camera – as early as 1929, but it had been used sparingly by the major studios which, with good reason, thought it had little more than novelty value. (Its chief limitation was that the color values were somewhat distorted.) By 1932, however, Technicolor had a three-strip system ready which offered far more accurate color reproduction, and Disney at once saw its advantages. *Flowers and Trees* had been partly made as a black-and-white film. This footage was scrapped and the whole thing was done again in color. It was premiered at Grauman's Chinese Theater in Hollywood along with Irving Thalberg's production of *Strange Interlude*.

By today's standards, *Flowers and Trees* is a strange mixture of charm and absurdity. A romance between two young trees is disrupted by a crabby tree stump who initiates a fire that threatens the whole forest. Birds puncture clouds so that rain falls and douses the fire. The stump is destroyed and the two young lovers are married, with a glowworm for a wedding ring, while neighboring flowers celebrate their nuptials. Whatever weaknesses or strengths this cartoon may have had were overshadowed by the fact that it was in color. Color made it a valuable property and, from that point on, all Silly Symphonies were fully chromatic. Walt Disney made an advantageous deal with Technicolor which gave him exclusive rights to the three-color process, as far as animation was concerned, for the next two years. For the time being, the Mickey Mouse cartoons continued to be in black and white – but the Symphonies took full advantage of the new possibilities. Almost at once they became more inventive. *Flowers and Trees* was followed by *King Neptune* and *Babes in the Woods,* both of which display tighter structure and livelier action than anything previously seen in this series.

One factor which contributed to their inventiveness was the addition to the staff, in 1932, of Albert Hurter. Hurter, a Swiss-born artist, had learned the art of animation at the Barre studio in New York. After spending some time in the Southwest (he was passionately devoted to the desert landscape), he set up a commercial art studio in Los Angeles and then, probably at the instigation of Ted Sears or one of the other New York exiles, joined the Disney staff. From the very beginning of this association Hurter had a special position at the Studio, Disney realizing that his gift was for producing what became known as "inspirational drawings." This is to say that he spent his time developing visual ideas for future projects and improvising on themes which might trigger the

Lullaby Land, 1933, top, presents a child's dream adventures in a landscape metamorphosed from the patchwork quilt that covers his bed. The following year, in *The Goddess of Spring,* center, Disney artists attempted to revive the myth of Pluto and Persephone. *Music Land,* 1935, bottom, offered a twist on the Romeo and Juliet story, in which the son of the King of the Isle of Jazz falls in love with the daughter of the Queen of the Land of Symphony

The layout drawing, opposite top, for *Old King Cole,* 1933, gives some idea of the detail that went into every scene of a Silly Symphony. Another layout drawing, opposite bottom, this one for *The Wise Little Hen,* 1934, illustrates the scene in which Donald Duck made his debut. He is discovered dancing a hornpipe on the deck of a somewhat decrepit barge, right

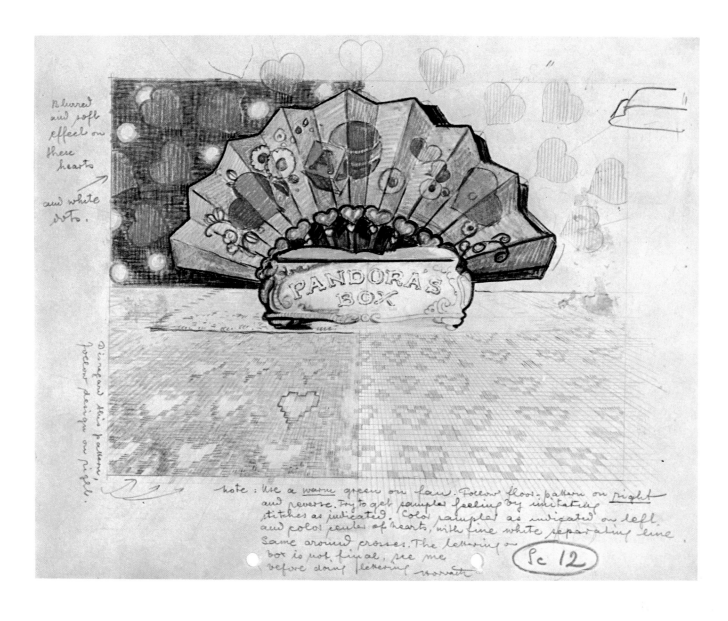

Blurred and soft effect on these hearts and white dots.

Diagonal this pattern, follow design on right.

note: Use a warm green on fan. Follow floor pattern on right and reverse. Try to get sampler feeling by imitating stitches as indicated. Color sampler as indicated on left and color center of hearts, with fine white separating line. Same around crosses. The lettering on box is not final, see me before doing lettering. *Horvath*

Pc 12

7 7/8"

DONALD DUCK

134   9

imaginations of story men or animators. Neptune's court in *King Neptune* and the gingerbread house in *Babes in the Woods* both reflect his influence. He had been trained in Europe and his drawings were imbued with the spirit of the gothic fairy tale. This added another dimension to the native American vigor of the Disney product. As the Studio continued to evolve toward more ambitious projects, Hurter's influence was felt more and more strongly.

In 1933, Hurter designed the settings and main characters for what turned out to be the greatest Disney success up to that time – the famous *Three Little Pigs*. It is hardly necessary to recapitulate here either the plot or the success of Frank Churchill's hit tune, "Who's Afraid of the Big Bad Wolf?" The movie was a smash. Theaters retained it week after week, and its impact reflects the fact that it went far beyond any of the earlier Symphonies in terms of plot and character development. The story line is so strong that social commentators have seen it as an archetypal parable about the Great Depression. (Disney insisted that it was intended as entertainment and nothing more, but the film had such a mythic ring to it that it invited interpretations of this sort.) The animation was excellent and the characters had a real existence of their own – something which, to that date, had been achieved only with Mickey and Minnie. Just one thing marred the movie. In one section, the Big Bad Wolf approached the brick home of the Practical Pig in the guise of a caricatured Jewish peddler. Humor at the expense of ethnic stereotypes was not uncommon in Hollywood at the time, but this gag represented a serious lapse in taste even by the elastic standards of the period. Later, when *Three Little Pigs* was rereleased, this section of the movie was revamped to eliminate the offensive element.

The following year, 1934, saw the production of several excellent Silly Symphonies, including *The Tortoise and the Hare*, *The Grasshopper and the Ants*, and *The Wise Little Hen* – all of which were moral fables and showed just how proficient the Studio had become at structuring a story and establishing character. *The Tortoise and the Hare* put Aesop into modern dress as the rakish hare loses his race to the tortoise against a milky landscape that is typical of these early color cartoons. This milkiness – at times it resembles smog – resulted from the fact that Emil Flohri mixed a great deal of white pigment with his paint and water. In *The Grasshopper and the Ants*, the grasshopper is a particularly well-established character (his theme song is "The World Owes Me a Living") keyed to the voice talent of Pinto Colvig. Colvig – a former circus clown – was a musician and a member of the gag team, but his greatest claim to fame is that he provided the voice of Goofy, who had had his first supporting role in a 1932 cartoon, *Mickey's Revue*.

The Wise Little Hen introduced another voice talent and a new character who, within a year, was to challenge Mickey as Disney's star attraction. This character was Donald Duck, and the man who provided him with a voice was Clarence "Ducky" Nash. Until Disney discovered him, Nash had worked for a milk company, entertaining children with his animal

A general view of the Hyperion Avenue studio, c. 1933

A group photograph taken at the Studio in the mid-thirties, about the time that staff expansion was picking up momentum

Walt looks on as Mary Moder, Pinto Colvig, and Dorothy Compton rehearse "Who's Afraid of the Big Bad Wolf?" Composer Frank Churchill is at the piano

A promotional vehicle and theater marquees advertising Mickey Mouse

imitations. One of these imitations evolved into Donald's ill-tempered quack and made his voice known all over the world.

Donald Duck had a relatively modest role in his first screen appearance, making his debut as a dyspeptic creature, living on a ramshackle houseboat, who feigned a bellyache every time the Wise Little Hen asked him for assistance. (In this first incarnation he was drawn by Art Babbitt and Dick Huemer, who had finally joined the Disney animation staff.) Donald's bill was a little longer than it is today, but he had the same voice, the same sailor suit, and the same irascible temperament. He quickly made the jump to costarring roles in Mickey Mouse pictures such as *Orphan's Benefit,* irritating everyone on the screen but endearing himself to the audiences. Many animators found the Duck difficult to work with, but two in particular – Dick Lundy and Fred Spencer – had a way with him, and they must be given much of the credit for developing him into a star.

We might remark at this point that the idea of animators being "cast" for certain characters was becoming quite common. Animators tend to think of themselves as actors who "perform" with their pencils, and, given this concept, it was only natural that some animators should have a better touch with certain roles and certain types of business than with others. Just as Ub Iwerks had given Mickey his initial impetus, so Donald found benefactors in Spencer and Lundy, and Pluto and Goofy began to develop as major characters largely because certain artists had strong feelings about them and the way they should behave. Pluto owed much of his evolving importance to Norm Ferguson. For a 1934 cartoon, *Playful Pluto,* Webb Smith devised a sequence in which Pluto becomes entangled with a sticky ribbon of flypaper. Ferguson took this sequence and turned it into a classic of comic animation. The man who had a real feeling for Goofy was Art Babbitt. Babbitt knew how to make the most out of any situation that the Goof might find himself in, and this led to more and better situations being invented for him. In this way the Goof developed from a bit player with a funny voice into the full-fledged idiot star of the mid-thirties.

Mickey, meanwhile, had become a national symbol, and as such he was expected to behave properly at all times. If he occasionally stepped out of line, any number of letters would arrive at the Studio from citizens and organizations who felt that the nation's moral well-being was in their

Lillian and Walt Disney at home with their pet chow

Walt and Mickey pose with Will Hays

hands. It was becoming harder and harder to find comic situations for Mickey that would not give offense in some quarter. Eventually, he would be pressured into the role of straight man, but the gradual change had not yet eroded the core of his personality, and the Mouse cartoons of the mid-thirties were consistently inventive while becoming increasingly sophisticated. The strides made by the Disney Studio between 1928 and 1934 were quite extraordinary. The story department came up with better and more fully developed ideas and the animators implemented them with increased skill. They had learned that for a character to seem real he had to have real weight – had to be seen to obey the laws of gravity (or to deliberately defy them if that was what the situation called for). This was not an easy thing to achieve. To take a single example, to make Goofy appear to have real weight, an animator like Art Babbitt had to understand exactly how gravity would affect the character's singular walk – part lope, part shuffle.

In Mickey's early days, he had expressed his reactions in terms of elaborate "takes" – throwing his whole body into a response so that there

Lunch at the Paramount commissary, 1934. Disney is seated with veteran animator Walter Lantz. Standing are Gary Cooper, left, and Walter Winchell

Disney's growing success abroad can be gauged from this French comic and this Bulgarian poster for a film presentation at the Royal Theater in Sofia

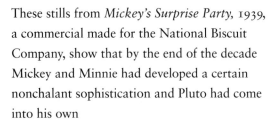

These stills from *Mickey's Surprise Party*, 1939, a commercial made for the National Biscuit Company, show that by the end of the decade Mickey and Minnie had developed a certain nonchalant sophistication and Pluto had come into his own

For *Playful Pluto*, 1934, Webb Smith devised and Norm Ferguson animated a scene in which Pluto becomes entangled with a strip of flypaper. A classic of its sort, this sequence demonstrates how Disney artists could take a simple situation and build on it in such a way that the humor arose directly from the personality of the character

Poster, 1933

JOSEPH M. SCHENCK
PRESENTS
WALT DISNEY'S
MICKEY MOUSE
"MICKEY'S PAL PLUTO"
PLUTO
PLUTO
UNITED ARTISTS PICTURE

In *Orphan's Benefit*, 1934, Donald Duck came into his own. His efforts to entertain a group of children are frustrated by the malicious behavior of the audience, which causes him to dissolve into helpless rage

could be no doubt about the fact that he was surprised, angry, happy, or whatever. By the mid-thirties, Disney artists had learned how to convey a shift in mood by a subtle change of expression on a character's face or by an almost imperceptible alteration of physical attitude. And as the Disney team perfected its skills it continued to expand, drawing to itself talented young men who were attracted by the spectacular advances that had already been made.

One nonaesthetic factor made the Disney Studio especially attractive to young artists in the 1930s. The Great Depression was at its height, and there were not too many markets they could turn to. Ward Kimball's story is typical:

"I was going to art school in Santa Barbara and I thought I wanted to be a magazine illustrator. . . . This was the Depression and you had to make a little bread anywhere you could find it, so on Saturday mornings I would pick up four or five dollars at the local Safeway store. I'd have to get there by 5 A.M., rain or shine – or rather fog – and hack lettuce. . . . After I thawed out my fingers, I'd go back and paint showcards. . . . When I was through with this, about 9:30, I'd go across the street and up a block to the Fox Arlington Theater which, every Saturday morning, featured the original Mickey Mouse Club. . . . I was paid three dollars to rehearse and lead about ten kids who played instruments and did a short band march number at the beginning of the program. . . .

"About this time, I saw my first Disney color cartoon – *Father Noah's Ark,* a Silly Symphony – and I was amazed at the movement and the artwork. Rarely did you see a Technicolor live-action picture – maybe John McCormack singing partly in color – but here was this full-color *Father Noah's Ark.* Wow! I began to see that this was no ordinary, run-of-the-mill cartoon stuff. The Disney gags were funnier and there seemed to be one every few seconds. . . . The Disney cartoons had a realism that no others had – the giraffes ran like giraffes and the chipmunks and squirrels scampered like chipmunks and squirrels. Not only that, the faster animals caught and passed the slower ones – which I had never seen done before.

"Then along came *Three Little Pigs* with its hit tune which was played over and over on the radio. . . . Many of the other studios were reaching into their bag of old silents and rereleasing them with new sound tracks by people like Jelly Roll Morton and Fats Waller, to which they would add a few ratchets and honks and slide whistles – and that was supposed to be a sound cartoon – but Disney cartoons made a real honest attempt to integrate sound and picture.

"In 1934, when I'd been going to art school for two years and money was real tight, one of the instructors at school said, 'Kimball, you make a lot of funny drawings and it seems to me you ought to work for a man like Disney.'

"Well, to drive all the way to Los Angeles during the Depression was tough – gas was twelve cents a gallon. So my mother says, 'Okay – I'll take you into Los Angeles and bring you back just this once.' So I loaded my portfolio with paints and sketches. Well, nobody had ever come to

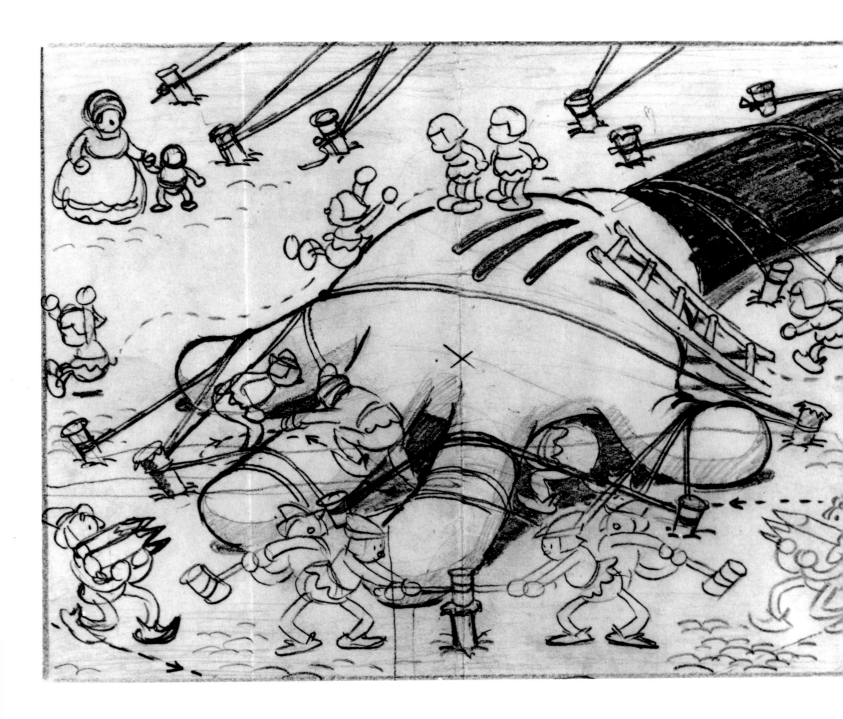

Gulliver Mickey, 1934, is one of several
cartoons that make Mickey the hero of a
children's classic

In this layout drawing for *Gulliver Mickey,*
Mickey's dream self takes leave of his sleeping body

Scene 3.   OHUH HELLO ROBIN ... YA' FASCINATE ME!

Who Killed Cock Robin?, a Silly Symphony of 1935, gives the old nursery rhyme a new twist. Robin, below, it turns out, is not dead, but has merely been wounded by Cupid's arrow. The triumph of the cartoon is Jenny Wren, left, the object of Robin's passion, who is a thinly disguised caricature of Mae West. Even Walt Disney seems to have been satisfied with this polished and sophisticated little production, and it is said to have influenced him to go ahead with *Snow White and the Seven Dwarfs*

SCENE 2.

The Cookie Carnival, a Silly Symphony of 1935, is a bizarre little masterpiece full of humorous invention. As the title suggests, it concerns a holiday in Cookie Land, the high point of which is the election of a queen. In this variation of the Cinderella story, the prince is a poor hobo, right, and the heroine a heart-broken cookie who has been left out of the parade because she does not have a suitable costume. The action proceeds in a rapid-fire sequence of hilarious visual puns, and the witty, baroque imagery probably owes a great deal to the imagination of Albert Hurter

Broken Toys, another Silly Symphony of 1935, has W. C. Fields and other Hollywood characters appear in the guise of discarded dolls. The main plot involves a sailor doll who performs an emergency operation to restore the sight of a dainty little creature who has lost her eyes

(SUPER·SPEED ACTION →)

Mickey's Service Station, 1935, was the last
Mickey Mouse cartoon to be made in black
and white. Pegleg Pete, the perennial villain,
brings his car in for a checkup because he
has been hearing a squeak. Mickey, Donald,
and Goofy rip the car apart looking for the
source of the offending noise. It turns out
to be a cricket which has concealed itself in
the vehicle, but our heroes do not discover
this until the car is a wreck.

A typical enough plot, it affords all the
main characters ample opportunity to display
their usual foibles. Mickey is doggedly persistent in an ineffectual sort of way, Goofy is
characteristically incompetent, and Donald's
propensity for rage is tempered only by his
latent cowardice

Generally recognized as one of the classics of Disney animation, *The Band Concert*, 1935, was the first Mickey Mouse cartoon to be made in Technicolor. Mickey is discovered in the park of a small Midwestern town, directing an orchestra through a program of popular classics. He embarks on a spirited version of *The William Tell Overture,* but events conspire to disrupt the performance. Most troublesome is Donald Duck, in the guise of a street vendor, who again and again leads the orchestra astray by playing "Turkey in the Straw" on an unending succession of fifes which are concealed about his person.

As the orchestra approaches the storm section of the overture, a more serious problem arises. A tornado, which seems to have been conjured up by the music, approaches the town. The twister picks up the entire orchestra – along with Donald, a farm house, and assorted vegetation – sending everyone and everything spinning in the air. Mickey holds the performance together by sheer willpower, and the piece comes to a rousing finale, with musicians hanging from trees and anything else that has been left standing.

It is interesting that the disruptive Duck plays Mickey's theme from *Steamboat Willie,* suggesting that Donald has taken over the role of mischief-maker from the Mouse

In the early thirties, Mickey and the other Disney characters were already being adapted for use in all kinds of merchandising operations. Dozens of companies manufactured items under license from the Studio. At least two were saved from bankruptcy by their Disney franchises

Disney's with a portfolio of his work before. So I come in and here I am, just turned twenty, and I come to the front office on Hyperion Avenue and ask for a job."

Kimball began work as a Disney apprentice on April 2, 1934. Within five years he would become one of the Studio's top animators.

The expansion of the Studio can be illustrated in another way. In 1929 and 1930, additions were made to the front, rear, and one side of the original structure on Hyperion Avenue. In 1931, a two-story animation building was erected. In four years, the Studio grew from 1,600 square feet of floor space to 20,000 square feet.

Mickey Mouse and Mary Pickford

3 Hyperion Days

On January 12, 1936, the *New York Times* published an interview head-lined "H. G. Wells in Close Up." The author of *The Invisible Man* had a few comments to make about the film industry. "Many do not realize that all Hollywood studios are so busy that they keep very much to them-selves. Consequently, Chaplin never visited the Disney studios. Imagine, Charlie and Walt Disney, those two geniuses, never met! I took Charlie there. Disney has the most marvelous machinery and does the most inter-esting experiments. Like Chaplin he is a good psychologist and both do the only thing in film today that remains international."

Four days after the *Times* story, on January 16, René Clair was reported by the *New York Journal* as saying that the outstanding figures in the movies at that time were Charlie Chaplin and Walt Disney. "The reason is," he explained, "that they have no outside interference. They act as their own producer, director, and even attend to their own stories and musical scores. Their artistry is sublime."

Two months later, on March 13, the *Tulsa Tribune* quoted Thornton Wilder as telling a lecture audience, "The two presiding geniuses of the movies are Walt Disney and Charlie Chaplin." Ten days after that, Mary Pickford told a reporter for the *Boston Post,* "There is only one Walt Disney. . . . He is the greatest producer the industry has ever turned out."

On May 25, the *New York Journal* carried some outspoken opinions expressed by the composer Jerome Kern. "Cartoonist Walt Disney," said

Kern, "has made the 20th century's only important contribution to music. Disney has made use of music as language. In the synchronization of humorous episodes with humorous music, he has unquestionably given us the outstanding contribution of our time. In fact I would go so far as to say it is the only real contribution."

Harper's Bazaar, dated November 1 of that same year, printed an article titled "Boom Shot of Hollywood," by Janet Flanner, Paris correspondent for the *New Yorker*. "Certainly the sanest spot in Hollywood," she observed, "is that studio exclusively devoted to the creation of delicate deliriums and lovely lunacies – the fun factory of Mickey Mouse, Miss Minnie and Mr. Walt Disney, Incorporated. Visitors are rarely admitted. Withdrawn to a safe distance from the rest of the movie maelstrom, the Disney plant is remotely located in one of those endless suburban settings of Barcelona bungalows, pink roses and red filling stations that makes southern California so picturesque. The studio looks like a small municipal kindergarten with green grass for the children to keep off of and, on the roof, a gigantic glorious figure of Mickey to show them the best way. . . . With hysteria the seeming law for movie making, it's a wonder Mickey and Silly Symphonies succeed in this world at all, since the place where they're made is as sensible as a post office. Law and order reign there, without seeming unattractive, side by side with Minnie, Madam Clara Cluck, Donald Duck and Elmer the Elephant who, all Rabelaisian in spots but solidly moral at heart, are doubtless easier to get along with than the other big stars in the movie game."

Disney, then, did not lack for influential admirers, and the list could easily be extended. Arturo Toscanini, for example, saw *The Band*

Concert six times and invited its producer to visit Italy. Sergey Eisenstein, the greatest of Soviet directors, pronounced Mickey Mouse America's most original contribution to culture.

Mickey, though still a star, was rapidly becoming a symbol, representing some concept of comedy that was to all appearances universal. In 1934 Harold Butcher, New York correspondent for the *London Daily Herald*, had written, "After a quick trip around the world . . . I have returned to New York to say that Mickey Mouse has been with me most of the way. On the Pacific, in Japan and China, at Manchouli – suspended precariously between Siberia and Manchukuo . . ."

From England, in 1935, came the report that the Queen and the Duchess of York had selected Mickey Mouse chinaware as gifts for six hundred children. That same year, Mickey Mouse cartoons were used to test RCA's television system and the League of Nations voted its approval of Mickey.

The Disney merchandising operation was by now a multimillion-dollar enterprise. The *American Exporter* informed its readers that, "beside the 80 licensees in the U.S. who are manufacturing merchandise bearing the likeness of Mickey Mouse or some other of the Walt Disney characters, there are 15 in Canada, 40 in England, 80 on the European continent and 15 in Australia. Kay Kamen, Inc., representing Walt Disney Enterprises, has branch offices in Toronto, London, Paris, Copenhagen, Milan, Barcelona, Lisbon, and Sydney.

"U.S. exporting manufacturers who are now exporting merchandise under Walt Disney license include Hickok belts, Lionel electric toys, Ingersoll watches, Dennison paper goods, Seiberling latex rubber dolls and Oak toy balloons.

"England is making a Mickey Mouse marmalade. Other products include cutlery, soap, playing cards, candy, bridge favors, wristwatches, toothbrushes, socks, shoes, garters, slippers, umbrellas, hot water bottles, lamps and sheets."

The same publication estimated that exports of Disney-licensed products would exceed $5,000,000 for 1935. The *New York Telegraph* reported that total sales were up to $35,000,000 a year. Cartier offered a diamond bracelet bearing the likeness of Mickey for a mere $1,150. More significantly, both Lionel trains and Ingersoll watches were virtually saved from bankruptcy by their Disney franchises (two million Mickey Mouse watches were sold in a single eight-week period).

Donald was by now seriously challenging Mickey's preeminence, and when the Studio announced his first birthday, the *New York Times* devoted a serious editorial to the growing popularity of the irascible duck, wondering if he might not replace Mickey in the affections of the public. Dozens of other papers echoed the question.

As for Disney himself, he was learning to field the questions that come with fame. Always he was suitably modest. "I do not draw, write music or contribute most of the gags and ideas seen in our pictures today," he told the *Times*. "My work is largely to supervise, to select and shape material, to coordinate and direct the efforts of our staff."

Disney with Stan Laurel and Oliver Hardy

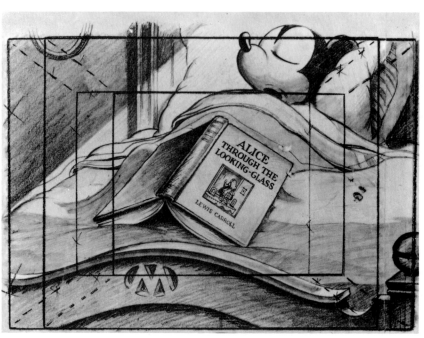

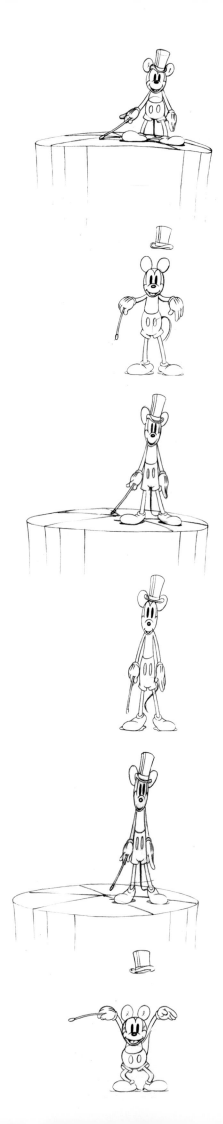

Thru the Mirror, 1936, is a witty improvisation on one of the Lewis Carroll themes that had fascinated Disney since the time of the Alice Comedies. Right: Dick Lundy's animation drawings for a sequence in which Mickey impersonates Fred Astaire clearly show how flexible Mickey's body had become

Moving Day, 1936, provides Goofy with some of his finest moments, pitting him against a piano with a mind of its own. This sequence, animated by Art Babbitt, is a sustained and inspired piece of nonsense. Comedy is distilled from the situation with a close regard for character that would have been unthinkable even two or three years earlier

Another reporter asked Disney how it felt to be a celebrity. "It feels fine," he replied, "when being a celebrity helps get a choice reservation for a football game. . . . As far as I can remember, being a celebrity has never helped me make a good picture, or a good shot in a polo game, or command the obedience of my daughter, or impress my wife. It doesn't even seem to help keep fleas off our dogs and, if being a celebrity won't give one an advantage over a couple of fleas, then I guess there can't be that much in being a celebrity after all."

So much for Disney the public figure, but what of Disney the man? How did his colleagues see him?

Jack Cutting recalls that Disney seemed mature beyond his years and, at times, very serious. "I always felt his personality was a little bit like a drop of mercury rolling around on a slab of marble because he changed moods so quickly. I believe this was because he was extremely sensitive. . . . He could grasp your ideas and interpret your thought rapidly. You didn't have to give Walt a five-page memo – he understood the point right away. . . .

"Although Walt could exude great charm if he was in the mood, he could also be dour and indifferent toward people – but this was usually

Moving Day also presents Mickey with a
number of problems, including a struggle with
a trunk that will not stay closed

Moose Hunters, 1937, presents Mickey,
Donald, and Goofy in a series of typically
disastrous confrontations with wildlife

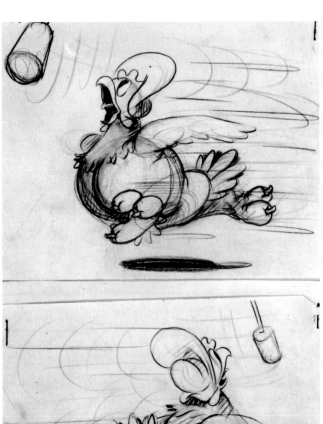

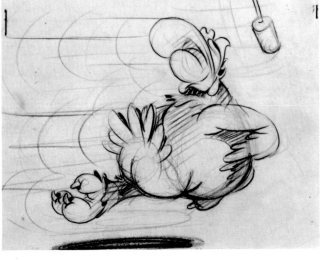

Mickey's Amateurs, 1937, offers a blend of entertainment and near catastrophe

Pluto co-starred in such movies as *The Beach Picnic* and *Society Dog Show,* both released in 1939. The top drawing is by Fred Moore

Above: *Mickey's Circus,* 1936, presented Mickey in a role that was a natural for him – the ringmaster. Right: a Fred Moore study for *Brave Little Tailor,* 1938. Bottom: a scene from *A Gentleman's Gentleman,* 1941. For a brief period during the early forties, Mickey was given ears that worked in perspective

because he was preoccupied by problems. Sometimes you would pass him in the hall, say hello, and he would not even notice you. The next time he might greet you warmly and start talking about a new project he was excited about. You might not understand what he was talking about at first, because he didn't always give you a preamble on the subject. If you didn't pick up on his chain of thought quickly, he would sometimes look at you as though you were slow-witted, because when he was excited about an idea it was clear to him and he assumed it was to everyone else.

"The people who worked best with Walt were those who were stimulated by his enthusiasm. . . . More than once, when he was in a creative mood and ideas were popping out like skyrockets, I have suddenly seen him look as if he had been hit in the face with a bucket of cold water. The eyebrow would go up and suddenly reality was the mood in the room. Someone in the group was out of tune with the creative spirit he was generating. Then he would say it was difficult to work with so-and-so."

These creative moods were often exercised at the "sweatbox" sessions which were so essential a part of the Studio routine (the projection rooms at Hyperion Avenue were not air-conditioned – hence the name sweatbox). As soon as a sequence was animated and shot as a pencil test, it would be run in one of these projection rooms. Disney would be in attendance along with animators, story men, the director, and anyone else concerned. (Sometimes people from outside the production team would be invited in to give a layman's opinion.) The sequence under consideration would be subjected to an intense analysis in an effort to see if it could be improved in any way before it was sent off to the inking and painting department. Sometimes, instead of pencil tests, it would be a "Leica reel" that was under consideration. The Leica reel (another Disney innovation) provided a way of projecting story continuity drawings in synchronization with whatever part of the sound track had been prerecorded, thus giving at least a rough idea of how the final movie might look and sound. In any case, Disney would always lead these discussions and generally had valuable contributions to make.

"He always had the answers," says Dick Huemer. "He would go right to the middle of the problem and there would be this nugget that he'd pull out. Damnedest thing! You'd kick yourself and say, 'Why didn't I see it? There it is!' But he had an instinct for it, and I think the instinct was based on the fact that he always considered the common man's viewpoint. . . . Aside from his genius, he was just a down-to-earth guy."

Marc Davis is one of the many Disney artists who has emphasized his employer's readiness to gamble everything on an idea as one of the key factors in the growth of the Studio. "He was not afraid to risk every penny, go into hock, hire 150 people and wonder how he was going to meet the payroll. He did this all his life. He felt money is good only because of what you can do with it. Without him, I can't see animation having become much of a business because, for the most part, the other studios were either followers or they were just filling up programs. Almost anything they did that was half-way good was acceptable. But Walt was trying to make a little jewel out of each one of these things."

Studying penguins as an aid to animation: standing, left to right, Walt Disney, Albert Hurter, Leigh Harline, Frenchy de Trémaudan, Clyde Geronimi, Paul Hopkins (behind Geronimi), Hugh Hennesy, Art Babbitt, Norm Ferguson, and Bill Roberts. Seated, Dick Huemer and Wilfred Jackson

Frank Churchill conducts a recording session. Disney and Wilfred Jackson are seated at the extreme left. The clarinetist to Churchill's left is Pinto Colvig

Ted Sears

Disney listens as three members of his story team display their versatility: Webb Smith, piano; Ted Sears, violin; and Pinto Colvig

Jim Macdonald and Ed Forrest record sound effects

Of course, if you were a young and inexperienced animator you were not privy to the vital sweatbox conferences. "Word would dribble down to you," Frank Thomas remembers, "that someone had decided to do such-and-such to your scene. Milt Kahl and I once wrote a song – 'If I Should Die, Please Bury Me in Sweatbox Four' – because that's where all the big meetings were held and then we could find out what was going on."

Young artists joining the Studio usually started by learning to do in-between drawings. Ward Kimball remembers that the Studio was still a small place in those days. "The in-betweening department was down in the semibasement. . . . We called it the bullpen and in the summer you had to strip to the waist, it was so damn hot. . . . By five o'clock I was always exhausted. . . . I would get on a Big Red streetcar and, on those hot summer evenings, I sometimes would fall asleep leaning on the window and watching the loose screws twist in and out of the wooden window frames."

It was not every night, however, that an in-betweener could leave work at five o'clock. Apart from the overtime – which seems to have been plentiful – there were also art classes, which had become an integral part of the Studio schedule. As far back as 1931, Disney had decided that his artists would benefit from further training, and he arranged for some of them to take an evening class at the Chouinard Art School (Les Clark recalls that, since not all of them had cars, Disney himself would often drive them to school). The class these Disney artists attended was taught by a young man named Don Graham, who was soon to have an important role in the Disney organization. Graham remembers that for most of

Above: a pastel drawing for *Water Babies*, 1935. Opposite, top: a scene from *Cock of the Walk*, 1935, a Silly Symphony which includes clever parodies of Hollywood dance routines. Opposite, bottom: a story continuity sketch for *Toby Tortoise Returns*, the 1936 sequel to *The Tortoise and the Hare*

the 1931–32 school year he worked one night a week with a group of about fifteen Disney artists in his regular class.

"Walt, of course, picked up the tab. In the fall of 1932, Art Babbitt, one of the top animators at the Studio, convinced Walt that instead of sending his men across town to Chouinard, it would be far wiser to conduct classes at the Studio, where there could be more control of attendance.

"On November 15, 1932, the great Disney Art School was born in the old sound studio at Hyperion. First it was just two evenings a week, with some twenty or thirty men each evening. In a matter of three or four weeks, it became necessary to divide these classes. Phil Dike was called in and between us we worked these two evenings a week until 1934. During this period James Patrick, a talented young artist, was also employed for a few months as a teacher. The attendance during these two years averaged better than fifty men a session. . . .

"In 1934, the nature of the school changed its character completely. Dike was put in charge of the color coordination of all production work which went through Technicolor. . . . I was employed on a three-day and two-night basis. During the first year of this period I was trained in the sweatboxes under the direct critical eye of Walt and the directors. The evening school was put on a five-evenings-a-week schedule. Eugene Fleury and Palmer Schoppe filled in the evening schedule with me. A new training department was instituted in the daytime. . . .

"At about this time, Walt announced his intention of making *Snow White*, which implied a vast expansion of the animation department. Early in 1935, he came to me and said, 'I need three hundred artists – get

Above left: several Disney shorts exploited caricature, but Will Rogers had to be taken out of *Mickey's Polo Game*, 1936, after his death in a plane crash. Above right and opposite: *Mother Goose Goes Hollywood*, 1938, includes portraits of Groucho Marx, Katharine Hepburn, Laurel and Hardy, and W. C. Fields

them.' And thus began a huge campaign of recruitment. Ads in all the newspapers up and down the West Coast, then on a national basis, and even opening up an office in the RCA building in New York City, where I spent three months looking at portfolios. . . .

"When the new training department was instituted, in 1934–35, the new employees were brought into the Studio in small groups, usually a dozen or so at a time. They were given from six to eight weeks to demonstrate their potential. . . . Usually I would work with them the first two weeks, every day, eight hours a day, utilizing a human model. Then their day would be devoted a half day to drawing, a half day to production problems. They were also encouraged to attend the evening school, which soon became extremely active, with a nightly attendance of about 150. Under George Drake's supervision, many authorities on various aspects of animation, drawing of characters, layout and background problems, et cetera, were called in to lecture and instruct."

Typical of the kind of instructional material used was a book assembled by Ted Sears and Fred Moore. This contained model sheets, indicating how the main characters should be drawn, photographs of humans and animals in action poses, and detailed analyses of the personalities of Mickey, Donald, Goofy, and Pluto. The following, written by Sears, is a typical example:

"Mickey is not a clown . . . he is neither silly nor dumb.

"His comedy depends entirely upon the situation he is placed in.

"His age varies with the situation . . . sometimes his character is that of a young boy, and at other times, as in the adventure type of picture, he appears quite grown up. . . .

A title card for the 1935 cartoon *On Ice*, top, and a background painting for *Mickey's Fire Brigade*, also released that year

Many fine artists – Charles Philippi, Hugh Hennesy, Tom Codrick, and others – made layout drawings for Disney during the thirties. Their work often displays a high standard of draftsmanship, as in these examples from *Thru the Mirror,* 1936

Mickey, Donald, and Goofy worked against
these spectacular backgrounds in a 1937 short,
Clock Cleaners

Pan shots – takes in which the camera moves across a panoramic background – necessitated elongated paintings like this one for *Three Blind Mouseketeers*, 1936

Background paintings for *Modern Inventions,*
above and opposite top, and for two other
1937 cartoons, *Pluto's Quinpuplets* and *Don
Donald,* the latter of which was Donald's
first solo vehicle

"Mickey is most amusing when in a serious predicament trying to accomplish some purpose under difficulties, or against time. . . . When Mickey is working under difficulties, the laughs occur at the climax of each small incident or action. They depend largely upon Mickey's expression, position, attitude, state of mind, etc., and the graphic way that these things are shown. . . .

"Mickey is seldom funny in a chase picture, as his character and expressions are usually lost."

Before giving hints on how to draw the Mouse, Fred Moore added his own thoughts on Mickey's personality:

"Mickey seems to be the average young boy of no particular age; living in a small town, clean living, fun loving, bashful around girls, polite and clever as he must be for the particular story. In some pictures he has a touch of Fred Astaire, in others of Charlie Chaplin, and some of Douglas Fairbanks, but in all of these there should be some of the young boy."

Moore's drawing hints include the following suggestions:

"The body to be drawn as somewhat pear-shaped, fairly short and plump. . . . The body should be pliable at all times. . . . If Mickey were taking a deep breath we would give him a chest. If he were sad, we would loosen chest and droop shoulders, etc. The body should be thought of as having a certain volume, so when it is stretched it should grow thinner. . . .

"The shoes are fairly large and bulky – a medium between hard and soft – flexible enough to help animation, but stiff enough to be shoes. . . . Mickey is cuter when drawn with small shoulders, with a suggestion of stomach and fanny – and I like him pigeon-toed."

Moore also added some suggestions to be kept in mind by the apprentice when drawing Minnie:

"Minnie seems cuter with her skirts high on her body – showing a large expanse of her lace panties. This skirt should be starched and not hang loose. . . . Her mouth could be smaller than Mickey's and maybe never open into so wide a smile, take, expression, etc. Her eyelids and eyelashes could help very much in keeping her feminine as well as the skirt swaying from the body on different poses, displaying pants. Carrying the little finger in an extended position also helps."

Clearly, these hints are rather elementary and were intended mainly for the recruits being processed by Don Graham's training program. The fact that so much critical attention was being lavished on these apprentices did not mean, however, that the senior animators were being ignored. Their work was always subject to the appraisal of Walt Disney himself. He had, sometime earlier, instituted the practice of issuing credit ratings on many of the cartoons. These would be sent to the director and to each of the animators. Individual scenes would be rated "A," "B Plus," and so on, and these ratings would be accompanied by extensive comments in which Disney indicated where and how he thought each sequence could have been improved.

In December 1935, ratings were issued for a Silly Symphony titled *Cock o' the Walk*. This film was directed by Ben Sharpsteen, to whom Disney addressed the following remarks:

Backgrounds for some 1938 shorts: *Polar Trappers,* above and opposite top, *Boat Builders,* far right center and bottom, and *Ferdinand the Bull*

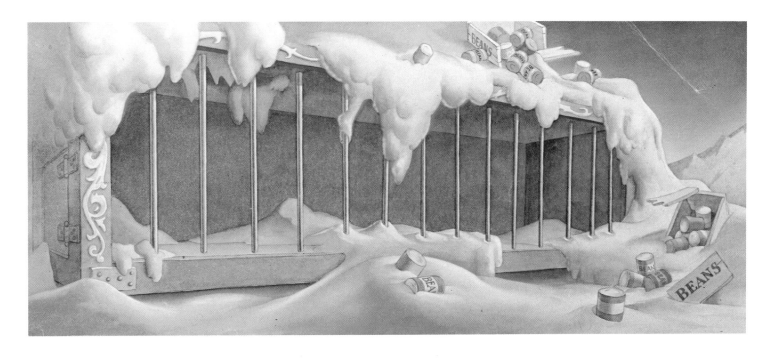

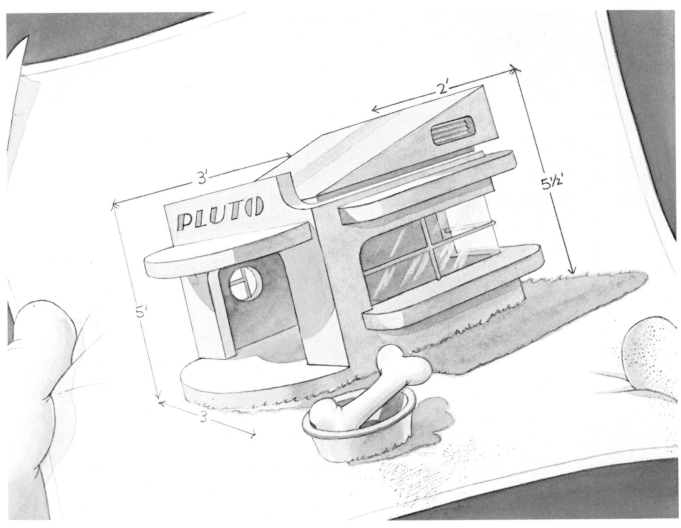

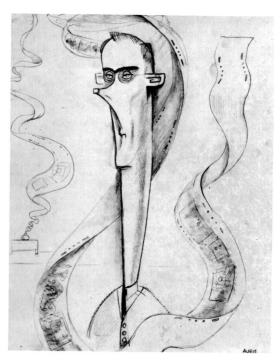

Walt Kelly, of *Pogo* fame, was a Disney artist for several years. In the drawing above he portrays, left to right, an invented character, himself, Ward Kimball, and Fred Moore. Caricature was practically a way of life at the Studio. Center is T. Hee's version of Norm Ferguson. Right is Aurie Battaglia's caricature of layout artist Ken O'Connor

Paintings for a 1939 release, *Donald's Lucky Day,* and for *Pluto's Dream House,* 1940

"The direction is fine from a technical standpoint. Some of the technical scenes and setups were well planned but the direction of the action is very poor from a personality and interest-building angle. The main fault with the story lies with the director and the story men. Without a doubt the animators would have gotten a better result if the story had been properly worked out and if the director had taken the story and treated it from a fantastic comical angle . . . instead of having so many scenes that paralleled human actions."

The following are extracts from some of the comments aimed at animators who worked on this film:

"The actions, as they were given by the director, have been carried out, but the true spirit of the character of the hens is lacking. Instead of waddling, they run. There are certain things which, if handled properly, would have made the action typical of a humanized hen and would have expressed more personality and interest to the audience. . . .

"I would suggest that you concentrate more on caricature, with action; not merely the drawing of a character to look like something, but giving your character the movements and actions of the person you are trying to put over. Remember, every action should be based on what the character represents. . . .

"Something was started in this scene which is what we are striving for. This is doing things in the dance which humans are unable to do. I mean the pullet on the rooster's muscles and the juggling from side to

Donald's Nephews, 1938, introduced the indefatigable Huey, Dewey, and Louie

By the late thirties, Donald had all but eclipsed Mickey in popularity. Examples here are from two 1938 shorts, *Donald's Golf Game,* top, and *The Fox Hunt,* center. At bottom is one from the following year, *Donald's Cousin Gus*

After a cartoon was completed, story continuity drawings were stapled into books – often with surprising results. This group from *Fire Chief,* 1940, gives a marvelous sense of movement

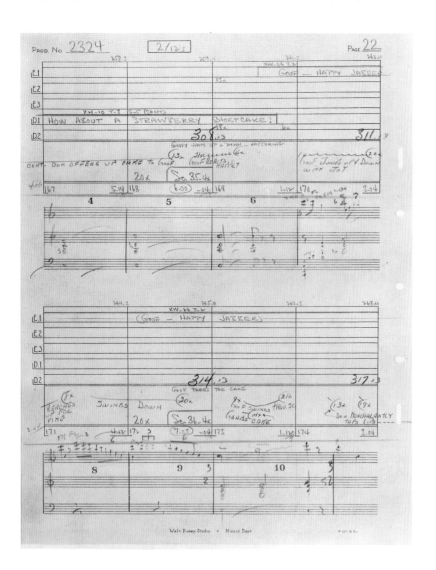

side, but it was passed over before we had a chance to build it up into anything funny."

Seen today, *Cock of the Walk,* with its brilliant parodies of Busby Berkeley dance routines, seems one of the best cartoons of its period. In view of this, the severity of Disney's remarks seems extraordinary, but we must keep in mind the fact that he was trying to make each one of these films into a little jewel. He believed in pushing his animators as far as he would push himself. We should note, too, that by 1935 he was deeply involved in the planning of *Snow White* and was, therefore, very concerned with establishing the standards that would be required to make a success of his first animated feature.

Considering the level of activity maintained at the Studio, it is amazing that anyone found any time for leisure. In fact, a nearby vacant lot provided Disney employees with a suitable playing field for softball games, which, with volleyball, became popular lunchtime activities. Disney seldom joined in these sports but, apparently because of his friendship with Spencer Tracy, he did take up polo.

Jack Cutting, who played with him, recalls that he went about taking up polo by first finding out who at the Studio could ride a horse. He then hired Captain Gil Proctor, formerly a cavalry officer and a member of

Some idea of the complexity of making an animated film can be gathered from these "bar sheets," which govern the entire sound track of a movie, showing exactly where every accent should fall. At different times they have taken different forms, but this example is quite representative.

Above each bar, the film footage is noted, providing a convenient general reference. The three upper staves – E1, E2, E3 – are devoted to instructions for the three effects tracks. Immediately below these – D1 and D2 – are staves carrying the words to be spoken on the two dialogue tracks. A description of the action that will be seen on screen occupies the center section, along with scene numbers and other material, while the music is transcribed onto the lower half of each bar sheet

Donald's Vacation, 1940

Left, top: *Donald's Lucky Day*, 1939; bottom:
The Autograph Hound, 1939

HELD POSITION

A 1939 cartoon, *Goofy and Wilbur,* above, was the Goof's first solo outing. Later he starred in a series of comic instructional films such as *The Art of Self Defense,* 1941, top right, and *How to Swim,* 1942

SCENE 17 - Goof enters gym thru door, broad shouldered, wears towel wrapped around head, bathrobe on. Removes three bathrobes, last one on coat hanger, and towel, is disclosed with narrow shoulders, etc.

Goofy in *Mickey's Amateurs,* 1937

the Army polo team, to coach his recruits. After some reading and black-board instruction, they began to practice on a field in the San Fernando Valley. At first, practice was held two mornings a week, very early, so that everyone could be at the Studio by 8 A.M. In the summer there were further sessions after work and then serious competition on weekends. Initially, the play was between two Studio teams, but eventually Walt and Roy (who also played) bought a string of quality ponies and began to play with Tracy, Will Rogers, and other celebrities from the movie colony.

Aside from family life, polo seems to have been Disney's only form of recreation at that time. The Disney family, like the Disney Studio, was growing. By 1936, Disney had two daughters – Diane and Sharon.

Above left: the Studio polo teams: Walt Disney's in the light jerseys, Roy's in the dark. Above right: Walter Wanger, left and Walt Disney right, 1934 or 1935, at the old Riviera Polo Grounds. Below left: Spencer Tracy, Walt Disney, James Gleason, and Frank Borzage. Below right: Spencer Tracy and Walt Disney

II Feature Animation

4 Snow White: The First Feature

The initial success of Mickey Mouse and the Silly Symphonies did not satisfy Disney for long, and as early as 1934 he began to think seriously about making a feature-length animated film. Two important considerations prompted him to this line of thought. One was a question of simple economics, namely, that no matter how successful the short cartoons were, they could never make very much money. They might share billing with the main feature – they often did – but film rental was determined by running time, not popularity, so the revenue from these shorts would always be limited. Beyond this, Disney was anxious for an opportunity to work within an expanded format – a structure that would allow for more elaborate and leisurely character development, that would give him a chance to evolve more complex plot ideas and greater naturalism. In 1926, Max Fleischer had made a five-and-a-half-reel cartoon titled *Einstein's Theory of Relativity,* but nobody had made an animated feature that could compete on equal terms with live-action pictures, and most people in the industry thought that to do so successfully would be virtually impossible. After all, the reasoning went, the kind of cartoon antics that can make us laugh for seven or eight minutes would become very boring if we were exposed to them for seventy or eighty minutes at a time. Disney, as usual, was at least one jump ahead and had no intention of merely extending his established gag routines to fit into a larger format. He was planning to take a fairy story and bring it to the screen with a kind of magical realism that was beyond the reach of live-action movies.

As everyone knows, the story Disney chose for his first feature was *Snow White and the Seven Dwarfs.* (It may be recalled here that the first movie he had ever seen, on a newsboys' outing in Kansas City, was a silent version of *Snow White.*) At first he referred to his new project as the "Feature Symphony," and to some extent it was an extension of the Silly Symphony concept, music playing an important part in its structure. But it was much more besides. No one can say just when Disney began to think about *Snow White,* but by the summer of 1934 his ideas were beginning to take concrete form. An exploratory outline, dated August 9 of that year, includes the following discussion of the dwarfs:

> The names which follow each suggest a type of character and the names will immediately identify the character in the minds of the audience:

Scrappy	Doleful	Crabby
Happy	Wistful	Daffy
Hoppy	Soulful	Tearful
Sleepy	Helpful	Graspy
Weepy	Bashful	Busy
Dirty	Awful	Dizzy
Cranky	Snoopy	Snappy
Sneezy	Goopy	Hotsy
Sneezy-Wheezy	Gabby	Jaunty
Hungry	Blabby	Puffy
Lazy	Silly	Strutty
Grumpy	Dippy	Biggy
Dumpy	Graceful	Biggy-Wiggy
Thrifty	Neurtsy	Biggo-Ego
Nifty	Gloomy	Jumpy
Shifty	Sappy	Chesty
Woeful	Flabby	

The same outline elaborates some of the possibilities seen for the dwarfs:

SLEEPY: Sterling Holloway. Falls asleep in midst of excitement, in middle of sentence, and so forth . . .

HOPPY-JUMPY: Portrayed by Joe Twerp, the highly excitable, nervous radio comic who gets his words mixed up (flews nashes ry bichfield). He is in constant fear of being goosed but is not goosed until last scene.

BASHFUL: Portrayed by Buelow, a unique radio personality with a very funny bashful laugh, halting delivery and very funny way of misplacing the word "though" . . .

HAPPY: Portrayed by Professor Diddleton D. Wurtle, whose wild Ben Turpin eyes are reinforced by one of the funniest tricks of speech in radio . . .

Before embarking on their first feature-length film, Disney artists needed experience in animating the human figure. A 1934 Silly Symphony, *The Goddess of Spring,* was designed to test their skills in this area. Meanwhile, rough versions of characters for *Snow White* began to appear at the Studio

SNEEZY-WHEEZY – GASPY: Asthmatic inhalations and exhalations of every breath. . . . Dapper . . . nimble dancer – quick movements stopped in midair by embryonic sneeze. . . . Always trying nutty cures and diets . . .

BIGGY-WIGGY – BIGGO-EGO: Portrayed by Eddie Holden, in his character of Hipplewater. A pompous, oily-tongued know-it-all . . .

AWFUL: The most lovable and interesting of the dwarf characters. He steals the drinks and is very dirty . . .

As *Snow White* went into production, Disney artists were asked how they thought the dwarfs might look and behave. These sketches are representative of the suggestions they made

These ideas were probably dictated by Disney. Anyone familiar with *Snow White* will realize that the dwarfs were destined to go through many changes before they reached the screen, but we can see that certain characteristics were already beginning to take shape (it should be pointed out that not all the performers named in these descriptions contributed to the eventual movie – but they did provide Disney with a concise way of describing a personality). This early manuscript also lists a number of possible songs for the film – including "Some Day My Prince Will Come" – indicating that a good deal of thought had already been devoted to this aspect of the subject. The outline differs from the final version in a number of ways so that, for example, Snow White is envisaged passing through a whole sequence of enchanted places before the woodland animals lead her to the dwarfs' cottage. These include the Morass of Monsters and the Valley of the Dragons, which are self-explanatory, as well as Upsidedownland and Backwardland (where birds fly tail first and trees have their roots in the air) and the Sleep Valley ("vast poppy fields, slumbrous music from the wind soughing through the trees"). The Queen is described as being "stately, beautiful in the way of a Benda mask." We are told that she is cool and serene. Only in her emotional climaxes does she erupt to full fury (a note in parentheses urges study of Charles Laughton in *The Barretts of Wimpole Street*).

BASHFUL DWARF ALWAYS
TYING BEARD IN KNOTS –
SNOW WHITE UNTIES IT
FOR HIM –

Another outline, this one dated October 22, 1934, includes a complete breakdown of the cast of characters. We can see from this how quickly things were beginning to develop:

SNOW WHITE: Janet Gaynor type – 14 years old.

THE PRINCE: Doug Fairbanks type – 18 years old.

THE QUEEN: A mixture of Lady Macbeth and the Big Bad Wolf – Her beauty is sinister, mature, plenty of curves – She becomes ugly and menacing when scheming and mixing her poisons – Magic fluids transform her into an old witchlike hag – Her dialogue and action are overdramatic, verging on the ridiculous.

THE HUNTSMAN: A minor character – Big and tough – 40 years old – The Queen's trusted henchman but hasn't the heart to murder an innocent girl . . .

PRINCE'S HORSE: This gallant white charger understands but cannot talk – like Tom Mix's horse Tony – The Prince's pal.

MAGIC MIRROR: The Queen's unwilling slave – Its masklike face appears when invoked – It speaks in weird voice.

This outline also includes another set of descriptions of the dwarfs – not dissimilar to the earlier ones except that the names have become more settled. Already they include Happy, Sleepy, Doc, Bashful, and Grumpy. Sneezy has been temporarily ousted by Jumpy, and Dopey has yet to be christened.

By the fall of 1934, then, the cast was pretty well established in Disney's mind. A story team was being built up, and we may presume that Albert Hurter and Joe Grant were beginning to work on character design. Very soon, more detailed outlines began to circulate – mimeographed sheets

that dealt with specific scenes and situations. These kept everyone in touch with progress and doubled as invitations to submit ideas and gags that would contribute to the development of the plot.

For the cartoon shorts Disney had introduced a bonus system whereby anyone suggesting a gag that was used in the picture received five dollars and anyone providing an idea that formed the basis for an entire cartoon received a hundred dollars. This system was adapted to the new situation, and an outline dated November 2, 1934, includes the notation, "We shall distribute, from time to time, various sequences and situations to be gagged up as the story develops. . . . The following sequences between Snow White and the dwarfs are now open for ALL POSSIBLE SUGGESTIONS AND GAGS."

Parts of the plot had already taken recognizable shape, as the following extracts show:

Snow White is going through the woods alone, discovers the home of the Seven Little Dwarfs, who are all away working in a mine – digging for gold and jewels. OPPORTUNITIES OFFER THEMSELVES HERE AS TO HOW SNOW WHITE MIGHT BE LED TO THE HOUSE

As ideas began to clarify, model sheets and articulated sculptures were prepared

Snow White proceeds to straighten up the house. We show her picking garments off the floor, making beds, washing the dishes. THE BIRDS MIGHT HELP. THEY COULD BRING IN FLOWERS AND VASES, CARRY OUT COBWEBS FROM THE CEILING OR RAFTERS. *SOME GOOD GAGS COULD BE USED HERE TO SHOW SNOW WHITE AND THE BIRDS BUSY FIXING UP THE HOUSE FOR THE DWARFS' RETURN . . .*

All props and the interior of the house want to be of a quaint, old-time nature, such as the dwarfs would have about them. The proportion of the dwarfs to Snow White is about one-half her size, so be governed by that in using utensils, chairs, tables, and so forth. . . .

The circular continues in this vein and ends with the reminder, "PLEASE DRAW UP ALL SUGGESTIONS AND GAGS *READY FOR COLLECTION THURSDAY, NOVEMBER 8, 1934.*"

On November 19, members of the production staff received a two-page memo which was headed, "Time and general sequences of *Snow White* as described by Walt." This gives a synopsis that conforms quite closely to the version that eventually appeared on screen, diverging from the final form mostly in that it includes several episodes that were later eliminated. That same day, another circular went out, accompanied by a letter from Disney which read, in part, as follows:

GAG OUTLINE sequence DWARFS DISCOVER SNOW WHITE.

Please read through the following outline carefully. . . . Study the gag action and dialogue possibilities of each section of this sequence and try hard to give some helpful suggestions. If you don't like any particular section of business, *please say so* and, at the same time, try to suggest something that might be better. . . . There are good gag possibilities through this sequence – let's see if we can't make the most of it.

Thanx, Walt

What followed was a series of notes and questions relating to how the dwarfs might react to finding Snow White asleep in their house. So far as one can gather, the response to these invitations was usually enthusiastic. Someone, for instance, might come up with a suggestion of possible dialogue for Doc ("You're a pot-bellied old Hop Toad." "He's a I'm a whose a belly potted old flop load – a hop todied old – a hop jellied pot pode – a jot jellied – a . . ."). Ideas were gathered and weeded out, then marshaled into some kind of usable structure. Within a matter of three or four months, *Snow White* had developed from the embryonic stage and was beginning to take shape as a viable endeavor.

The story at least was taking form. There was, however, a great deal more than story involved in a pioneering project of this kind. The Disney artists would be dealing with problems that neither they nor anyone else had confronted before.

There were, to start off with, several purely technical problems. All animation drawings up to this point had been made on sheets of paper measuring 9½ by 12 inches – layouts and backgrounds also being geared to these dimensions. The drawings were then traced and painted onto celluloid sheets of exactly the same size before being sent to the camera department, along with the appropriate backgrounds. The camera could be adjusted to photograph the entire setup – minus the margins – or a small part of it if a close-up effect was required. The area to be photographed was designated as the "field" (rectangles drawn on many of the layouts illustrated in this book are indications of field size). The size of the animation paper determined the largest possible field size, which was known as "five field." As soon as production of *Snow White* got under way, it became evident that this field size would be inadequate for much of the animation involved. A scene in which Snow White was to appear with all seven dwarfs, or with fifty animals, would – if they stuck with the old animation paper – mean that each character had to be drawn on a minute scale, making the animator's task extremely difficult, if not impossible. To overcome this problem, a new field size – "six-and-a-half" – was introduced, which meant that a complete new series of animation boards, sliding cel boards, checking boards, and inking and painting boards had to be designed, built, and installed; and animation cameras had to be adapted to shoot this new field size. Even so, certain long trucking shots demanded characters who would appear so small on the screen at some point that even this modification would be inadequate to the animator's needs. To get around this, a method of reducing drawings photographically was devised – a mechanical solution that allowed the artist to work on a convenient scale.

Another limitation that animation had run up against was its inability to produce a real illusion of depth. When a camera moved into a setup which consisted of a painted cel held tightly against a flat background, scale distortions were inevitable. Take, for example, a situation where a character stands in a meadow with mountains in the background. In reality, as one approaches that character, he will appear to become bigger, but the mountains will remain about the same size because they are so far away. When the camera moves in on a flat representation of the same scene, both the character and the mountains will appear to increase in size at exactly the same rate. In the short cartoons this had not presented a serious problem because such situations seldom arose, and when a little distortion did creep in it was not really noticeable in the context of quick-fire gags that were sweeping the audience along; but feature films required a much greater regard for naturalism. Flat backgrounds might still be adequate for most scenes, but from time to time a real illusion of depth would be necessary. William Garity, head of the camera department, was given the job of developing a multiplane camera – one that could shoot simultaneously several layers of action and background, layers that were separated in such a way as to produce an accurate sense of depth. (At about the same time, Ub Iwerks was working on a similar idea at his own studio.)

Albert Hurter's studies were vital to the concept of the story that began to emerge

The opening scenes of *Snow White* establish the movie's theme and atmosphere with great economy. The Wicked Queen, her magic mirror, the Prince, and Snow White herself – little better than a servant in her stepmother's palace (see overleaf) – are all introduced. The threat to the little princess's life is introduced without delay and made graphic by a close-up of the box in which her heart is to be placed

As Snow White flees into the forest, trees and fallen logs become monsters that seem to threaten her. The Disney artists tried to see the world through her frightened eyes, turning it into a nightmare

The Queen entrusts her huntsman with the task of murdering Snow White. Once in the forest, however, he is overcome by the princess's innocence and drops to his knees to beg her forgiveness. Clever use of shadows and camera angles adds to the drama of the scene

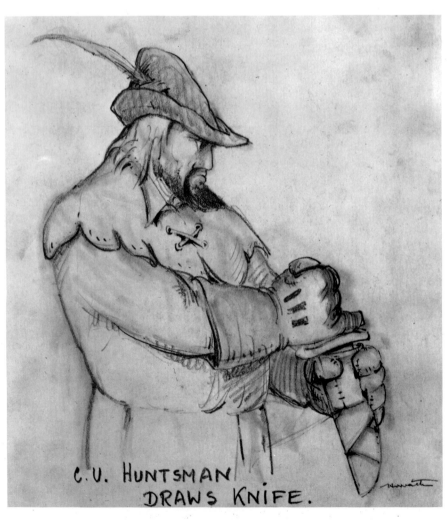

C.U. HUNTSMAN DRAWS KNIFE.

It is difficult to estimate exactly what kind of schedule Disney had in mind for the production of his first feature. The closing months of 1934 saw great progress in story planning, but was he ready to proceed at full speed? The indications are that the initial burst of energy was followed by a period of more cautious exploration. Technical problems could be solved – we can assume that that aspect of the project did not worry him unduly – but what about the animators? Were they ready to handle the demands that would be placed on them by a movie of this sort?

One serious consideration was that they had very little experience in animating the human form. Toward the end of 1934, several animators were put to work on a Silly Symphony titled *The Goddess of Spring*, which retold the Greek myth of Persephone. The character of Persephone – if not exactly a prototype – was certainly conceived with Snow White in mind. Because of Don Graham's art classes, Disney artists were now better equipped to deal with human anatomy, but animating a young woman still presented great difficulties. Les Clark, one of those assigned to this project, had his sister pose for him as an aid to drawing Persephone, but he was still disappointed with the results. Disney told him not to worry, that it was unreasonable to expect immediate success with so ambitious a project. The experiments continued.

The year 1935 saw a high point in the development of animated shorts at the Studio, and this must have provided the impetus to push *Snow White* into full production. The caricatures of Hollywood personalities in a cartoon titled *Broken Toys* were highly sophisticated, and Disney is said to have been particularly happy with the way in which Jenny Wren's character was established in *Who Killed Cock Robin?* These Silly Symphonies, and others like them, indicated that the time was ripe. Disney's veteran animators were coming into their prime and younger artists were catching up fast (soon Don Graham's recruiting system would bring many talented apprentices to the Studio). Character design was well advanced by now, and the animation team began to take shape. Dave Hand was assigned the task of supervising director (which meant he was the man responsible for seeing to it that Disney's instructions were carried out). Bill Cottrell, Wilfred Jackson, Ben Sharpsteen, Larry Morey, and Perce Pearce were named as sequence directors (each of them taking responsibility for specific sections of the movie) while Ham Luske, Bill Tytla, Fred Moore, and Norm Ferguson were made supervising animators (in charge of the quality of the actual animation). Then came the task of "casting" the artists.

Since animators think of themselves as actors with a pencil, the process of casting them for a production of this magnitude was a sensitive one. Moore, Tytla, Fred Spencer, and Frank Thomas were assigned to the dwarfs. (Moore's charm and Tytla's vigor would both be needed for these characters; Spencer had a sure touch with broad comedy and Thomas was one of the most promising of the younger artists.) The Queen as she first appears – an evil beauty – was given to Art Babbitt. After her trans-formation, she would be drawn by Ferguson. Three younger animators – Milt Kahl, Eric Larson, and Jim Algar – were put in charge of the ani-

Adriana Caselotti, the voice of Snow White

mals who befriend Snow White. Snow White herself, the most difficult and crucial character of all, was consigned to Ham Luske and Grim Natwick. Luske specialized in character development and thus was a natural for the heroine. Natwick – who also drew the Prince – was a strong draftsman, chosen because of his ability to deal with the human figure.

Layout also presented new problems, and the layout team, headed by Hugh Hennesy and Charles Philippi, found itself confronted with a considerable challenge. Layout artists not only determine the spaces in which an animator must work, they are also in a sense responsible for deciding how the film will look when it reaches the screen. They take on many of the tasks which in a live-action movie would be handled by the art director, the director of photography, and the film editor. An animated film must, in effect, be cut in advance, since animation is so costly that the producer cannot afford to shoot extra footage. Every edit is determined at the layout stage (with the collaboration of the director and, sometimes, the story team). Camera angles and lighting are also determined in layout, as are final decisions about the character of the setting in which the action is to take place. This art direction aspect was especially important in *Snow White*, where it was necessary to maintain an atmosphere of fairy-tale quaintness. Much of the preliminary design work to this end – the bizarre furnishings of the dwarfs' cottage, for instance – was done by Albert Hurter, but it was the layout artists' responsibility to make these inventions work within the final context of the film. Color was an important consideration. In the interiors, it was keyed down to give them an aged look (Gustav Tenggren's elegant watercolor studies had an important influence on their eventual appearance). Everything had to be carefully designed so that the characters would read clearly against their backgrounds.

By the spring of 1936, production of *Snow White* was in full swing. Story conferences were being held almost every day and each scene was discussed and analyzed down to the last detail. Fortunately, a stenographer was present at all these meetings, so that a complete record exists. The following, for example, are extracts from a session dated Saturday, June 27, 1936. The transcript notes that it lasted from 8:45 A.M. to 1:00 P.M. and that those present were Walt Disney, Frank Churchill, Charles Philippi, Joe Grant, Bill Cottrell, Larry Morey, and Bob Kuwahara. The conference dealt with the sequence in which the Huntsman, having taken Snow White out into the woods, was supposed to kill her. The meeting began with Morey running through the continuity for the scene (we can imagine that the group was surrounded by storyboards) while Churchill played the musical score on the piano. Disney then led off the discussion:

"I feel that what Snow White says to the little bird should have a double meaning – such as, 'Are you a little orphan?' In other words, have the conversation with more contact to her present predicament. . . . She is stooped over [this little bird], which gives you a swell position for the knife in the back. Let the menace come in while she is still with the bird – just at that point, with some connection there where she kissed the

bird and the bird perked up and flew away – it has a connection for the Huntsman to soften. It would be tying it together. Maybe instead of expressing the menace musically you ought to stay with her and let the menace come in. . . . The Huntsman comes along – he is a threat all during the thing – and Snow White is there with the little bird, which is very innocent – such a sweet girl as she to have picked up a little bird and then someone going to knife her. Get the contrast in there."

At this point, Philippi suggested that the little bird could start chattering and fly away – giving her a reason to turn around. Disney disagreed.

"That is too direct. I want the thought where she has kissed the bird and the Huntsman softens – that is a good contrast."

Disney wanted to develop the scene in such a way that it would show how the Huntsman loses his nerve.

"That is what we want to build. A shot of the bird flying away and the knife is right over her back and – just as she watches the bird go away – the knife drops . . . and she turns on around and looks and he immediately pleads with her. That would be better than a long bunch of dialogue. . . . You have your set-up there – the morning sun and Snow White dressed in her prettiest dress and being taken into the woods. . . . You know what to expect – you know that he is to kill her."

Clearly, the scene under discussion falls into the category of melodrama, but seldom had melodrama been subjected to the process of intensive refinement that we can see at work in these story conferences. If we consider *Snow White* from an artistic viewpoint, what is of special interest is not the fact that Disney selected melodrama as a storytelling form – evidently it was a genre he understood and felt was appropriate to the subject matter – but rather that he exposed it to this process of refinement. His overall approach was determined by his own predilections and by the taste of his prospective audience. What gave the film its impact was his obsessive drive for perfection.

Another typical conference was held on December 22, 1936, on the Hyperion sound stage. Twenty-nine people – mostly animators and animation directors – were present to discuss the dwarfs' personalities, but the main feature of this meeting – which lasted from 7:00 P.M. to 10:20 P.M. – was Disney's incredibly detailed shot-by-shot description of the movie, which seems to have been a virtuoso performance, as the following extract shows.

"We fade in on the sunset and hear the dwarfs coming home from the mine. They are marching home against the setting sun, singing the marching home song, which is the 'hiho' song that has a whistling chorus. We have a little sequence of these guys going over picturesque spots – mushrooms and roots of trees. There are little gag touches in there. We fade out on this sequence into the next sequence of Snow White, with a candle in her hand, and the animals following her upstairs. . . . She sees all these cute little beds, all seven, and she is pleased. These beds are hand carved and she reads the names on them, and she thinks they are little children. . . . Doc, Bashful, Grumpy, Dopey, Sneezy, Sleepy . . . and when she reads on

Snow White is befriended by woodland creatures who take her to the dwarfs' cottage. Assisted by the animals, Snow White cleans the cottage and then – exhausted by her experience – falls asleep across several of the dwarfs' beds

Overleaf: backgrounds were painted in low-keyed colors to emphasize the antique character of the cottage

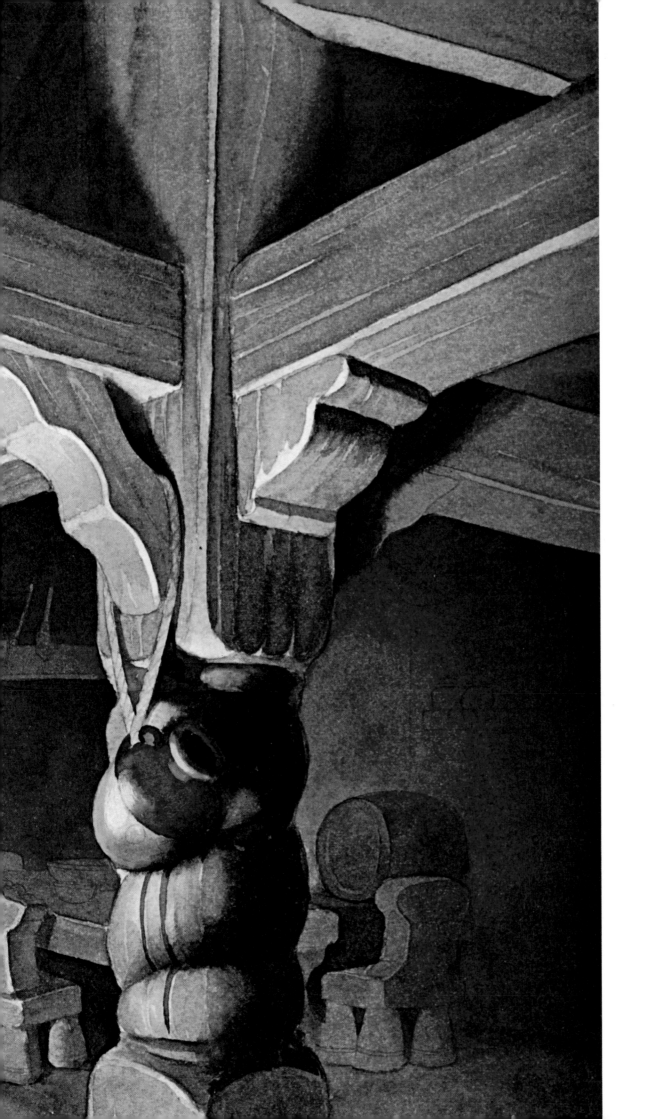

to Sleepy she says, 'I am a little tired myself,' and lies there on three beds and tries them all out. The animals see her get in bed and cover her up with a sheet as she goes to bed. The rabbits and deer and all the animals get in these beds and settle down for a snooze. You hear the offstage dwarfs singing the marching home song, and the animals dash and look out the window. They immediately scram out of the bedroom, run down out of the house, and hide. They anticipate these dwarfs coming. Then we pick up with the guys coming home, on up to Fred Moore's sequence where they come up to the bedroom to attack this monster."

What we can learn from this meeting is that *Snow White* existed in Disney's head as a very real thing and that he was determined it should reach the screen just as he had conceived it. There can be no doubt as to who was in control. *Snow White* was a team effort, but it is still clearly the creation of one mind.

These meetings were the medium through which Disney exercised his control over the movie, and they permitted him to keep everything under close scrutiny. The musical score, for instance, which would be vital to the total impact of the film, was in the capable hands of Frank Churchill, Ollie Wallace, Leigh Harline, and Paul Smith, but Disney had his own ideas about how it should help move the action along – ideas that were strongly held and remarkably sophisticated. On February 16, 1937, during a discussion of the dwarfs' entertainment, he made the following remarks:

"It can still be good music and not follow the same pattern everybody in the country has followed. We still haven't hit it in any of these songs. . . . It's still that influence from the musicals they have been doing for years. Really, we should set a new pattern – a new way to use music – weave it into the story so somebody doesn't just burst into song."

By the time *Snow White* reached the screen, its songs were indeed integrated with the story in a fresh and original manner. The way this was done anticipates the ingenuity with which Richard Rodgers and Oscar Hammerstein II incorporated songs into the structure of *Oklahoma!*, which premiered in 1943. *Oklahoma!* was hailed as a breakthrough, but it seems that Disney was already moving toward the same goals several years earlier. With music, as with so many other things, Disney was not satisfied to do things the way they had always been done, and he did not want *Snow White* to be a mere imitation of live-action musical comedies. His attention to musical detail can be gauged by the attention he gave to the dwarfs' entertainment. For this sequence he insisted that the music be as bizarre as the characters of the dwarfs themselves, and he instigated experiments in which "legitimate" and "illegitimate" instruments were blended to sound like no orchestration that had ever been heard before. This sequence also involved yodeling, and various performers – described as Swiss, cowboys, and hillbillies – tested for it, but none came up to Disney's standards. Eventually, this problem was solved from within the Studio. Someone asked Jim Macdonald, the sound-effects man, to try out, and though he had never yodeled before, his understanding of music and the demands of the sound track enabled him to provide exactly what was needed.

Snow White was the only feature in which transparent colors were employed for the background paintings. Later, gouache became the usual medium

MCU: Doc at sorting table - tapping
diamonds - gets sour note - tosses
diamond away - o.s.song continues

MCU: Bashful, Sneezy and Happy.
Bashful: "LOOK OUT - SHE'S MOVIN'!"
Happy: "SHE'S WAKIN' UP."
Sneezy: "WHAT'LL WE DO?"

MLS: Group. Doc: "HIDE!" Group
scrambles under bed - Dopey last.

While Snow White sleeps, the dwarfs conclude
their day's work at the mine and head for
home. Mistaking the princess for a monster,
they are set to kill her, but – just in time –
they see that she is a girl and hide in confusion

At the mine, Dopey places two huge diamonds
over his eyes like spectacles. The diamonds'
facets create this frightening image

Snow White insists that the dwarfs wash up
before they eat. Grumpy, even more reluctant
than the others to submit to this humiliation,
undergoes a forced scrubbing

Voice talent was, of course, an important contributing factor to the success of the whole project. The most difficult voice to cast was the heroine herself, and Disney had a loudspeaker installed in his office so that he could hear singers auditioning on the sound stage without having to see them (he did not want his decision to be influenced by their looks). Finally, Adriana Caselotti – a young woman with some operatic training – was chosen.

Live actors were also filmed as an aid to animation. The problem with animating humans is that everyone instinctively knows how a man or woman moves, so that the least inaccuracy in the way they are drawn is immediately apparent. Nobody has ever seen a real-life Mickey Mouse or a real-life Dopey. Snow White, however – as well as the Prince and the Queen – presented a different kind of challenge. Years earlier, Max Fleischer had devised a method of filming live actors and using the results as a guide for his animators. This system, known as rotoscoping, yielded gestures and mannerisms that could never be invented. Now actors were brought to Hyperion Avenue (the performer cast as Snow White went on to achieve fame as the dancer Marge Champion), and they would act out a piece of "business" in front of the cameras – often under the direction of the animators themselves. This action would then be tranferred to a series of photostats which the animator could use for reference. The artist could, in fact, have simply traced the figures from the photostats, but this was seldom done because the characters had to be adapted in order to be consistent with the remainder of the animation. Instead, a kind of gentle caricature was employed, so that gestures and poses became slightly exaggerated. This system served the animators well, and they continued to use it in later movies.

The character of Snow White was an enormous challenge in many ways. Frank Thomas, recalling just one of the details that went into establishing her screen image, reports that when the cels came back from inking and painting, Snow White looked pale and anemic. "She had no color in her cheeks. So they tried painting color on there – which made her look like a clown. One of the girls said, 'Walt, can we try putting a little rouge on her cheeks?' He said, 'What do you mean?' So she took out her makeup kit and put some rouge on the cel and it looked keen. Walt said, 'Yeah, but how the hell are you going to get it in the same place every day? And on each drawing?' And the girl said, 'What do you think we've been doing all our lives?' He said, 'You mean to tell you can put that in the same place on the girl's face no matter how she turns?' . . . They just knew where it ought to go and, without any kind of guide, they made Snow White up on each cel – so there's this lovely little tint on there. That's how much we cared."

Disney's perfectionism can be illustrated by another Frank Thomas story. As mentioned earlier, Thomas was assigned to work on the dwarfs, and one of his scenes called for Dopey to do a little hitch step to catch up with the others. "This was on the story board, not my idea. So I had him do a hitch step. Walt said, 'Hey, that's good – we ought to use that hitch step all through the picture.' Of course a lot of stuff had been

After supper, the dwarfs put on an entertainment. In a sequence animated by Fred Moore, Dopey experiences some difficulty while attempting to balance on Sneezy's shoulders

Warned that the Queen (who has used magic
to transform herself into an old hag) has
reached her victim, the dwarfs set off to the
rescue. They are too late to save Snow White,
who has already bitten the poisoned apple,
but they pursue the Queen up into the mountains, where a storm is raging

The Queen attempts to send a boulder crashing down on the dwarfs, but lightning strikes the crag she is perched on and she is hurled to her death. The dwarfs return to the lifeless body of Snow White and sadly place her in a crystal casket. She remains there through a full cycle of the seasons until, finally, the Prince arrives to wake her with a kiss

At a Disney premiere: Marlene Dietrich, top, Judy Garland, center, and Charles Laughton with Elsa Lanchester

animated by then, so he called all the scenes back for hitch steps to be added. The guys came over to me and said, 'Was that goddamn hitch step your idea?' That kind of thing would often happen. You'd be well into a picture when a better idea would come along – and you'd back up and change everything that had been done."

Although much of the production work on *Snow White* was jammed into the final ten or twelve months, it was the result of more than three years of concentrated effort by Disney himself – three years in which he faced new problems almost daily. The whole venture was an enormous gamble from the very first. The industry was convinced that he had bitten off more than he could chew, and hints of impending disaster were commonplace both in the trade papers and the national press. During this period, the Studio staff expanded to more than one thousand, many of whom were directly involved in the feature project. Some names have been mentioned, but literally hundreds of other artists and technicians were involved in all kinds of capacities, from painting backgrounds to devising special effects. (How, for example, do you make a painted stream look like a stream or a painted rainstorm like the real thing?)

Finally, at a cost of close to $1,500,000, *Snow White* was completed. Four days before Christmas, 1937, it was premiered at the Carthay Circle Theater in Hollywood. The audience was studded with celebrities. It was the kind of opening of which Disney had always dreamed. The reviews were sensational. *Snow White* was an overnight success, justifying all of Disney's hopes for it and impressing itself on the imagination of the Western world.

Snow White is distinguished by two seemingly opposed characteristics: economy of construction and extravagance of invention. Disney's training in the field of cartoon shorts had taught him how to tell a story without wasting a single foot of film. There is nothing in *Snow White* that does not contribute either to developing character or to moving the plot forward. (Two fully animated scenes – the dwarfs eating soup and building a bed for Snow White – were deleted at the last moment as superfluous.) Yet this does not lead to a feeling of spareness, because crammed into this framework is a profusion of detail that is almost overwhelming. The fruits of three years' work by hundreds of talents are compressed into eighty-three minutes of action, imagery, music, and dialogue.

The songs are memorable and, like everything else, contribute to the movement of the story. As for the animation, the character of each dwarf is firmly established – each is a distinct individual. The development of the Queen is excellent, both before and after her transformation into the witchlike crone. The Huntsman is effective, and the birds and animals function well as a kind of Greek chorus. Snow White occasionally seems a little too much like a twentieth-century coed, but she has great charm and easily wins our sympathy. The only real failure is the Prince, who seems wooden and lacks character (Snow White deserves a better consort). Above all, the entire movie manages to sustain the ambience of timelessness which is so essential to the fairy-tale genre.

Shirley Temple presents Walt Disney with a special Academy Award incorporating one large and seven little Oscars for his production of *Snow White*

Some critics have found the film simplistic and therefore not worthy of serious consideration, but this approach is in itself simplistic. *Snow White* has the elemental quality of folklore – questions of right and wrong are understood in advance – which dictates a certain directness of approach that would be merely banal in most live-action pictures. But the character of animation is quite different from live action in that it permits virtually total control of every detail of every situation that may arise. Nothing need be left to chance, and in the case of *Snow White*, nothing was. Disney lavished such loving care on every aspect of the film that it took on an imaginative density which makes it quite extraordinary.

Other critics have charged that *Snow White* is excessively frightening – suggesting that it might have a harmful effect on children. In fact, many episodes in the fairy tales of Hans Christian Andersen and the Brothers Grimm are far more terrifying, and ultimately scariness is justified by the nature of the story. In the case of *Snow White*, without the Wicked Queen there is no story, and by definition the Wicked Queen must perform misdeeds that inspire fear.

Snow White and the Seven Dwarfs may have provided Walt Disney with his finest moment. There was an element of luck in Mickey's success (admittedly, Disney tended to make his own luck), but his first animated feature was a triumph of a different order. No happy accidents were involved. Disney walked into the project with his eyes wide open, knowing the risks involved and convinced that they were worth taking. *Snow White* was a conscious effort on his part to advance the art of animation to a new level of sophistication – a level that everyone else had thought was beyond reach.

5 Pinocchio

Snow White and the Seven Dwarfs may have provided Disney with his finest moment, but *Pinocchio* is probably his greatest film. It shares in all the qualities that made the first feature such a success and adds to them a technical brilliance that has never been surpassed.

Pinocchio opens with a stunningly effective shot – the camera pulling back from a large white star, panning across the tiled roofs of a sleepy European village, then closing in on the lighted window of Geppetto's cottage. It is the kind of shot that has become familiar enough in live-action movies since the advent of power-operated zoom lenses, but taken within the context of its own period, and within the history of animation, it is innovative and spectacular. Nor is it just a piece of flashy showmanship. It serves to capture our imagination and draw us into the atmosphere of the story before a single word has been spoken.

Disney's early success had resulted from his grasp of the potentials of the sound film. By the time of his first feature films, he had evolved a method of storytelling which relied primarily on visual means. Next to animation itself, camera movements provided his team with its chief narrative devices. Disney continued to make expert use of music and sound, but his greatest achievement was the creation of a visual language that was totally convincing and extremely flexible.

Some critics have suggested that this visual language is marred by being backward-looking – leaning heavily on the illustrational styles of the nineteenth century. This seems an unreasonable objection; given the subject matter of films like *Snow White* and *Pinocchio*, what idiom could have been more appropriate? Disney's obsession with naturalism seems anachronistic if one places him alongside Picasso (especially considering that the Spaniard was the senior by twenty years). At the same time, however, Picasso's fidelity to largely traditional media – such as the stretched canvas with its built-in limitations – might be considered anachronistic when compared to Disney's pioneering of the art of animation. Disney's great contribution was to break free of the static image. We might have seen interiors resembling Geppetto's workshop in old prints, but never before had we been able to penetrate these spaces and move about within them. Disney's imagination, the skill of his artists, and the technological magic of the motion picture camera made this possible.

The multiplane camera had seen only very limited use in *Snow White,* but *The Old Mill,* a short released in 1937, demonstrated its full potential, and it was employed extensively throughout *Pinocchio.* Disney now had the ability to produce a convincing illusion of depth. The only drawback was the expense involved in operating the multiplane. A single scene – in which the camera zooms down on the village with the school bells ringing and pigeons circling down and down until they are among the houses – cost $45,000 (equivalent to perhaps $300,000 today). The scene lasts for only a few seconds. To offset outlays of this kind, Disney technicians managed to create some simpler devices, which they used whenever they would not detract from the quality of the film. One sequence, for example, shows a steamer crossing an expanse of calm ocean. It was made by pulling a single cel, on which the boat was painted, across a background, with smoke effects trailing behind it and distortion glass over the water. Disney was immensely proud of this scene because it was so simple – yet so effective that at the premiere it received a round of applause.

More often than not, however, Disney's quest for perfection led to more rather than less expense. Figaro the kitten had a highlight airbrushed onto him on every single cel he appeared in. Most producers would have looked on this as unnecessary, even absurd. Disney thought it might improve his film, so he did it. The result of this attitude was an animated movie of unprecedented lavishness.

As has been seen, *Snow White* evolved rather gradually. With the experience of this one feature behind him, Disney seems to have felt that he need not be quite so cautious, and production of *Pinocchio* was put into top gear. Things did not work out according to plan, however, and after six months he called a halt to the project and put everyone on new assignments until the problems had been ironed out.

The primary dilemma centered on the character of Pinocchio himself. Should he be treated as a puppet or as a small boy? Until this issue was settled, very little could be done. Book illustrations of the story tended to show Pinocchio as essentially puppetlike, and this seems to have influenced

Walt Disney in action: a sequence of photographs taken at a *Pinocchio* story conference

Geppetto's workshop

PINOCCHIO

One of Gustav Tenggren's watercolor studies
for *Pinocchio*

Some of Albert Hurter's early sketches
for *Pinocchio*

Many models were made to guide the animators.
Live-action footage was shot for the same purpose; the example shown here was used as an aid
for a sequence featuring the Fox and the Cat

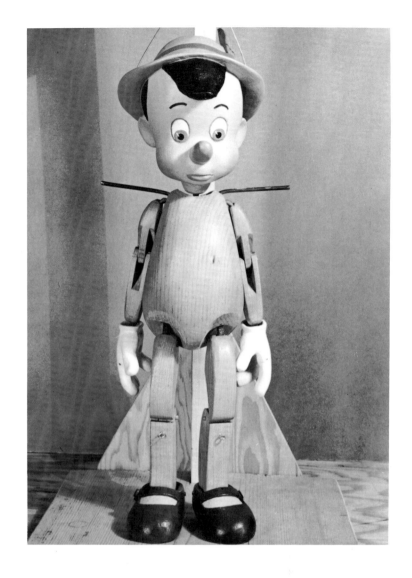

At the beginning of *Pinocchio*, the Blue Fairy brings the hero to life and appoints Jiminy Cricket to be his conscience

This panoramic background was painted for
the opening of *Pinocchio*

Jiminy Cricket in Geppetto's workshop

the animators' first efforts. Frank Thomas, Milt Kahl, and Ollie Johnston were assigned to the character, and they animated about 150 feet of film, using the speeded-up voice of Ted Sears as a sound track. Disney was not happy with the results. After further experimentation, they went ahead with a more boylike version of Pinocchio (except in the scenes, animated by Thomas, where he is still on strings) and found a child's voice which fitted with this interpretation. A further snag was Jiminy Cricket's personality, which became more and more important as the story developed, until he had usurped many of the functions originally intended for Pinocchio. The nominal hero of the film was soon reduced to speaking dialogue that did not go far beyond "Why?" and "Why not?" He was a total naive – the Blue Fairy had brought him to life and he had the innocence of a baby. The animators had to show that everything was a completely new experience for him, and this had to be evident in every movement he made. The success of the film hung on their ability to handle this formidable task.

Jiminy Cricket, drawn by Ward Kimball, Woolie Reitherman, and Don Towsley, presented another kind of challenge. Being a very small character (his physical size contrasts with the importance of his role in the film), he was difficult to animate except in close-ups. The artists rose to the occasion, making him so expansive a character that he seems larger than life. In contrast to the Cricket stands one of the villains of the piece, the puppet master Stromboli. Animated by Bill Tytla, Stromboli is an enormous, muscular presence who fills the screen with his infamy. His every gesture is a threat. Tytla, as we have remarked, was an

Geppetto, delighted with his new son, sends Pinocchio off to school. Before he gets there, however, Pinocchio is sidetracked by the Fox and the Cat, who persuade him that the theater offers more glamour. Soon he finds himself co-opted into Stromboli's puppet troupe

Stromboli, animated by Bill Tytla, is
perhaps the greatest of Disney villains –
totally consumed by rage and evil

Stromboli shuts Pinocchio in a wooden cage. The Blue Fairy rescues him, but not before he tells her a series of lies – only to discover that, with each lie, his nose grows longer and longer, eventually sprouting branches and leaves

Succumbing to temptation once more, Pinocchio, accompanied by the jaded street urchin Lampwick, finds himself on Pleasure Island. The image of Lampwick eating the ultimate club sandwich did not appear in the released version of the film

exceptionally gifted animator, and this was an ideal assignment for him. It is probable that no one else could have built this character to the same point of menace. Stromboli is a man whose anger combines with physical strength to keep him in a constant state of explosive agitation. (At the premiere, W. C. Fields was heard to say, "He moves too much," but Fields was noted as a harsh critic.)

Perhaps more likable, but in the villains' camp nonetheless, are the Fox and the Cat, who are slyly determined to lead Pinocchio astray for the sake of a fast buck. Animated by Norm Ferguson and John Lounsbery, these characters – like Stromboli – seem to be in constant motion, but it is motion less governed by rage. The cunning of the Fox and the stupidity of the Cat turn them into a kind of vaudeville team that keeps moving to hold the attention of the audience. The Fox knows just when to throw a knowing glance and the Cat is a malicious dolt with an instinct for mischief. Neither is subject to the eruptions of sheer evil that determine Stromboli's personality. They are self-made villains. He is a force of nature.

Geppetto, handled largely by Art Babbitt, is the least interesting of the main characters. He is asked to function on a single, fundamentally

Pinocchio and Lampwick engage in an orgy of self-indulgence which comes to a sudden end when the two revelers discover they are turning into donkeys

sentimental emotional level, thus presenting the animators with very little challenge. Fred Moore was luckier in his assignment, treating Lampwick, the cocky street kid, as something of a self-caricature. Monstro the whale is suitably fearsome, and two small creatures, Figaro the kitten and Cleo the goldfish, add a touch of charm to the proceedings. Live-action footage was shot as an assist to the animation of several characters, notably the Blue Fairy, whose brief appearances are very effective.

Once again, Albert Hurter's influence is felt throughout the film, both in terms of character design and in the profusion of quaint detail that crowds the background of almost every scene. Gustav Tenggren contributed many line-and-wash studies which greatly affect the look of the movie. The multiplane camera and the visual complexity of the film as a whole presented the layout team with great opportunities which they eagerly seized. Under the direction of Charles Philippi and Hugh Hennesy, with important contributions by Ken Anderson, the art of layout was carried to new heights of inventiveness. Many of the layout drawings are extremely beautiful, and the same can be said of the background paintings. For *Snow White,* backgrounds had been painted mainly with transparent washes, but in the case of *Pinocchio,* while something that resembles a classic watercolor technique is adhered to, opaque pigment came into general use. For multiplane shots, all but the bottom layer was painted onto glass, and oil paint was used for this purpose.

Many character models, some fashioned from clay and some from wood, were made to assist the animators. The artist could refer to these models, turning them so that they could see at a moment's notice just how Jiminy Cricket, for example, would look from any angle (in this respect the models served a purpose similar to that of the live-action footage, and they could be used for characters who could not be shot in

Chastened by his experiences, Pinocchio sets out to find Geppetto – a search which takes him under the sea

Eventually Pinocchio and Geppetto are
reunited in the belly of Monstro the whale

Escaping from the whale, who gives furious chase, Pinocchio is washed ashore, seemingly dead. But he recovers, and, having proved himself brave, truthful, and unselfish, is soon changed into a real boy by the Blue Fairy. Joyfully, Figaro the kitten dives into the fish-bowl and kisses Cleo the goldfish

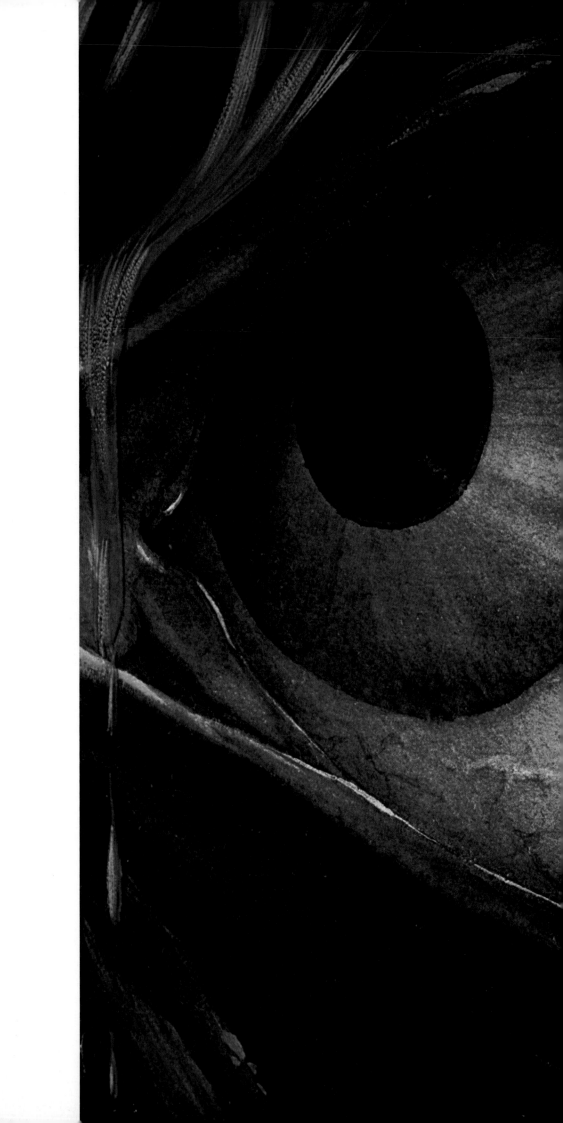

Jiminy Cricket and the whale's eye

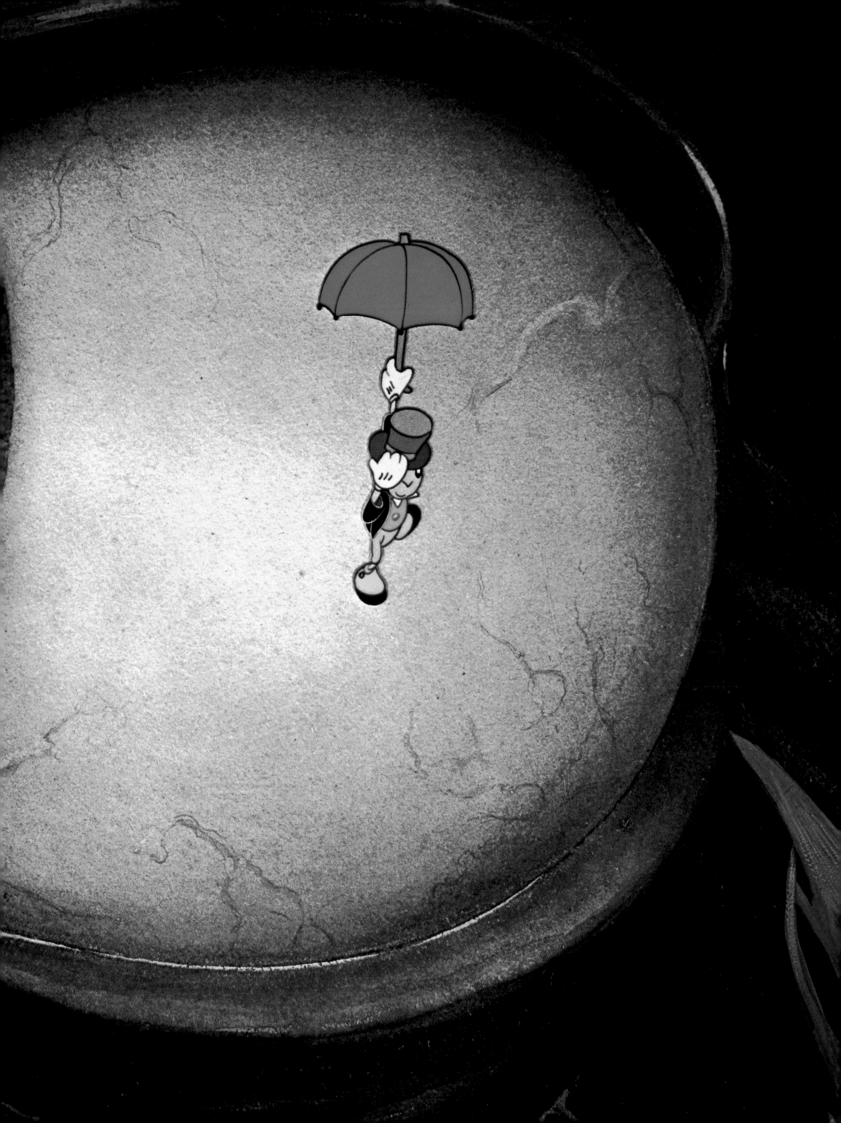

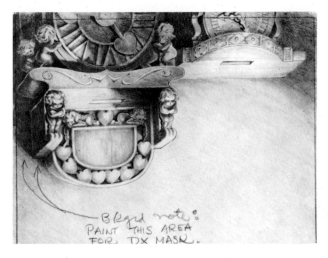

Blegd note:
PAINT THIS AREA
FOR TX MASK.

NOTE TO PAINTER— ADD SPIDERWEBS AS INDICATED IN SC. 26·28 ETC.

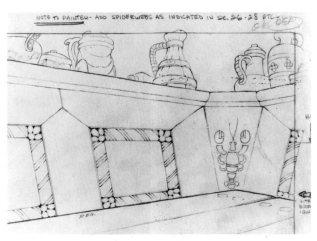

The layout drawings for *Pinocchio* were made with great attention to detail. Often more than one artist worked on a single layout, the first making an outline drawing, and another adding the tonal rendering. Although never intended for public display, many of these drawings are very beautiful

live action). The special effects in *Pinocchio* are particularly striking – live-action rain is incorporated into one scene – and it is impossible to overlook the effectiveness of the musical score, highlighted by such songs as "Give a Little Whistle" and "When You Wish upon a Star" – both composed by Leigh Harline with lyrics by Ned Washington.

The plot of *Pinocchio* required extensive adaptation to make it suitable for the screen – far more radical changes being made than had been necessary for *Snow White*. Once again Disney was charged with frightening children, but compared with Carlo Collodi's original, his version of *Pinocchio* is quite restrained. He kept just enough of the element of horror to make the story effective. Certainly, the scene in which Pinocchio's nose grows longer as a result of each of his lies triggers a deep response, as does the sequence in which he and Lampwick are transformed into donkeys.

Although the reviewers welcomed it with enthusiasm, *Pinocchio* was not an immediate box-office success. The film was released in February 1940, five months after the outbreak of war in Europe, and it may be that the public was not in the mood for a fable of this sort. Not that *Pinocchio* was a frivolous movie. On the contrary, despite the happy ending, it presents the blackest vision of any animated feature produced during Walt Disney's lifetime. It is also Walt Disney's masterpiece.

Pinocchio was not the only thing on Disney's mind during the period from 1938 to 1940. Two more major film projects – *Fantasia* and *Bambi* – were already under way, and, in addition to this and a full schedule of short cartoons, Disney had decided to build a new studio. On August 31, 1938, a deposit was made on a fifty-one-acre site in Burbank, near the Los Angeles River, in the same general area as the Columbia Ranch and the studios of Warner Brothers and Universal Films. New buildings, designed by Kem Weber, a leading Los Angeles architect of his generation, were erected and others were brought from Hyperion Avenue. The move to Burbank began in August 1939 and was completed by the following spring.

Background paintings, opposite and overleaf,
followed the letter and spirit of the layout
drawings, above, adding the dimension of color

The atmosphere of *Pinocchio* owed a great
deal to the effectiveness of the background
paintings

Operating the multiplane camera crane. The technician at the upper left is Card Walker, who later became president of Walt Disney Productions

When the new studio was nearly ready, Walt Disney took his father on a tour of the premises. According to legend, Elias, the former carpenter and contractor, was evidently a little disturbed by what he saw. "Walter – what can it be used for?" he asked. His son, taken aback, said, "It's a studio – where I work." Elias persisted: "No, Walter, what can it be used for?" Suddenly, it dawned on Walt that what his father wanted to know was what the property could be used for if the studio failed. "Now this would make a perfect hospital," said Walt, improvising. For the rest of the tour, the Studio became a hospital. The master filmmaker showed his father where the operating rooms could go, extemporizing upon the advantages of the wide corridors and the advanced air-conditioning system. His father left a happy man.

Elias's worries were not entirely unfounded. In April of 1940 Walt had found himself so short of operating capital he had been forced to offer stock to the public for the first time; thus, an artistic high in his career corresponded with an economic low.

Completely sure of himself, however, Disney refused to cut back on his ambitious production schedule.

6 Fantasia: The Grand Experiment

The new emphasis on feature film production did not mean that Disney had lost his special affection for Mickey Mouse, but Mickey was losing ground to Donald and this prompted Disney, in 1938, to plan a comeback for him. The vehicle he chose for this purpose was *The Sorcerer's Apprentice,* an ancient fairy-tale motif which Goethe had employed as the basis for a very popular poem; Disney's immediate inspiration was Paul Dukas's orchestral work of the same title, written in 1897. This popular piece of program music seemed to provide an ideal score for the Mickey project. Its running time made for a film about twice the length of the average cartoon short, thus allowing for leisurely storytelling and substantive character development. Anxious to lend his production as much prestige as possible, Disney sought the services of Leopold Stokowski. Stokowski, maestro of the Philadelphia Orchestra, had long admired Disney's work and was delighted to make himself available. In fact, he involved himself so intensely in the project that it soon began to develop into something far more ambitious.

The idea that evolved was for a full-length feature film which would take the form of a concert of orchestral pieces conducted by Stokowski and illustrated by the Disney artists. Eventually, in November 1940, it would be released under the title *Fantasia,* but for the time being it was referred to as "the Concert Feature."

The first thing to be decided upon was the program of music that

would form the basis of this film. While Stokowski was instrumental in the process of selection, the final choice would have to be dictated by visual considerations, and therefore it was imperative that Studio artists be involved from the first. Disney called in Joe Grant and Dick Huemer (he knew that Huemer was an opera buff and that Grant's experience in character design would be invaluable) and had them listen to hundreds of pieces of music in order to evaluate them in terms of their potential as a basis for animation. It had been decided that a narrator would be needed to link the various episodes of the film, and Deems Taylor, known to millions as music commentator on the Metropolitan Opera radio broadcasts, was chosen for this role and to assist in the process of selection. The field was narrowed down to a dozen or so possible compositions, and Grant and Huemer began to investigate the story potential inherent in each of these.

Eventually, the film was broken down into seven main parts, the first being an introduction which culminated with Stokowski's orchestral arrangement of Bach's *Toccata and Fugue in D Minor.* Next came excerpts from Tchaikovsky's *Nutcracker Suite;* then came *The Sorcerer's Apprentice,* followed by Stravinsky's *Rite of Spring.* The fifth piece was Beethoven's Sixth Symphony, the "Pastoral." Then came "Dance of the Hours" from Amilcare Ponchielli's opera *La Gioconda.* The final selection combined Mussorgsky's *Night on Bald Mountain* with Schubert's "Ave Maria."

It has sometimes been suggested that in making *Fantasia* Disney was courting the intellectual community, but this does not seem consistent with his character or his goals. There is every reason to believe that he

Deems Taylor, wearing glasses, and Leopold Stokowski at the Studio. With Disney, they discuss the storyboard for *The Sorcerer's Apprentice* and inspect the multiplane camera. In the right-hand photograph, they visit the ink and paint department

Left: shooting live action for *Fantasia*; center: Stokowski in the Disney paint laboratory; right: dummy musicians used for silhouettes in the film are loaded onto a truck

was always careful to keep the mass movie audience in mind. If intellectuals praised his work, that was an added bonus, nothing more. With the exception of the Stravinsky piece, all of the final selections for *Fantasia* fell into the category of popular classics – tunes with which many people would be familiar. In this respect, *Fantasia* is reminiscent of some of the Silly Symphonies.

Disney did not have pretensions toward high culture. Nor did he claim any extensive knowledge of classical music, though, according to his daughter Diane, he enjoyed it tremendously. He certainly understood fully how music could be integrated into his movies. Everything he produced from *Steamboat Willie* on supports this. *Fantasia* should not be seen as a totally new development – a play for cultural respectability – but as a culmination of everything that had gone before.

Nonetheless, the concert character of the movie and the fact that Stokowski and Deems Taylor were associated with it raised certain expectations, and Disney went to great lengths to live up to them. He planned the film for a special wide screen but had to abandon this scheme for financial reasons. He also developed a sound system utilizing seven tracks and thirty speakers, which anticipated stereophonic sound and even some of the characteristics of Dolby sound. Stokowski himself handled the sound mixing for this multitrack system, and the results were, to judge by contemporary accounts, quite spectacular. Unhappily, the system was prohibitively expensive and was installed only in a few first-run theaters. For general distribution, the sound was remixed for more conventional equipment.

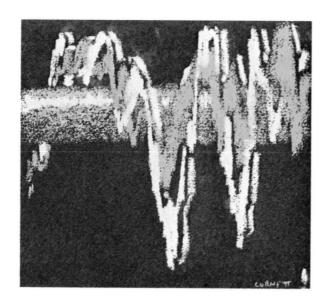 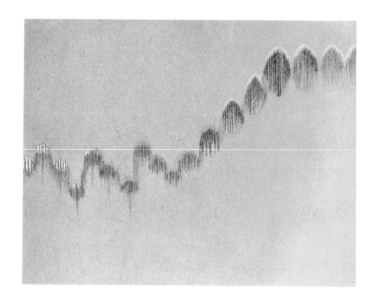

The film opens with a brief introductory section in which Deems Taylor sets the scene; then the *Toccata and Fugue* begins. Visually, this segment provided a field day for the Disney effects department (as did a later interlude which introduced the sound track as a character). When *Fantasia* was in production, more than sixty people worked for the effects department, and they were given the task of interpreting the patterns of Bach's music in terms of abstract and semiabstract forms. This was a new area of experimentation for them, and, under the circumstances, they did a creditable job. Their notion of abstraction owed more to Art Deco design motifs than to modern painting, but it is consistently inventive. The main criticism that can be made is that whereas the music is very formal and rigorous, the animation is rather lighthearted and stylized, emphasizing the melodic highlights of Bach's themes rather than the harmonic richness. Quasi-surrealistic images are used at times when a more strictly abstract interpretation might have been more appropriate.

Despite its flaws, this opening section of the movie does command one's attention and was a bold attempt to do something that had not been done before.

The *Nutcracker Suite* is ballet music, and Disney's artists treated the section of the film it underpins as a kind of animated dance sequence. The first two movements of the suite were dropped and the order of the others rearranged so that a continuous story could be constructed, leading off with "Dance of the Sugar Plum Fairy." Dragonfly sprites dart among flowers, touching them with wands so that they sparkle with

Hundreds of pastel studies were made of the *Toccata and Fugue* segment of *Fantasia* and for the "sound track" interlude, both of which used abstract forms to illustrate musical ideas

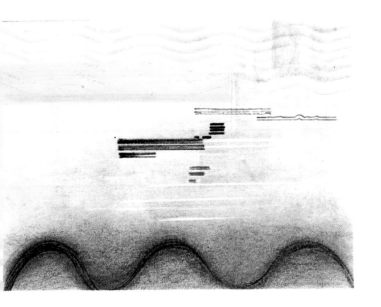

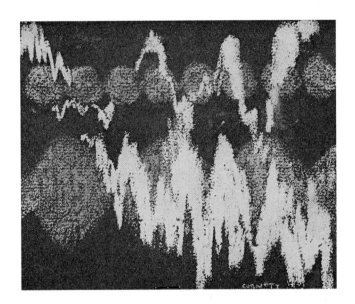

tiny beads of dew. Buds open and more fairies are awakened. The atmosphere is one of great delicacy. (Airbrush work and special transparent paints contribute greatly to the sense of lightness.)

The next movement, "Chinese Dance" – animated with great wit, principally by Art Babbitt – is one of the high spots of the movie. A group of humorously choreographed mushrooms moves through a solemn routine with almost ritualistic movements. One, smaller than the rest, has great difficulty following the steps of its associates.

"Dance of the Flutes" follows, with blossoms drifting down to the surface of a stream, where they are transformed into tiny ballerinas. A breeze picks them up and sends them skimming out across the surface of the water and among the branches of overhanging trees, until they are swept over a cascade and vanish from sight.

As the fourth movement, "Arab Dance," opens, bubbles rise to the surface from the spot where the blossoms vanished. The camera fades into the depth of the stream and there, among a forest of water plants, exotic fish – some gold and some black – perform an aqua ballet. As the sequence ends, the light fails and bubbles again begin to rise to the surface.

A thistle in the form of a Cossack bursts from the largest bubble and "Russian Dance" begins. More thistles join in, whirling with orchids that resemble girls in peasant costume. Music and dancing become faster and faster, then freeze to a final tableau.

This segment concludes with "Waltz of the Flowers." Autumn fairies move among the trees, touching leaves which take on their fall colors and drift with the wind. The fairies touch milkweed pods which burst,

Disney artists transformed Tchaikovsky's
Nutcracker Suite into a nature ballet featuring
spectacular effects animation and delicate
airbrush work

releasing their seeds, which become yet another kind of dancer, complete with bouffant skirts and sleek black hair. Frost sprites appear and skate across the surface of the stream, transforming it to ice as snow begins to fall, covering the landscape.

A technical tour de force, the *Nutcracker Suite* section succeeds admirably within its own terms, allowing the effects department to display its skills and making imaginative use of multiplane shots. It features some extraordinary animation and picks up on the romantic flavor that had colored so many of the Silly Symphonies, transforming that sensibility into something substantial enough to provide a base for bravura performances by all concerned.

Disney had planned *The Sorcerer's Apprentice* as a spectacular showcase for Mickey, and it became exactly that, the whole project being developed with great care and attention to detail. Under Jim Algar's direction, nothing was left to chance. Story sketches were made in full color, and some of the Studio's top animators were put on this assignment (Bill Tytla, for example, and Les Clark, who had been drawing Mickey for ten years).

Mickey is portrayed as a young magician, the disciple of a great Wizard who, bored for the moment with his own powers, leaves Mickey in charge of the subterranean cavern where he practices his arcane craft. Mickey has been ordered to fill the large water vat in the cavern, but the ambitious apprentice discovers that the Wizard has left his magic hat behind and decides to take advantage of this. Donning the hat, he brings a broom to life and directs it to carry the water. The broom marches to the well, fills a wooden pail with water, and starts on its appointed task. Satisfied with the success of the spell, Mickey settles down in the Wizard's chair to take a snooze. Soon he is dreaming that he is high above the earth, far out in space. His powers have become so great that he can control the paths of stars and planets, and comets change their course at his bidding. Next he is standing on top of a towering crag, conducting the waves of the ocean. With a gesture worthy of Stokowski, he beckons to the breakers to smash against the base of a rock. He repeats the gesture and waves break over the top of the crag, drenching the dreaming apprentice and startling him from his reverie.

He awakens to find that the cavern is awash. The broom is following his instructions with too great a zeal and has already brought thousands of gallons of water from the well, threatening to cause a disastrous flood. Mickey orders it to stop, but his magic powers have vanished, and the broom mechanically continues its task. In desperation, Mickey attacks it with an axe, only to see the broom split into many brooms, all of which continue with dogged perseverance, sweeping him aside and swamping the cavern. The water gets deeper and deeper. Furniture is afloat. Mickey seeks safety on a gigantic book of spells, which is soon sucked into an iridescent whirlpool. The apprentice seems on the point of losing his life when, suddenly, the Wizard appears at the top of the stairway. A single gesture from him and the waters subside. Everything returns to normal. Mickey, chastened, is left to clean up the mess.

The Sorcerer's Apprentice presents Mickey as
a neophyte magician dabbling with spells he
cannot control

As *The Sorcerer's Apprentice* moves toward its climax, Mickey finds himself quite literally out of his depth

With this story, Mickey had certainly come a long way from *Steamboat Willie*. The fantasy of controlling the universe is not something that one would have suspected of Minnie's old sweetheart, not even of the conductor in *The Band Concert*. Yet one of the things that has always given Mickey's personality a certain depth was his true-to-life tendency to indulge in fantasy (and, more often than not, his fantasies would clash with some pressing reality). The Mickey of *The Sorcerer's Apprentice* is the same old Mickey, but the circumstances he finds himself in encourage him to indulge in more grandiose dreams. The magnitude of his fantasy and the absurdity of the reality with which he finds himself in conflict enable us to learn something more about Mickey's psychology. As a magician he is a failure, but he succeeds in something much more important – for the first time he becomes a fully rounded, three-dimensional character.

Although told in an amusing way, *The Sorcerer's Apprentice* presents psychological ideas that are very basic to the human condition. Technically, like everything else in *Fantasia*, the segment is superb.

Rite of Spring heralds an abrupt change in mood. Disney saw Stravinsky's ballet music as providing the score for nothing less than a portrayal of the creation of the world (and certainly the insistent rhythms are suggestive of primeval forces). In later years, Stravinsky expressed displeasure

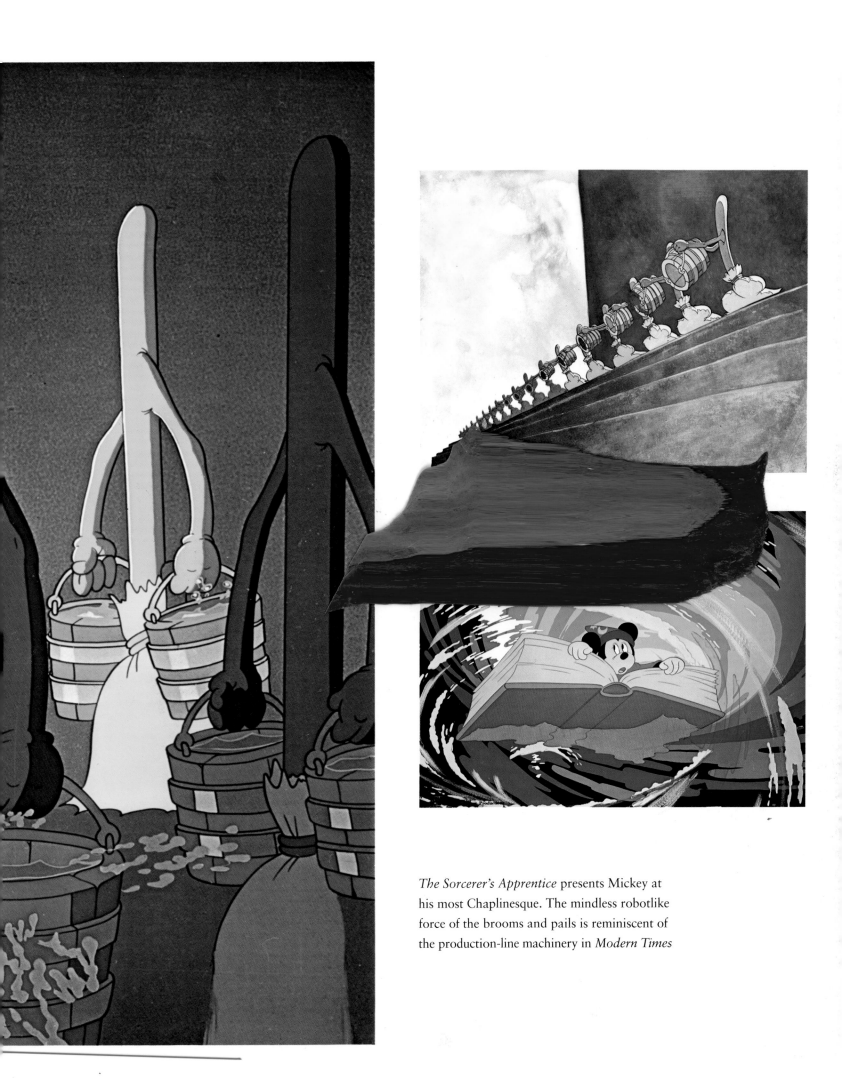

The Sorcerer's Apprentice presents Mickey at his most Chaplinesque. The mindless robotlike force of the brooms and pails is reminiscent of the production-line machinery in *Modern Times*

with the way his music had been used, but this seems to relate mostly to alterations in the orchestration that may have been made without his permission; there is no reason to suppose that he was dissatisfied with Disney's overall concept. He visited the studio and saw the storyboards that had been prepared. Photographs taken during the visit suggest that he was not unhappy with them.

This segment begins with visions of a time when the earth was still a molten mass, and it carries the story of evolution to the point at which the dinosaurs disappeared from the face of the planet. Millions of years are telescoped into a few minutes. We see mountain ranges thrown up by gigantic volcanic convulsions; then primitive forms of marine life emerge from the oceans and learn to live on dry land. Later, huge reptiles roam the surface of the earth and engage in titanic battles to the death. Eventually, a massive drought turns whole continents into deserts.

Unfortunately, all this is not too convincing on the screen. The formation of the earth is treated imaginatively by the effects department, and the emergence of life in the sea is handled with delicacy; after that, however, the story becomes crudely melodramatic. Dinosaurs are transformed into ham actors. When they fight, theatrical lighting is used, as though the action would not seem dramatic enough by itself. The music overpowers the imagery, which finally seems far too schematic.

The next segment, set to the "Pastoral" symphony, is difficult to judge objectively. It has considerable charm, yet its visual character seems to have very little to do with the true nature of Beethoven's music.

This can be explained in part by the fact that the Arcadian scenes which make up this segment were originally intended for a much lighter piece of music – an excerpt from Gabriel Pierné's *Cydalise*. The rhythms of the Pierné selection proved to be too persistent to support the subject matter (the animators needed some pauses and legato passages). Disney decided to switch to the Beethoven work – apparently against Stokowski's better judgment.

Visually, this segment owes a great deal to the stylized decorative and illustrative idioms of the thirties – it passes before the viewer like an animated mural for some fashionable restaurant. The backgrounds are extremely elegant and pleasing (Art Riley, Claude Coats, and Ray Huffine must share credit with the layout team of Ken Anderson and Hugh Hennesy), combining gently curving forms with an innovative use of color.

The best scene comes near the beginning, when flying horses resembling giant butterflies glide in above the lake before settling on the surface of the water. This has a wonderful sense of poetry which only animation could supply. Much of the action concerns flirtations between centaurs and centaurettes. The former – a hybrid species combining football players and cart horses – seem rather clumsy, but the centaurettes, styled by Fred Moore, display a certain adolescent charm, looking like high school coeds who have undergone some unlikely transformation.

Good comic interludes are provided by Ward Kimball's Bacchus and his drunken unicorn-mule. Toward the end, Zeus, aided by Vulcan, stages

In *Fantasia,* Stravinsky's *Rite of Spring* is used to underscore the story of the earth's prehistory, including the age of the giant reptiles

a thunderstorm for his own amusement. Night falls and Artemis appears in the sky to launch an arrow of fire from the bow of light formed by the new moon.

It is difficult to give an adequate idea of Disney's interpretation of "Dance of the Hours," but we might begin by saying that it is possibly the best – and certainly the funniest – segment of the movie. The animators, who included John Lounsbery, Howard Swift, and Hugh Fraser, were given the task of developing a parody of classical ballet featuring hippos, elephants, ostriches, and alligators. The result is hilarious. A hippo in a negligible tutu does pirouettes as though she weighed no more than a feather. Alligators swoop down from behind pillars, the inherent menace of their species amplified by choreographic fantasy and clever camera angles. Elephants hide timidly behind flimsy architectural elements, and ostriches perform entrechats with an inspired absence of grace. Gravity and reason are denied in a triumph of insanity. Directed by T. Hee and laid out by Ken O'Connor, "Dance of the Hours" is a classic of comic animation.

Fantasia concludes with *Night on Bald Mountain* and "Ave Maria." As technical achievements they are extraordinary, but emotionally they are unsatisfying. The concept of this segment is a simple contrast of good and evil. To Mussorgsky's dramatic music, witches ride demonic steeds and tormented spirits rise from the grave to join the Devil on top of a jagged, rocky peak. The special effects in these sequences are excellent, and Bill Tytla's Devil is realized with enormous vigor. At dawn, the ghosts return to their resting places and, to the strains of "Ave Maria," a procession moves slowly toward a Gothic chapel.

Most of the great monuments of Christianity – whether Chartres Cathedral or the King James Version of the Bible – were the products of years of patient labor. To expect the Studio artists to come up with something even remotely comparable while working to specifications and under deadline pressure is unfair; yet anything less in this area does not seem worth attempting.

Fantasia is a film with great merits and great faults. Structurally, it owes very little to anything that preceded it in the history of the cinema, and Disney deserves great credit for breaking so boldly with precedent. His artists deserve praise for some of the finest animation that has ever reached the screen.

It has been said that *Fantasia* was ahead of its time, and in certain respects this is true (the popularity that the film continues to enjoy bears this out). In other ways, it was very much of its time. For the most part, its imagery belongs essentially to the pre-World War II era, as does Deems Taylor's commentary.

The film has had many critics. Frank Lloyd Wright visited the Studio while it was in production. Invited to lecture the staff as part of the art education program, he was shown sections of the movie and was out-

A pastel drawing for the "Pastoral" segment. Such pre-production studies are sometimes referred to as "concept art"

From the top down: Disney and Igor Stravinsky discuss the score of the composer's *Rite of Spring;* Disney and sequence director T. Hee (in shirtsleeves) with Stravinsky and choreographer George Balanchine; Julian Huxley inspects a *Fantasia* model, watched by Disney and astronomer Dr. Edwin Hubbel; members of Associated American Artists visit the Studio – left to right, George Biddle, Reeves Lewinthal, Thomas Hart Benton, Ernest Fiene, Grant Wood, and George Schreiber

Early studies for the "Pastoral" segment of *Fantasia* betray influences reaching back to the nineteenth-century Symbolist movement (see overleaf)

The version of the "Pastoral" segment that reached the screen owed a good deal to Art Deco idioms

"Dance of the Hours," as interpreted by the
Disney artists, became a hilarious parody of
classical ballet

FOLDER Dance of the hours reel ①

Fantasia concludes with *Night on Bald Mountain* and "Ave Maria," a presentation of the conflict between Good and Evil

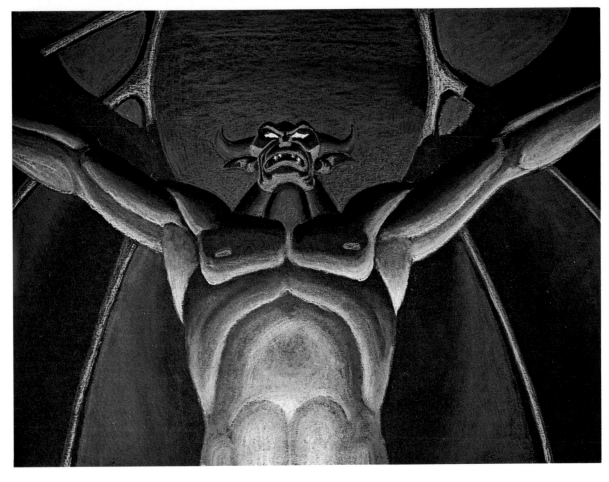

spoken in his dislike for it. It was absurd, in his opinion, to illustrate music. He felt that Disney should take a long vacation and reconsider his position.

If we try to assess *Fantasia* objectively, we find that two segments – *The Sorcerer's Apprentice* and the animal ballet of "Dance of the Hours" – have a universal appeal. Each of the other segments has merits of one kind or another, but they are not held together by the aesthetic coherence that is evident in *Snow White* and *Pinocchio*. The viewer is asked to make too many taste adjustments during the course of the movie for it to be a complete success.

Nonetheless, *Fantasia* is an amazing piece of filmmaking, one that will continue to fascinate audiences. For all its faults, there have been few movies in the entire history of cinema to compare with it in terms of boldness of concept and brilliance of execution.

Top: artists Art Riley, left, and Ray Huffine at work on *Fantasia* backgrounds. Center: Retta Scott, an animator who worked on the "Pastoral" segment. Bottom: working on study for *Rite of Spring*, Woolie Reitherman consults a model of a dinosaur

7 Dumbo and Bambi

Cinematically, *Snow White*, *Pinocchio*, and *Fantasia* were blockbusters. The two features that followed – *Dumbo* and *Bambi* – were a little different in character. *Bambi*, except for its final climactic scenes, is a rather low-keyed movie. The Disney artists took great pains to establish the tranquillity that – according to the scenario, at least – prevails in the forest under normal conditions. This led to a lyrical approach which is quite distinctive and separates *Bambi* from all other Disney movies. *Dumbo* is a delightfully unpretentious picture, relying almost entirely on charm and humor rather than on spectacular effects.

Like *Pinocchio*, *Fantasia* did not have a great financial success at the time of its first release, and *Dumbo* was conceived as a way of recouping some of those losses. It was made for a fraction of the cost of the two preceding releases, yet its earning potential would prove to be at least equal to theirs. Multiplane shots and other expensive effects were kept to the bare minimum that would assure good production values, and the story was told as simply and directly as possible, with the emphasis placed on humorous character development. In many respects, this represented a shift back to the spirit of the cartoon shorts. After the demands of the first three features, *Dumbo* was practically a vacation for the Disney artists, and they clearly enjoyed themselves on this project. It is probably the most spontaneous animated feature that the Studio has ever produced. Audiences responded well to it, and the film brought in much-needed revenue (only the fact that it was released just two months before Pearl Harbor prevented it from having an even greater impact).

Dumbo is the story of a baby elephant who discovers that he can fly. Adapted for the screen by Joe Grant and Dick Huemer, the film has a number of highlights. The circus parade and the scenes with Dumbo and the clowns have a splashy vigor spiced with the kind of knockabout humor that benefited greatly from the expertise of the veteran animators. The older elephants, caricatured as gossipy women, feature fine animation by Bill Tytla and John Lounsbery. Perhaps the most original sequence of the movie is the one in which Dumbo and his friend Timothy Mouse get drunk and see pink elephants – brilliantly animated by Hicks Lokey and Howard Swift. This leads directly to the scenes in which Dumbo learns that he can fly, a discovery which is prompted by the raucous encouragement of Ward Kimball's quartet of hipster crows.

Disney's own involvement with *Dumbo* seems to have been less than it was with the earlier features. This is not to say that he was uninterested in the project – he was, of course, involved in the important story conferences, and all decisions were still subject to his approval – but he was not aiming for a new plateau of achievement in this film and clearly felt that much responsibility could be delegated to members of his staff.

All was not well at the Studio, however. Along with continuing financial difficulties, Disney found himself confronted by labor unrest. By 1941, unionization was firmly established in most of the other Hollywood studios, but it had not yet made inroads into the animation industry.

This is not the place to discuss the pros and cons of the dispute that led to picket lines going up outside the Studio, but the strike itself cannot be ignored since it did have a significant effect on future productions. In retrospect, it seems inevitable that some kind of unionization would have come about sooner or later, but Walt Disney refused to accept this. The strike was a bitter one and left deep wounds. As a direct or indirect result of it the Studio lost some excellent animators, as well as much of the freewheeling atmosphere that had typified it in the thirties. The Age of Innocence was over.

By coincidence, the theme of *Bambi* focuses on the passing of a state of innocence (man invades the forest, bringing terror and destruction to the animals who live there). Disney had begun preparatory work on *Bambi* as early as 1937, before the release of *Snow White*, but for various reasons it did not reach movie theaters until 1942. By its very nature, it was a project that could not be rushed, and the Studio's economic problems impeded the progress of the production. Disney's strongly held ideas about how *Bambi* should be made dictated that the film would have to be very expensive, and rather than cut back on production values, he waited until he was able to make the movie that he wanted. While *Fantasia* was eating up the company's resources, *Bambi* was cut back to a skeleton crew and did not return to full production until *Fantasia* was finished.

The prevailing mood of this film (until the climax, at least) is one of

Top: Joe Grant and Dick Huemer at work on the script of *Dumbo*. Center and bottom: while researching Dumbo, Disney artists spent time sketching at the Cole Brothers' Circus

Some of the most inventive animation for *Dumbo* was done by Ward Kimball, who drew the hipster crows

lyricism. Humor is blended with the lyricism, but it is humor of a very gentle variety and does not interrupt the mood. The forest becomes a character in the movie, every bit as important as any of the animals. Its response to weather (as in the raindrop sequence with its effective use of multiplane shots) and to season (as in the autumn montage) is as much a part of the story as any of the things that happen to Bambi and his friends. Much of the credit for this should go to Tyrus Wong, who keyed the background styling.

Great emphasis was placed on naturalism in the making of *Bambi*. Special art classes – an extension of the existing training program – were instituted so that Rico LeBrun could instruct the animators in the finer points of drawing animals. Real deer were kept on the lot as models for the artists. Books of photographic studies and innumerable model sheets were compiled, along with analyses of animal action and thousands of feet of live-action material to be used for reference.

The *Bambi* unit departed from the usual Disney procedure of casting specific animators for specific characters. This time the film was simply broken down into sequences and scenes, and any artist might be asked to draw any character. Because of this, the art classes and other aids had a special importance.

Technically, *Bambi* had a great deal to commend it. Much patient work went into it, and we might single out the contributions of the art direction team, headed by Tom Codrick, and the animation of Frank Thomas, Milt Kahl, Ollie Johnston, Eric Larson, and Retta Scott. But, for all the effort and skill, *Bambi* is ultimately unsatisfying – especially by the standards Disney had set for himself in his earlier features. The artists cannot be faulted. The problem lies with the interpretation of the story, perhaps with the story itself. In earlier Disney films – both shorts and features – the fact that animals take on human characteristics and have human voices is not disturbing since they exist in a world of their own which is governed by its own rules (as we have already noted, this links them to a tradition that has its roots in Aesop and Aristophanes). We are not surprised, for instance, when Pinocchio is seduced from the straight and narrow by a fox and a cat, for they are clearly caricatures of human types and the story unfolds in a fantastic dimension which we recognize as a metaphor for reality rather than as a naturalistic portrayal. Even the animals and birds in *Snow White* do not disturb us by their intelligent behavior. Within the framework of the fairy tale, it seems quite acceptable, and only relatively small demands are made on them – they are not even asked to speak. Prior to *Bambi*, Disney's use of humanized animals had always been within the limits of established idioms.

Bambi, however, is something quite different. This film aims for a kind of naturalism which falls outside the borders of fantasy and fairy tale – yet it presents an owl on friendly terms with baby rabbits who, in the real forest, would be his victims, and we are asked to believe in deer that speak the language and share the emotions of the humans who are supposed to be their enemies. It is very difficult to reconcile these contradictions.

Voice talents involved in the making of *Dumbo* included Sterling Holloway, left, who played Ol' Doc Stork, and Verna Felton as one of the gossipy elephants

Dumbo – opposite and overleaf – follows the career of a young elephant from the night he is delivered by stork at the winter quarters of the circus to the day he learns he can fly and to his "arrival" as a national celebrity

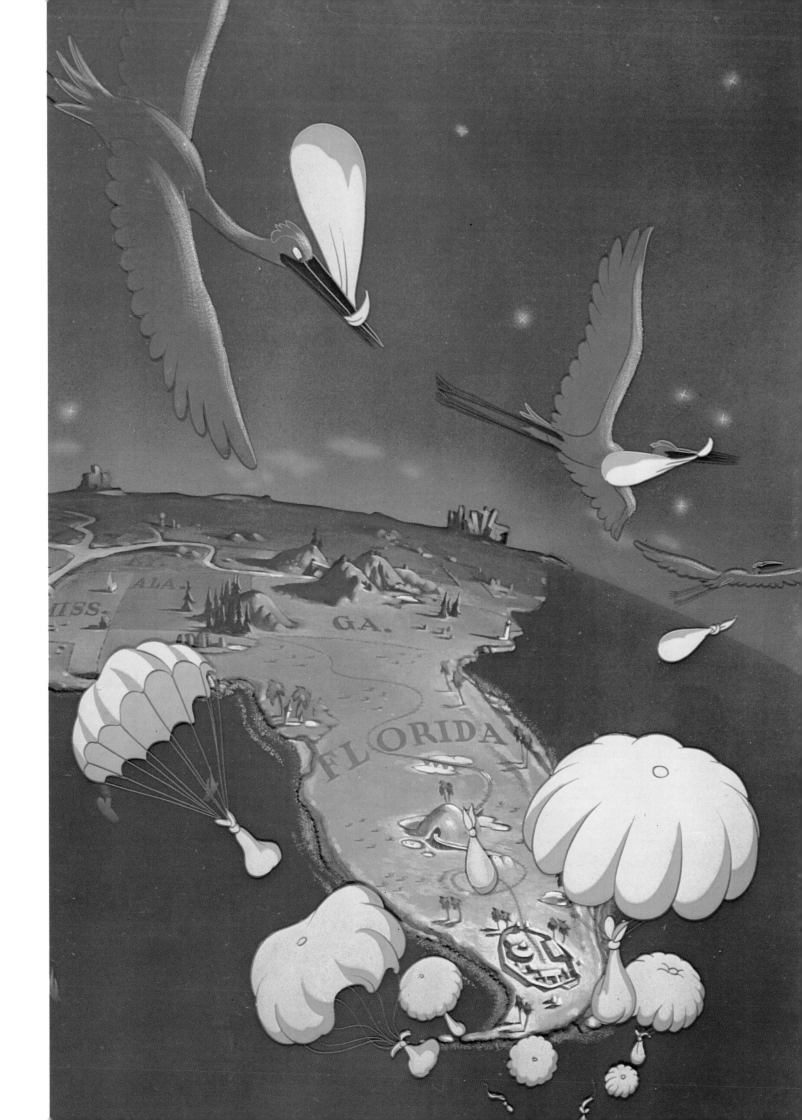

Circus clowns in *Dumbo*

At the end of the film, the circus train carries Dumbo over the mountains and to the bright lights of the big city

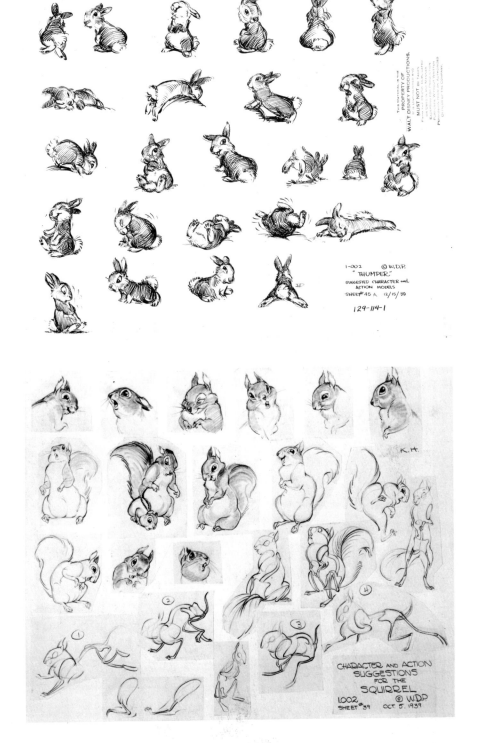

Preparatory work for *Bambi* included elaborate studies of animals in action

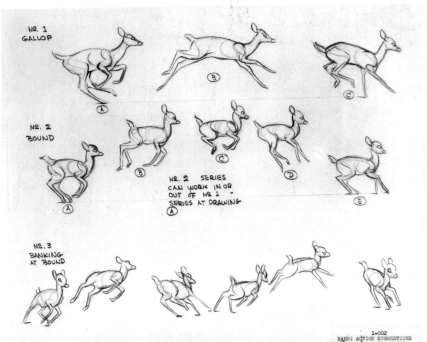

In *Bambi*, Disney artists aimed for a degree of naturalism
quite unprecedented in the history of the animated film

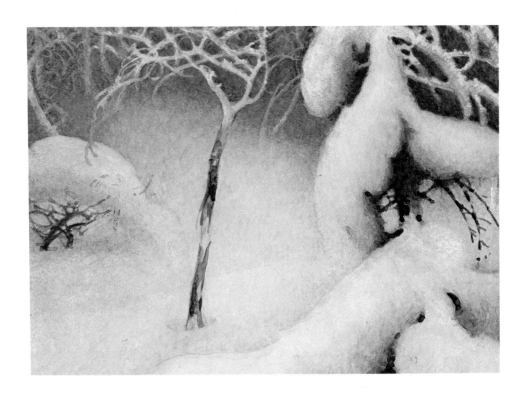

Bambi and his father in the snow

Background treatments for *Bambi* were
conceived to sustain a lyrical mood

The most sympathetic characters are those, like Thumper the rabbit and Flower the skunk, who are used mostly for humorous relief. They seem to belong to the Disney mainstream and work well in those terms.

Yet despite its shortcomings, *Bambi* is an important movie. Along with the four preceding feature films and the short cartoons of the thirties, it gave the Studio a tremendous reservoir of idioms and techniques. The Disney artists could now handle everything from the broad stylization of Mickey or the Goof to the naturalism of Faline. They had learned how to create any atmosphere they might need, and the multiplane camera allowed them to use space in new and complicated ways. The Disney paint laboratory had developed hundreds of new colors to extend the possibilities of animation in still another way.

Bambi also marked the end of an era. The expansion that began in the early thirties reached a peak and leveled off about 1940. By the time *Bambi* reached the screen, the armed forces were already depleting the Studio's ranks. Unionization precluded the possibility of ever building the staff to the level of the early forties, and, in any case, the economic conditions that made so many artists available in the thirties were a thing of the past. This did not mean that Disney animation had no future – obviously, this was far from being true – but it is fair to say that the initial momentum was spent. For a while, the Studio would have to coast – capitalizing on its past achievements, working well within its capabilities, experimenting a little, and waiting for energies to be restored.

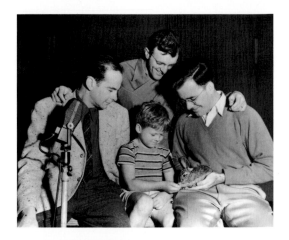

From the top down: special classes for *Bambi* artists were conducted by Rico LeBrun; animators Ollie Johnston, left, Milt Kahl, center, and Frank Thomas, right, pose with Peter Behn, the voice of Thumper; Frank Thomas sketches Faline

8 Interruptions and Innovations

America's entry into World War II had an almost immediate effect on Walt Disney Productions. In December 1941, part of the Studio was commandeered as quarters for an antiaircraft unit which stayed for several months. Before long, someone in the Navy realized that animation could be of great value in the presentation of training material. The Studio began to receive contracts from military and government agencies that led to the production of such titles as *Aircraft Carrier Landing Signals, Food Will Win the War, Automotive Electricity for Military Vehicles, Basic Map Reading,* and *Fundamentals of Artillery Weapons.* Since these productions had to be made as inexpensively as possible, extensive and clever use was made of "limited animation" techniques, in which camera movements and other simple devices were substituted for fully drawn animation. A more ambitious project was *Victory Through Air Power,* a feature-length film presenting the strategic bombing theories of Major Alexander de Seversky, made at Disney's expense but utilizing some of the techniques devised for the government-backed shorts.

Throughout the war period, Disney continued to produce short cartoons featuring Donald, Pluto, and Goofy (Mickey Mouse shorts were temporarily discontinued in 1942). Some of these were geared to the war effort or served a propaganda purpose. *Victory Vehicles,* for example, used Goofy to encourage Americans to conserve rubber and gasoline while *Der Fuehrer's Face* takes the form of a nightmare in which Donald imagines himself to be a worker in Nazi Germany. A still more extraordinary propaganda film, *Education for Death,* employed broad satire and powerful graphics to suggest that Germany's children had been schooled and disciplined into becoming a ruthless military machine.

The two most important commercial releases of the period – *Saludos Amigos* and *The Three Caballeros* – were themselves indirect products of the war. With Europe in turmoil, the Latin American market became increasingly important to American industry, including Hollywood, and it was with government sponsorship that Disney and a team of artists from the Studio traveled in 1941 to Argentina, Peru, Chile, and Brazil. Each of these nations provided the background for an animated short, and these episodes were then connected with documentary footage of the tour to create a "package" film released in 1943 as *Saludos Amigos.*

Perhaps the most interesting character to emerge from this mélange was José Carioca, the energetic, samba-loving parrot who would reappear two years later in *The Three Caballeros,* another package film featuring José, along with Donald and a Mexican rooster called Panchito, who sports a large sombrero and an itchy trigger finger.

The package film was not an ideal format for Disney artists, but it was a way of putting together feature-length releases at a time when wartime shortages and economic pressures made it impractical to produce full-length animated features. Some of these pressures continued after the war, and three more package films were released – *Make Mine Music* (1946), *Fun and Fancy Free* (1947), and *Melody Time* (1948). The first and third of these made use of the musical talents of recording artists such as Benny Goodman, Ethel Smith, and the Andrews Sisters, featuring them in animated segments that were sometimes comedic, sometimes semiabstract in a way that was reminiscent of *Fantasia. Fun and Fancy Free* featured just two animated story sections – "Bongo" and "Mickey and the Beanstalk" – though Jiminy Cricket was used in the introduction and incorporated into the linking live-action sequences.

For economic reasons, the Studio was coming to rely more and more upon live action and upon live-action/animation hybrids such as *Song of the South,* released in 1946. Although human actors carry the main body of the film's narrative, three Brer Rabbit stories are included as cartoon inserts and represent the best Disney animation of this period. In several scenes, live action and animation were combined very effectively.

By 1949, the Studio was almost ready to return to true feature animation. That year saw the release of *The Adventures of Ichabod and Mr. Toad,* which was still technically a package film but consisted of just two longish "featurettes" – more substantial than those in *Fun and Fancy Free* – linked only by the fact that the hero of each segment is prone to disaster. The "Toad" episode is based on Kenneth Grahame's *The Wind in the Willows* and is enlivened by fine character animation and some imaginative art direction. Unfortunately, the story is too compressed for any of the personalities to be fully explored. All of the action is there but not the leisurely pace of the original (it seems that Disney had intended the story to serve as the basis for a feature-length film but was forced to settle for this compromise version).

Walt Disney in Argentina

Der Fuehrer's Face, 1943, took the form of a nightmare in which Donald Duck found himself working in a Nazi munitions factory

During World War II, Disney characters were often used to illustrate matters of public interest. In *Victory Vehicles,* 1943, opposite, Goofy urged people to save scrap metal and gasoline

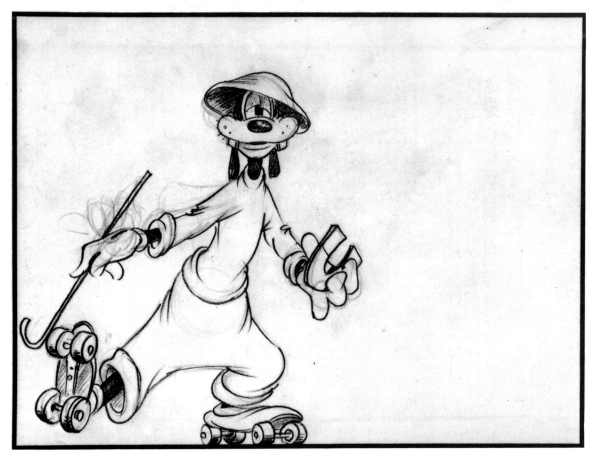

The 1943 package film *Saludos Amigos* included the story of Pedro the mail plane and introduced Donald's friend José Carioca

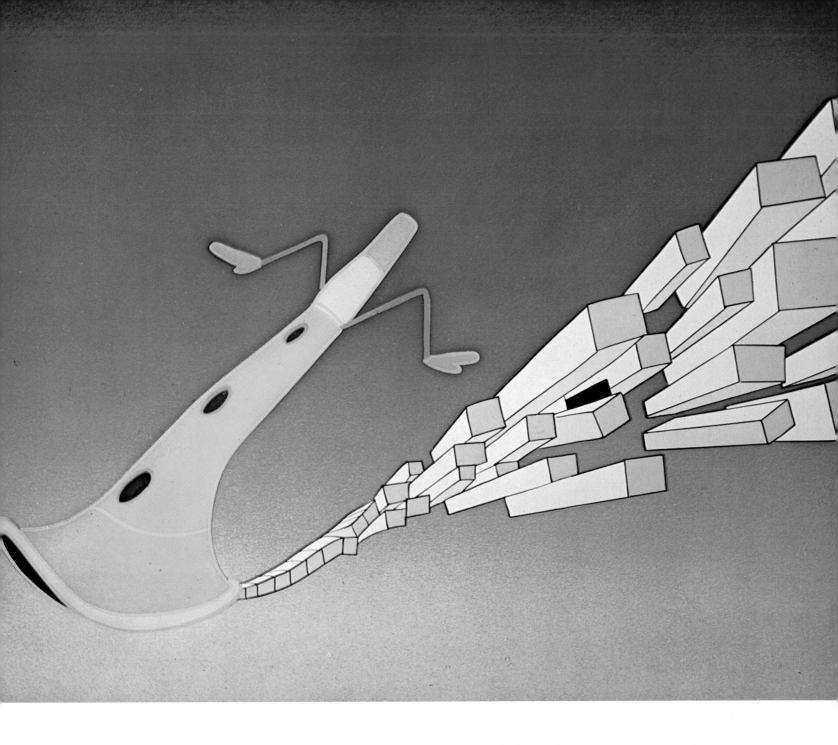

"After You've Gone" is a segment of the 1946 package film *Make Mine Music*

The animated portions of *Song of the South*, 1946, left, brought the animals of the Uncle Remus stories to life

Released in 1949, *The Adventures of Ichabod and Mr. Toad*, opposite, combined screen adaptations of two famous stories

The tale of Ichabod, based on Washington Irving's *The Legend of Sleepy Hollow,* is narrated by Bing Crosby. For the most part, it is presented in a rather pedestrian manner, but the final sequence, in which Ichabod Crane is pursued by the Headless Horseman, is outstanding, with the drama building to a fine pitch of excitement. *The Adventures of Ichabod and Mr. Toad* fell short of being a great movie, but it was a significant step toward regaining past glories.

The Studio was still producing short cartoons for theatrical release. (It continued to do so until 1956.) Donald and Goofy were now the biggest stars, each benefiting from character traits that made him easy to write for. Mickey made occasional appearances, but usually as a straight man, and Pluto continued to find himself in situations that derived from Webb Smith's 1934 flypaper gag. Important newcomers were Chip and Dale, highly territorial chipmunks who knew how to make Donald's life miserable. Besides these "character" cartoons, there were also occasional one-shot shorts like *Morris the Midget Moose* (1950) and *Susie the Little Blue Coupe* (1952), which went some way toward replacing the Silly Symphonies. Several skilled directors – Jack King, Jack Hannah, Bill Roberts, and Jack Kinney – specialized in short cartoons during this period, as did some first-rate animators, such as Bill Justice, John Sibley, and Bob Carlson.

On occasion, short subjects were accorded rather special treatment, as was the case with *Toot, Whistle, Plunk, and Boom* (1953). A highly stylized history of music, devised by Ward Kimball, this was the first CinemaScope® cartoon ever produced. A similar subject from the same year, *Adventures in Music: Melody,* was an experiment in 3-D animation.

Meanwhile, in 1950, Walt Disney released his first true animated feature since 1942. This was *Cinderella* – a project that had been in development for several years – and it was a success both at the box office and as a piece of imaginative filmmaking.

In spirit, it harks back to *Snow White and the Seven Dwarfs,* though with an added frosting of surface glamour and a greater reliance on gag routines. Cinderella, her stepmother, and the Prince are treated somewhat naturalistically while the ugly stepsisters, the Fairy Godmother, the King, and the Duke are essentially caricatures, but they all work well together. The animal characters are excellent. Lucifer the cat is a splendid villain, and the mice are consistently entertaining.

The backgrounds are less distinctive than those which added so much to *Snow White* and *Pinocchio,* but they are more than adequate, establishing a kind of French Provincial look. The well-constructed story consists of two parallel plots – one concerned with the human characters and the other with the animals – linked only by Cinderella herself. Songs in the film include "A Dream Is a Wish Your Heart Makes," "Bibbidi-Bobbidi-Boo," and "So This Is Love."

Cinderella succeeds because it remains faithful to the spirit of the original fairy tale while embroidering it with the kind of business that Disney understood better than anybody else. The next feature, *Alice in*

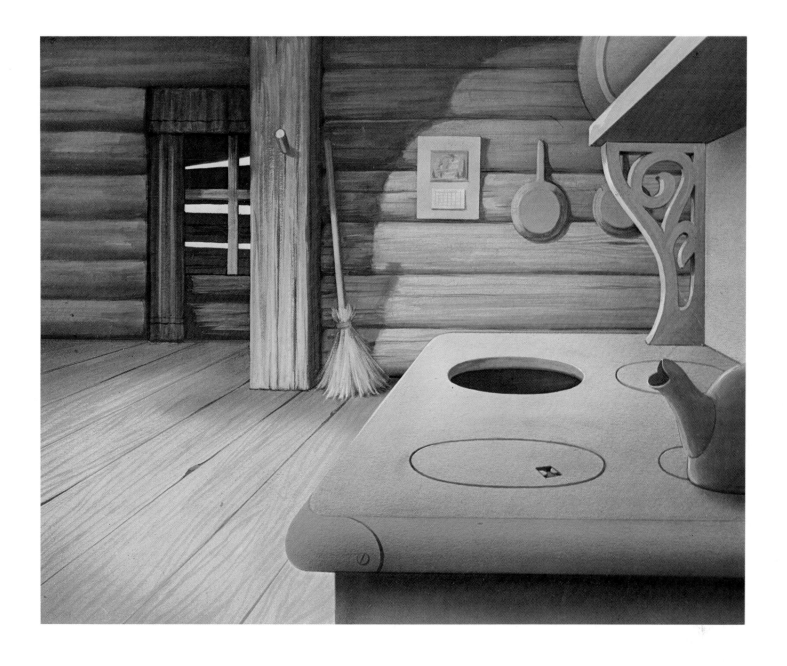

Much fine work went into the short cartoons of the forties, as in these examples of backgrounds from Donald Duck and Pluto vehicles

Left: *Slide Donald Slide*, 1949. Top: the 1950
short *Motor Mania* is one of several that take
an ironic look at the habits of the American
driver. Center: *Two Chips and a Miss*, 1952, a
typical outing for Chip and Dale. Bottom:
Toot, Whistle, Plunk, and Boom, 1953, is an
experimental short made in Cinemascope

Wonderland (1951), failed because it neither captured the unique atmosphere of Lewis Carroll's story nor displayed the authoritative Disney touch except in a few isolated scenes. Given the fact that the *Alice* shorts had provided him with his first success, it's hardly surprising that Disney had long cherished the idea of adapting the *Alice* books, first mentioning the idea while *Snow White* was in production. He worked at the idea intermittently for years, but it was no easy matter to translate Carroll's highly intellectual verbal humor into visual terms.

The movie has occasional moments of sharp surrealistic invention – the Mad Hatter's tea party is a memorable sequence – but for the most part it is a confusing hodgepodge of disparate story elements and stylistic inconsistencies. Carroll's fictional world is dislocated by inversions of reason but held together by the insane persistence of his own preposterous logic. Disney responded to the nonsense element in the *Alice* books but found no adequate cinematic equivalent for Carroll's erudite word games. Disappointed with the film, he blamed its failure on the heroine's "lack of heart."

Peter Pan, released in 1953, is an altogether more satisfactory picture – which incidentally provided a demonstration of just how expert the Disney animators had become at handling the human form. As in *Cinderella*, naturalism and caricature were skillfully blended.

Unlike *Alice*, Sir James Barrie's play adapted very well to the screen. If the movie has a weakness, it derives from the fact that there are too many characters to permit all of them to be developed adequately in the seventy-seven minute running time. The Lost Boys, for example, are potentially as interesting as the Seven Dwarfs, but they are individualized only in the crudest of ways. Even Peter and Wendy are a little sketchy. Captain Hook, meanwhile, emerges as a well-defined personality, and Tinker Bell, though her petulance becomes irritating, has an insistent presence.

Character development apart, the movie has a satisfying narrative flow, well-handled comedy routines, and more than its fair share of genuine magic moments in which the art of animation makes the impossible possible. The flying sequences are handled with great panache, permitting the viewer to imagine the excitement of defying gravity.

Peter Pan is not a masterpiece, but it is an enjoyable piece of entertainment that only the Disney Studio could have made. If Disney had had a problem making the overly inquisitive Alice believable, he had no such difficulty identifying with Barrie's boy who refused to grow up.

The year 1955 saw the release of *Lady and the Tramp,* Disney's first animated feature in CinemaScope. It was innovative in another way, too. Set in the recent past, the film deals with a kind of milieu Disney feature animation had not addressed until then – something rather close to our everyday world. (*Dumbo* had been set in the present, but the circus environment introduced an exotic element.) *Lady and the Tramp* unfolds in the suburbs of a medium-sized American city in the early years of the century, a setting compounded from vernacular elements that are still familiar today.

CinemaScope itself presented a challenge, especially to the layout artists. With a conventional aspect ratio, it is easy enough for a single

Cinderella was Disney's first true animated feature since *Bambi*. Released in 1950, it recaptured much of the spirit of the early features, modified by a new lightness of touch and an emphasis on surface glamour (see also overleaf)

Cinderella's Fairy Godmother prepares her for the ball

Disney's version of *Peter Pan,* 1953, is a
generally entertaining interpretation of Sir
James Barrie's stage classic

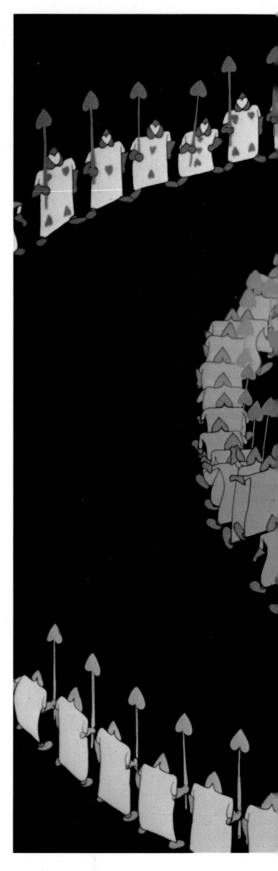

Released in 1951, *Alice in Wonderland* had some brilliant
visual touches but failed to capture the flavor of Lewis
Carroll's story

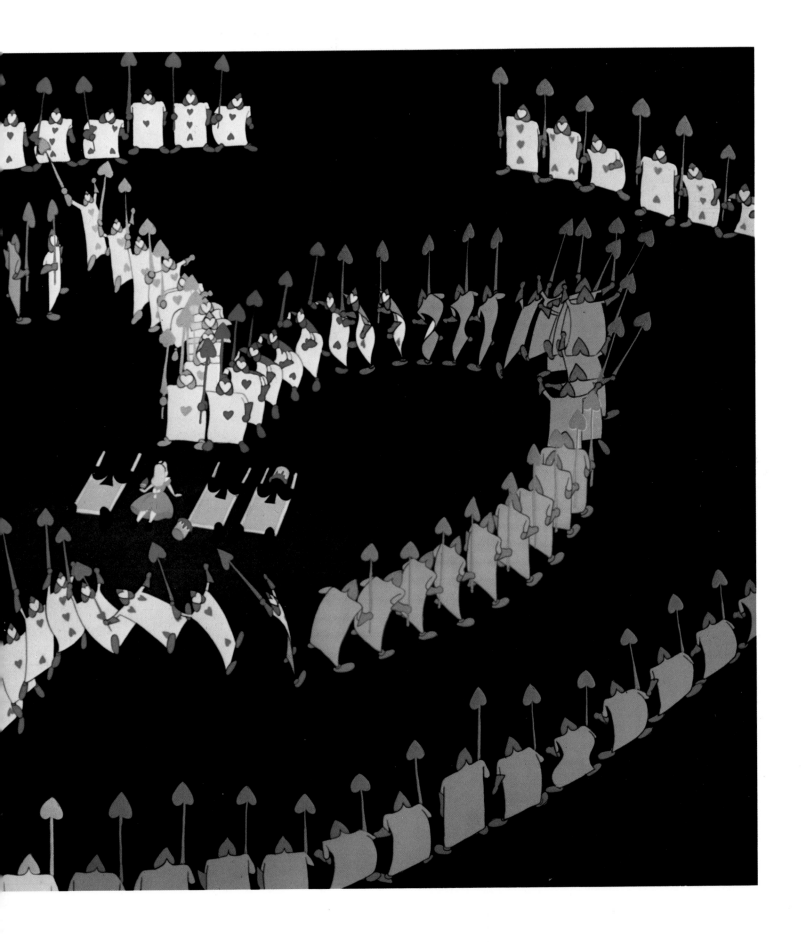

Released in 1955, *Lady and the Tramp* was
the first animated feature made in CinemaScope.
More significantly, it broke new ground in terms
of subject matter, setting a more informal tone
for future Disney movies

character to activate the whole screen, and characters can be closely grouped, which makes them easy to handle. CinemaScope provides a sense of space, but the stretched-out format makes it difficult for a single character to dominate the screen, and groups must be well spread out to keep the screen from seeming bare. Longer takes become necessary since the constant jump-cutting that is the norm in animated films would seem busy and annoying.

The Disney team overcame these difficulties remarkably well, and the animators did a fine job of grafting human personas onto the principal canine characters without losing the nuances of dog behavior that were necessary if the story was to be convincing. There are some well-executed action scenes – Tramp killing the rat comes to mind – and the movie introduced some memorable songs, including "Bella Notte" and "He's a Tramp." *Lady and the Tramp* and *Cinderella* were the strongest Disney animated features of the 1950s.

Lady and the Tramp was followed by another wide-screen feature – one that began with high hopes and ended in near disaster.

Sleeping Beauty was conceived as the most spectacular of Walt Disney's postwar productions. The artist Eyvind Earle was called in to devise background stylings somewhat remotely based on medieval tapestries and early Renaissance paintings, and the characters were designed to blend with these settings. Much care was lavished on planning scenes to make the fullest possible use of the Technirama® 70mm format. The multiplane camera would also be extensively used.

Unfortunately, *Sleeping Beauty* went into production at a time when Disney was preoccupied with both live-action films and also with his major project of the 1950s – Disneyland. Despite his ambitious plans for *Sleeping Beauty,* he seems to have had a difficult time immersing himself in the subject. As always, nothing could proceed without his approval, but because of his other concerns he often neglected the movie for weeks at a time. *Sleeping Beauty* took six years to complete. It finally reached theaters in January of 1959 and was greeted with almost universal disappointment.

The film has its good moments. The evil fairy, Maleficent, is one of Marc Davis's finest creations, and there is some splendid effects animation toward the climax, as the Prince fights his way to the castle. Against this must be set the fact that the hero and heroine are the merest of ciphers who often seem to become lost against the overelaborate and overstylized backgrounds. The Technirama format led to some static scenes, but a more serious problem was the fact that Disney did not succeed in transforming the story in the way he had metamorphosed *Snow White* and *Cinderella. Sleeping Beauty* refused to submit to his genius for recreating archetypal stories. While it was in production, his genius was at work elsewhere.

As far as animation was concerned, new formats like CinemaScope and Technirama 70 proved to be more trouble than they were worth. *One*

An *Alice in Wonderland* story conference: Winston Hibler, Ted Sears, Walt Disney, and Ed Penner.

Recording the voice track for *Alice in Wonderland:* Jerry Colonna, Kathryn Beaumont, and Ed Wynn

Six years in the making, *Sleeping Beauty*, 1959, marked a temporary return to the world of the fairy tale. Unfortunately, its highly stylized treatment tended to slow the action and interfere with character development

Hundred and One Dalmatians, released in 1961, made use of a technical innovation that would have a more lasting impact. Ub Iwerks, now in charge of special processes at the Studio, had been experimenting with Xerox photography as an aid to animation and by 1959 had modified a Xerox camera to transfer animators' drawings directly to cels, thus eliminating the inking process and preserving much of the spontaneity of the pencil line. This saved time and money and had a major effect on the way Disney animation would look for the next thirty years since the style of everything else had to match the style the system imposed on the cels so there would be no clash between, for example, characters and backgrounds. The new look would be graphic and linear, quite different from the tonal renderings so typical of the early features. (Eventually, the system was modified and made somewhat more flexible by the introduction of color xerography.)

One Hundred and One Dalmatians was an all-Xerox feature, with the old inking method being resorted to only in a few instances where a colored line was needed. In fact, the film would have been difficult to make without the Xerox camera. There are scenes in which literally dozens of puppies fill the screen – each of them liberally spotted – and to animate these scenes using traditional methods would have been a herculean task. The Xerox camera allowed the artists to circumvent the problem by animating one small group of puppies, then using the camera to repeat their actions, making sure, of course, that the repeat was not too mechanical.

Beyond that, the new technique made the animators' task easier and permitted them to concentrate on the real substance of the film – character development and story. Set in England, in the present, the movie starts a little slowly but comes vividly to life when Cruella De Vil – another of Marc Davis's delicious delinquents – enters the picture. The pace picks up and never flags as the story builds steadily to its climax.

As in *Lady and the Tramp,* the dogs and other animals are presented as human surrogates and work well as such. Some of the most interesting animation in the movie, however, was reserved for the humans, who were

One Hundred and One Dalmatians, 1961, was the first feature to use the Xerox camera – a device which gave the backgrounds a more linear and graphic quality and helped preserve the spontaneity of the animator's drawings. This film provides fast-moving entertainment and many good touches, including "quotations" from old Disney cartoons (seen on television), and Cruella De Vil, who is perhaps the best villainess in Disney's postwar movies

Released in 1963, *The Sword in the Stone*
brought to the screen Disney's version of the
boyhood of King Arthur

drawn with a looseness new to Disney features. Elbows and knees are not always where they should be according to anatomy books, but everything works. Cruella is especially memorable, her face a blend of death mask and fashion plate, perfectly expressing her character, which is at the same time evil and laughable.

With *One Hundred and One Dalmatians*, the Studio recovered much of its old assurance and arrived at a new idiom. A good deal of the credit for this should go to Ken Anderson, who was responsible for production design, and to Bill Peet, who developed the story. Interestingly, Walt Disney is said to have strongly disliked the look of the movie. The public approved and made *One Hundred and One Dalmatians* a resounding commercial success.

By the early sixties, the animation staff had been pared down to a fraction of what it had been in the heyday of *Pinocchio* and *Fantasia*. Increasingly, Disney relied on the group he referred to as "the nine old men": Frank Thomas, Ollie Johnston, Milt Kahl, Eric Larson, Marc Davis, Woolie Reitherman, John Lounsbery, Ward Kimball, and Les Clark. These veterans were the key animators, but their ranks were depleted when Davis, a brilliant draftsman, switched his attention to designing for Disneyland and Reitherman began to concentrate on directing. As the staff settled into a new rhythm, a policy emerged of having one feature-length movie ready for release every three or four years, with occasional special projects.

The next animated feature was not one of the Studio's better efforts. Released in December 1963, *The Sword in the Stone* presents the boyhood of King Arthur, concentrating on his education at the hands of Merlin the Magician. The film totally misses the tone of T. H. White's story, and while there are some amusing set pieces and the animation is as accomplished as ever, character development is weak. Merlin, instead of being awesome, is presented as a bungling nincompoop, thus destroying the essence of the plot.

The Jungle Book, which appeared four years later, was an altogether more satisfactory production. Based on Rudyard Kipling's tales about Mowgli, a human child brought up in the jungles of India, the movie took liberties with the original, but these were amply justified by the end results.

Part of the success of *The Jungle Book* derived from the skillful casting of voice talent. Voices for the animated features had always been chosen with care, but – with a couple of exceptions – voice talent had not played a major role in defining character. It would be easy enough to imagine Geppetto or Pinocchio with slightly different voices (though Cliff Edwards's Jiminy Cricket is another matter). In the shorts, by contrast, characters like Goofy, Donald, and Mickey himself were inseparable from the voice talents (Pinto Colvig, Clarence Nash, and Walt Disney, respectively) who had helped shape them.

The Jungle Book was the first animated feature in which, across the board, the voice talents were more than just appropriate. Phil Harris, George Sanders, Sterling Holloway, Louis Prima, Verna Felton, Pat

Voice talents – including George Sanders, Phil Harris, Louis Prima, Sterling Holloway, and Sebastian Cabot – played an important part in the production of *The Jungle Book*, 1967. This adaptation of Kipling's stories also features some of the best animation of the postwar period

O'Malley, and Sebastian Cabot were chosen to speak for the creatures of Kipling's jungle – all of them actors whose voices had very distinct personalities that would influence the approach the animators would have to take.

The two greatest successes of the film are Baloo the bear, whose voice belonged to Phil Harris, and Shere Khan the tiger, played by George Sanders. Harris knew how to dominate a recording session, improvising on the "script" supplied by the storyboards and building the character into something that felt real and alive. The animators had the challenge of entering this character and making him perform on the screen.

The typical Disney villain is menacing and comic at the same time. We must sense that he is a real threat, but unless we can laugh at him too, he could destroy the mood of the whole film. Shere Khan is a tiger stalking an innocent boy – not the usual stuff of humor – but Sanders's delivery, sinister and affected at the same time, had just the right edge to it. One regrets only that Shere Khan did not have more screen time.

The Jungle Book proved to be Walt Disney's last animated film. In the late fall of 1966, a routine medical exam revealed that Disney – a heavy smoker – was suffering from advanced lung cancer. One lung was removed, but six weeks later, on December 15, he died in his room at St. Joseph's Hospital in Burbank, directly across the street from the Studio. He was sixty-five years old.

The Jungle Book was not quite finished, but Disney had already left his mark on it through the influence of his story sense and his attention to production values. Combining first-rate animation, fine background paintings (styled by Al Dempster), lively songs, and crisp direction – as well as the voice talents already noted – *The Jungle Book* would be one of the best of the Studio's postwar films, a fitting memorial to the man who had virtually invented the animated feature.

9 The End of an Era

Before he died, Walt Disney had given the go-ahead – on the strength of a board of drawings by production designer Ken Anderson – for the next animated feature, which appeared, in 1970, as *The Aristocats*. This film blends the vernacular style of *One Hundred and One Dalmatians* with *The Jungle Book*'s developments in voice characterization, and the result is a frothy comedy that has enjoyed considerable popularity.

An aristocratic cat named Duchess (her voice supplied by Eva Gabor) and her three kittens become the objects of the evil designs of their mistress's butler. Stranded in the French countryside, they are befriended by an alley cat named O'Malley (Phil Harris again). The film follows their adventures as they make their way back to Paris, only to be confronted once more by the black-hearted majordomo. This time the villain gets his just deserts and Duchess and O'Malley live happily ever after.

The plot is full of amusing incidents and is enlivened by some well-established secondary characters, who include the country dogs Napoleon and Lafayette (Pat Buttram and George Lindsey) and a delightful pair of English geese (the voices of Carole Shelley and Monica Evans).

Winnie the Pooh and the Honey Tree (1966) and *Winnie the Pooh and the Blustery Day* (1968) are a pair of admirable featurettes made during this same period. (The first appeared while Walt Disney was still alive, and he had approved the idea of the sequel.) Apart from the unnecessary Americanizing of some of A. A. Milne's characters, the Disney artists

Starring Tigger, Eeyore and, of course, Pooh
Bear, *Winnie the Pooh and the Blustery Day*,
1968, is a charming featurette-length adaptation of an A. A. Milne story (see overleaf)

Scenes from *The Aristocats*, 1970,
which featured a villainous butler and
strong comic relief

dealt very capably with the difficult task of translating the original Christopher Robin stories to the screen. The second film is especially good, with imaginative animation of the book itself. (Wind and rain threaten to blow or wash the words from the pages.) Most of the characters are very well conceived, with Tigger perhaps the outstanding success.

Winnie the Pooh and Tigger Too (1974) and *Winnie the Pooh and a Day for Eeyore* (1983) were later additions to the series. The 1974 film maintained the standards of the first two adventures. The animation for the fourth episode in the series was not done at the Studio but was farmed out to another animation house, with mediocre results.

Following *The Aristocats*, it was decided that the animation department should tackle a classic story as its next feature. Ken Anderson suggested a new treatment of the Robin Hood legend, and the idea was received with enthusiasm. As soon as a broad outline of the script had been established, a remarkable array of voice talent was assembled. Peter Ustinov was signed to play Prince John, a vain and insecure lion who is the comic villain of the piece. Terry-Thomas was cast as his obsequious sidekick, Sir Hiss, a snake. Other voice assignments included Phil Harris as Little John, Andy Devine as Friar Tuck, Roger Miller as Allan-a-Dale, and Brian Bedford as Robin Hood.

Robin Hood, released in 1973, is distinguished by much fine character animation on the part of veterans like Milt Kahl, Frank Thomas, Ollie Johnston, and John Lounsbery, backed up by Don Bluth and other talented newcomers. Its weakness, perhaps, is that it is a film that places *too* much faith in the powers of character animation to carry the day on its own. Compared with earlier Disney treatments of classics, it is weak in the area of art direction and production values. More important, it does nothing of any real originality with the Robin Hood legend.

Ken Anderson said at the time that the idea of doing *Robin Hood* with animals was in part the result of a desire to recall the spirit of the animated segments of *Song of the South*. "It's the kind of thing we do best," he argued, and the rest of the animation staff was in general agreement.

A *Robin Hood* story conference with, left to right, writer Larry Clemmons, director Woolie Reitherman, art director Ken Anderson, and animator Frank Thomas

A scene from *Robin Hood*, 1973

There is no doubt that one of the things Disney animation does do best is to use animals as human surrogates. In order for this to be fully effective, however, it must be done within the context of a powerful allegory, and this version of *Robin Hood* is almost entirely lacking in allegorical power. Rather, it uses first-rate character animation to enliven conventional situation-comedy gags. It is not a bad film, but it does not live up to the potential of the subject.

It was almost four years before another animated feature appeared, and this time it was *The Rescuers*, based on stories by Margery Sharp. The plot involves Bianca and Bernard (the voices of Eva Gabor and Bob Newhart), a pair of noble-spirited mice who set out to rescue a young orphan from the clutches of a suitably avaricious villain named Madame Medusa (Geraldine Page).

The Rescuers is not one of the Studio's great animated allegories either, but it is a lively entertainment full of colorful characters and situations. It lacks a powerful central theme, but it does have villainous deeds, sadistic crocodiles, a souped-up "swampmobile," a grouchy albatross named Orville in the charter-flight business, a dragonfly called Evinrude, some hungry bats, hidden treasure, the Louisiana bayous, and a benevolent society that meets in the basement of the United Nations building. In short, the Disney animation staff was given a chance to have fun, and everybody concerned made the most of the opportunity.

The Rescuers was a transitional movie in that it was still made under the guidance of the old guard – Woolie Reitherman, Ollie Johnston, Frank Thomas, Milt Kahl, Ken Anderson, Larry Clemmons, John Lounsbery, Eric Larson – but it was the first feature to display a significant influence from the next generation of Disney artists. The list of character animators includes names like Ron Clements, Glen Keane, and Andy Gaskill, who would have important roles to play in the Disney animation renaissance of the eighties and nineties.

This changing of the guard was even more in evidence by the time *The Fox and the Hound* (1981) went into production. Woolie Reitherman was still there, as producer, and the project was very much his to the extent that he had championed the Daniel P. Mannix novel that the movie is based on. (One of Reitherman's sons had once raised a pet fox.) Larry Clemmons was on hand as dean of the story team, and Frank Thomas and Ollie Johnston did much of the developmental animation for the main characters. Most of the animation, however, was done by a youthful team that included Clements, Keane, and John Musker. Others listed in the credits for this movie were Don Hahn (assistant director) and Burny Mattinson (story), both of whom, like the three artists listed above, would contribute to the coming animation renaissance.

The Fox and the Hound tells the story of Tod, a fox, and Copper, a hound, who become childhood friends but grow up to find themselves face-to-face with the conventional prejudices of the adult world – a world in which foxes and hounds are not supposed to get along. The grown Tod (the voice of Mickey Rooney) is ready to overlook these prejudices.

Based on stories by Margery Sharp, *The Rescuers*, 1977, is a lively adventure yarn which once again benefits greatly from the voice talents employed, notably Eva Gabor (Miss Bianca), Bob Newhart (Bernard), and Geraldine Page (Madame Medusa)

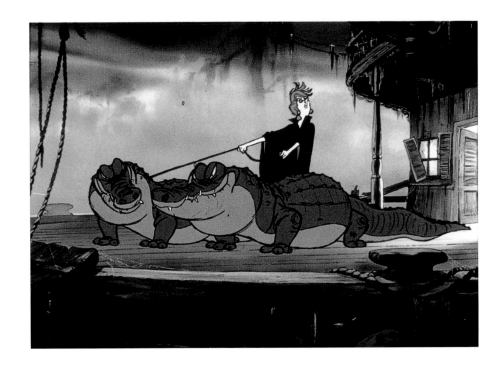

The Fox and the Hound, 1981, was a transitional
movie in that – despite important contributions
from studio veterans, especially at the planning
stage – it was carried out largely by younger
artists, some of whom would be key figures in
the Disney renaissance of the eighties and nineties.
Among the most gifted of the newcomers was
Glen Keane, who animated the bear in a
memorable fight sequence that was one of the
highlights of the movie

Copper (Kurt Russell) has serious doubts about maintaining the friendship. For a while, he grudgingly protects Tod from fox-hating hunter Amos Slade and his best hound Chief. Later, believing that Tod is responsible for Chief being wounded, Copper turns against his former friend. Only when Tod saves Copper and Slade from a bear does Copper embrace the friendship without equivocation.

The movie is full of solid characters, including Tod's mate Vixey (Sandy Duncan) and his mentor, an owl named Big Mama (Pearl Bailey). It is also enlivened by some strong action footage, notably the climactic fight between Tod and the bear. Brought to life by Glen Keane, the bear was a splendid achievement, one that gave notice that this was a young animator to be reckoned with.

Like most of the best Disney animated features, *The Fox and the Hound* also has a strong theme, rooted in the durability of true friendship and the blight of prejudice. Unfortunately, the theme is weakened because the relationship between Tod and Copper remains somewhat one-sided. Under Amos Slade's evil influence, Copper is so mindlessly obedient that the audience is left with the feeling that friendship is almost *forced* on him by Tod's selfless act – though in the end this misgiving is mitigated when Copper saves Tod's life with a selfless act of his own.

If the theme is not resolved as satisfactorily as it might have been, however, *The Fox and the Hound* is still an entertaining film, slight by the standards of some of its predecessors, but accomplished in what might be described as middle-period Disney feature animation style – the style that began with the animated episodes of *Song of the South*, evolved in the fifties, and prevailed for three decades during which time Disney animation was dominated by a handful of great character animators. *The Fox and the Hound* was a vehicle for the new generation of Disney artists, but they were still working in the shadow of their elders.

They needed to escape this formidable shadow. In the classics of the thirties and forties, Walt Disney had made bold use of camera movements, effects animation, and other technical devices, to enhance dramatic situations and advance the story. The films of the fifties, sixties, and seventies were different in that they were predicated, almost exclusively, upon the character animator's ability to breathe life into heroes like Peter Pan and Mowgli, heroines like Cinderella and Bianca, comic characters like Gus and Jaq (the mice in *Cinderella*), and villains like Cruella De Vil and Shere Khan. The other weapons in the animation armory were assigned to backup roles.

There were two principal reasons for this. An animated film could be made for less money if the production avoided expensive setups and elaborate effects. More important, the nine old men and the younger animators they trained had become extremely good at what they did. If creating believable human characters for *Snow White* had been a seemingly insurmountable challenge, by the fifties it was still a challenge but one that was approached with more than a decade of experience and acquired virtuosity.

Amos Slade's shack: one of the settings used
for *The Fox and the Hound*

It was almost as if the lead actors in the Disney repertory company –
the key character animators – had set out to demonstrate that they could
perform elaborate dramas on a bare stage if necessary. Scenery was
provided, but, as time went by, it became less and less significant to the
way the story was told. (*Sleeping Beauty* is the one big exception to this
rule, and in that instance the art direction almost suffocated the story.)

Not to put too fine a point on it, the animated features of the middle
period never reached the creative heights attained by *Snow White* or
Pinocchio, yet the least of them provides matchless examples of character
animation. Artists like Milt Kahl, Ollie Johnston, Frank Thomas, and
Marc Davis were to animation what Spencer Tracy or Charles Laughton
were to screen acting. Ward Kimball was animation's Ernie Kovacs. Eric
Larson was not only a superb animator but also as important a teaching
figure, in his field, as Lee Strasberg was in his.

These were the men who inspired and trained the new generation of
animators that began to come into its own in the early eighties. (A training program had been in place at the Studio since the early seventies.)

These younger animators were all too aware of the great skill of the men whose mantles they were assuming. They wanted to prove themselves worthy successors. At the same time, though, they wanted to show that they were capable of breaking the mold and creating something original.

They were looking for a major challenge, and they received it when Ron Miller – Walt Disney's son-in-law, who had become head of production – gave the go-ahead for *The Black Cauldron*, to be based on the five Lloyd Alexander books that make up his popular Chronicles of Prydain cycle.

At a time when there was a great interest in sword and sorcery fiction, this must have seemed like a good idea. The award-winning Alexander books had been very successful with a certain readership, offering exactly the blend of gothic creepiness, supernatural high jinks, cryptomythology, antic chivalry, chimeric violence, and pseudo-Celtic names that keeps young adult males glued to the pages of thick paperbacks with blond heroines, fierce dwarfs, and heavily muscled warriors on the cover.

In retrospect, however, this may have been exactly the kind of material the Disney animators should have stayed away from. To begin with, the subject matter may have had great appeal for that specific group, but it did not have the kind of broad appeal that would make it attractive to younger children or females of any age – important components of the audience for animated features. The plot was calculated to capture the imagination of young males, a category that included most key members of *The Black Cauldron*'s production team. The story team and the animators had little problem – at first, anyway – in immersing themselves in the adventures of Taran and Eilonwy as they pitted themselves against the evil forces of the Horned King. Free of the supervision of the generation of the nine old men, the new Disney artists were making a movie entirely for themselves.

That may have been where their problems started. By the time they ended, the Studio was under new management.

10　New Beginnings

At the time *The Black Cauldron* went into production, the Studio was desperately seeking a sense of direction and purpose that would permit it to thrive in the eighties. To compete with other studios, such as Warner Brothers, Paramount, Columbia, and Universal, it needed to reach segments of the market that Disney had not yet tapped.

It had been realized for some time that the Disney name could be a liability where certain types of films were concerned. Disney products had become identified almost exclusively with the family market, and that meant that young adults, in the fifteen to twenty-five age range, tended to stay away from movies with the Disney name attached to them, believing that they were strictly for children. Since the young adult category comprises more regular filmgoers than any other age group, it was important for the financial health of the Studio to reach out to it.

This problem was most pressing in the area of live-action films (see chapter 13), but the sense of demoralization that goes hand in hand with lack of direction was felt in the animation department as well, especially because this was a time of change in key personnel. The emerging generation was coming into its own but had not yet elected its leaders. Partly because of this, Don Bluth – among the most talented of the younger animators – had quit Disney in 1979 to form his own studio. There had been other departures, too.

In this context, *The Black Cauldron* was perhaps an overly ambitious production for the new generation to take on. In any case, the early enthusiasm for the project soon dissolved into bickering and backbiting. Production was divided up among several units, some of which hardly communicated with certain others as individuals battled for power. One result of this was that there was no clear directorial vision, and the finished movie lacked narrative and visual cohesion.

As difficult as it was, the period of *The Black Cauldron* brought some brilliant new talent to the Studio – young artists such as Andreas Deja and Ruben Aquino (who would become key animators in the renaissance of the eighties), and Tim Burton (who would go on to direct and/or produce such movies as *Beetlejuice, Batman, The Nightmare Before Christmas,* and *Ed Wood*).

Much of the new talent was coming out of the California Institute of the Arts, a school located in the hills near Los Angeles that had been partially built with money bequeathed by Walt Disney. Its animation department – with senior Disney animators serving as teachers and advisers – now nurtured budding artists, some on Disney fellowships, who often went on to the in-Studio training program. (CalArts is also home to programs intended to train artists for other branches of the film industry, as well as to one of the most prestigious fine arts departments in the country.)

Not all of the young artists coming to the Studio, from CalArts and elsewhere, were character animators. There were also effects animators, layout artists, and background painters, and this led to something of a rebirth of these departments, which is evident on-screen in *The Black Cauldron*. Imaginative effects and carefully constructed camera moves were used to carry the action forward, and the backgrounds were the best since *The Jungle Book*.

All this showed a nostalgia for the glory days of *Snow White* and *Pinocchio*. Unfortunately, that nostalgia was not reflected in story sense and overall vision. The production dragged on for years and seemed to become more confused with each passing day. As it finally limped toward a conclusion, the mood of uncertainty escalated, and the Studio was plunged into a state of turmoil, with various management and shareholder groups battling for control of the company. Eventually, in the fall of 1984, a new corporate team took the reins, with Michael Eisner (former president of Paramount Pictures) as chairman and Frank Wells (former vice chairman of Warner Brothers) as president of what would soon be renamed The Walt Disney Company. Eisner and Wells would prove to be a formidable team. Wells was a sound businessman, highly regarded on Wall Street and throughout the entertainment industry – a secure individual who preferred the respect of his peers to public acclaim. Eisner, on the other hand, would prove himself to be a creative and intuitive executive with a flair for publicity, able to provide the Disney organization with something it had lacked since Walt's death: visible leadership.

This was by far the biggest break with continuity in the company's history, but it was by no means a severing of ties with the Disney family since the new leadership had the strong backing of Roy E. Disney – son

Concept art for *The Black Cauldron*, 1985

A critical and commercial disaster, *The Black Cauldron* is a film that most of those involved with its making would like to forget. Despite its very evident shortcomings as a narrative, however, *The Black Cauldron* did display a high level of ambition that signaled the aspirations of the new generation of Disney animators

of Roy O. Disney and nephew of Walt – whose large block of shares had been used to tip the scales in favor of the Eisner/Wells team.

"Roy gave two conditions for his support," says Eisner. "One was that the company should not be broken up, which had been a threat of the early eighties, and the other was that we should give animation a fair shake."

The new executive team was voted in at a meeting of the board on September 24, 1984. Later that day, a celebration was held at the Lakeside Country Club, a stone's throw from the Studio, and during the proceedings, Eisner asked Roy Disney (who would assume the title of vice chairman) what role he would like to play in the company's future.

"Well," Disney recalls replying, "why not give me the animation department? I'll bet I'm the only guy around here who knows anything about it."

While Roy Disney had no hands-on experience in animation, he was a skilled filmmaker, and animation was in his blood. When he was a child, the Studio had been his second home. He had trained as a film editor – working on the *Dragnet* television series and on Disney's True-Life Adventures – before going on to produce nature movies and television movies of his own. He had grown up watching legendary animators like Fred Moore, Ward Kimball, and Norm Ferguson at work, and he had listened to his uncle discuss and describe upcoming projects with Walt's habitual enthusiasm and dramatic flair. Roy Disney knew a good deal about the possibilities of animated film and about the resilience of the Disney tradition.

Most people in and around the feature animation department believe very strongly that Roy Disney deserves credit for saving Disney animation from possible extinction. Certainly, he took control of the department when it was at its artistic and commercial nadir, nursed it back to health, and helped boost it to new creative heights. Had he not stepped forward at the critical moment, it is conceivable that executives whose backgrounds were exclusively in live-action films might eventually have decided that the animation department was a costly luxury the Studio could no longer afford.

"Roy was the hero," says producer Don Hahn. "Without him there might never have been *Beauty and the Beast* or *Aladdin*. He believed in animation, he understood it, and he fought for it."

Disney himself admits to having had some early doubts about the wisdom of his choice.

"The first thing I did," he recalls, "was to run the production reel of *The Black Cauldron*, which was close to being finished. I had heard there were problems, of course, but I wasn't prepared for what I saw. I looked at it and knew we were in deep trouble. There were bits that worked on their own, but they didn't hang together. The story got lost partway into the movie, and the movie was dark in an unrelieved kind of way, without the kind of light relief that's needed to make the bad guys palatable."

One of Michael Eisner's first executive acts had been to appoint Jeffrey Katzenberg – former head of production at Paramount – to the position of chairman of Walt Disney Pictures. It would be Katzenberg's responsibility, in tandem with Roy Disney, to determine the future of feature animation.

Top: When Michael Eisner became chairman of the Walt Disney Company, he set about reorganizing the Studio and transformed it into an entertainment industry giant. Center: As president of the Walt Disney Company, Frank Wells proved to be a skillful financial strategist, helping to lay the groundwork for the company's growth in the 1980s and 1990s. Bottom: Jeffrey Katzenberg played a key role in the renaissance of Disney feature animation during his decade as studio head

Like Disney, Katzenberg screened the production reel of *The Black Cauldron* and, like Disney, he was horrified by what he saw. Drawing on his experience with live-action movies, he announced that he would take the expensive production (it had cost about twenty-five million dollars at that point) into the editing room and recut it. Katzenberg did not realize (or perhaps care) that such a notion was looked on as sacrilege in animation circles. As explained in chapter 2, an animated movie is laid out on storyboards and preedited by layout artists and scene planners before animation ever begins. The idea that an executive would have the effrontery to *cut* a Disney animated feature seemed almost scandalous, and it appeared to augur badly for the future of the department. If the new regime was capable of committing such crimes against the nature of the medium, how could it be expected to support animation in the future?

In reality, it was the animation department that had created the monster. Katzenberg was merely trying to save what he could of a sizable investment in the only way he knew how.

"We had to get in there with a scalpel," he says. "I know this was very disturbing for some people, and I understood this, but I was not imposing my personal values on what [the animators] should or shouldn't be doing. I was responding to what I saw as our responsibility to the consumers – to the members of the public who vote at the box office."

Katzenberg managed to trim two or three minutes from the film, but it was too late to alter the overall conception.

Filmed in 70mm and released in the summer of 1985, *The Black Cauldron* received generally unfavorable reviews and did poor business. It does have its admirers, but few of them come from among the ranks of the artists who worked on the movie, most of whom look back on the production as a fiasco they would rather forget. It is difficult to find much to defend in the ineptness of the storytelling. The Horned King is a decidedly two-dimensional villain. There is little consistency about the character design, and the movie is weighed down by an excess of quasi-mythological claptrap. That said, however, it remains a watershed in the Disney canon if only because it represents an elevation of ambition on the part of the young animation artists.

The new regime did not close down the animation department, but it did move the animators out of the hallowed 1940 Animation Building, where most of the classics had been produced, and into a cavernous industrial structure several miles away in Glendale. (In time, the department would come to occupy several buildings in the industrial complex that was already home to the Imagineers of the Disney theme parks.)

"It seemed like a kind of warning," says Andreas Deja. "The old Animation Building was being turned over to live-action production. That was a signal that live action was to be the Studio's bread and butter. We were being sent out into the wilderness and told that it was time to get our act together. But at least we were given a chance."

It would have been a tragedy if the future of Disney animation had been determined by the failure of *The Black Cauldron*. In actuality, there was no immediate danger of this since Eisner had promised Roy Disney that feature animation would have its opportunity to prove itself. Even before *Cauldron* was released, Disney and Katzenberg had given the green light to another project. In 1982, when *The Black Cauldron* began to show signs of endemic chaos, several artists had asked to be taken off the production and were given the go-ahead to develop a project titled *Basil of Baker Street,* based on the book of the same name by Eve Titus. The principals behind this project were two veterans of the story department (Burny Mattinson and Dave Michener) and two relative newcomers who would play major roles in the animation renaissance (John Musker and Ron Clements). All four would receive director's credit.

Because production of *The Black Cauldron* was so attenuated, members of the *Basil of Baker Street* team had an unusual amount of time to hone their story so that what Katzenberg and Disney were presented with was a very complete and detailed set of storyboards. They liked what they saw and responded with cautious enthusiasm.

"What Jeffrey said," recalls Musker, "was, 'If you can make it in half the time you're used to, for half the money – go ahead.' "

Retitled *The Great Mouse Detective,* the movie was made on budget and in time to be released in July of 1986, just a year after *The Black Cauldron. The Great Mouse Detective* is a far less ambitious movie than its predecessor, but given its modest aims and budgetary restrictions, it is very successful – a thoroughly entertaining film that both pays tribute to earlier Disney masterpieces and points the way to triumphs still to come. Its only serious faults can be blamed largely on the cost cutting that had been demanded. The animation in a few scenes seems sloppy, as if it had been done hurriedly, and there are even instances of backgrounds occupied by static (nonanimated) figures.

Still, *The Great Mouse Detective* is enlivened by some excellent character animation – by the likes of Mark Henn, Glen Keane, Ruben Aquino, and Rob Minkoff – and displays many merits, not the least of which is an emphasis on storytelling that harks back to the glory days.

The story pits a mouse detective called Basil (not without Holmes-like mannerisms) and his sidekick, Dr. Dawson, against the archvillain Ratigan (splendidly realized around the perfectly cast voice of Vincent Price). Aided by Fidget – a peg-legged bat with a sadistic sense of humor – and assorted thugs, Ratigan schemes to kidnap Queen Moustoria and replace her with a clockwork dummy. To build this robot, Ratigan has kidnapped Hiram Flaversham, a master toymaker. It is Flaversham's daughter, Olivia, who begs Basil to take on the case of her father's disappearance. The characters they encounter during their adventures include a sappy hound called Toby (supposedly belonging to Sherlock Holmes himself), an overfed feline executioner named Felicia, and assorted riverfront ne'er-do-wells.

All of these characters, even the minor ones, are well drawn, with Ratigan and Fidget making memorable additions to the ranks of Disney bad guys. Just as importantly, they are woven into a well-thought-out plot that moves forward briskly, never loses sight of where it is going, and is eventually resolved in an entirely satisfactory manner. The movie is full of snappy dialogue and witty sight gags – the latter sometimes more

Made on a low budget, *The Great Mouse Detective,* 1986, proved to be a lively entertainment with strong characters and plenty of humor well integrated into the plot. It demonstrated that Disney feature animation was over its crisis and headed in the right direction. The panoramic layout drawing (center) is by Gil de Cicco

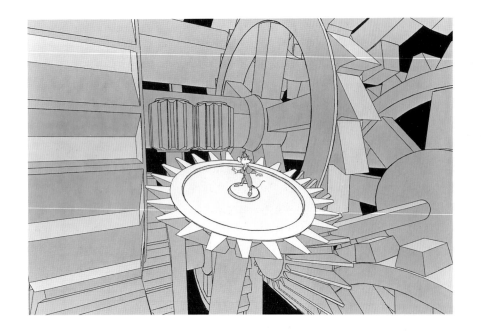

The climactic scene of *The Great Mouse Detective* made use of computer-generated imagery to bring to life the gears and escapements of the mechanism that drives London's Big Ben

reminiscent of vintage Warner Brothers cartoons than of earlier Disney features. It's true to say, in fact, that the new generation of animators had grown up admiring Looney Toons along with the Disney classics, and they were anxious to graft a hipper kind of humor onto the Disney main stem. (Disney had had its share of hip humorists – Ward Kimball, for one – but the wisecrack and the off-the-wall sight gag had found their true home at Warners, where they were nurtured by Chuck Jones, Friz Freleng, Bob McKimson, and others.)

The Great Mouse Detective also featured fine atmospheric backgrounds (some harking back to those painted for *Pinocchio*) and inventive camera work (which is another way of saying that the layout department was making a valuable contribution to the drama and texture of the movie). If the nine old men had come to emphasize character animation at the expense of everything else, the hungry young men and women who succeeded them looked for a new balance in which all departments made a major contribution to telling the story. In this regard, *The Great Mouse Detective* anticipated the major achievements of the Disney feature renaissance.

The film includes one spectacular sequence that depends in part on computer-generated animation. The Studio had had some experience with computer animation in the live-action science-fiction movie *Tron*, which appeared in 1982, but that was outside the feature animation department. The climax of *The Great Mouse Detective* takes place in the clock tower of the Houses of Parliament, with Basil, Olivia, and Ratigan dodging one another along with the cogs, flywheels, gears, and counterweights that drive the clock known to the world as Big Ben. It's a sequence that recalls the splendid 1937 Mickey Mouse short *Clock Cleaners,* but this time the machinery was animated with the aid of a computer, and the result was a mechanical ballet of a complexity and precision that greatly enhances the drama of the moment.

The Great Mouse Detective is a small-scale production, but – like *Dumbo,* another small-scale production – it is consistently entertaining and ultimately satisfying. The public responded to the movie and it turned a respectable profit. The feature animation department having justified its continued existence, new projects were put into development.

Peter Schneider – a young man with a strong theater background – was recruited by Roy Disney to run the department on a day-to-day basis, with the title senior vice president of feature animation. (In 1991 he became president of feature animation.) This was a crucial appointment because, for all the talent it contained, the department had been lacking in hands-on leadership. Schneider provided that leadership and brought a sense of focus. His sound theatrical instincts were soon felt at story meetings and other creative forums, but beyond that he became the person who adjudicated disputes, made difficult decisions, appointed personnel to key positions, soothed sore egos, and generally kept the wheels oiled so that animators and other artists could get on with making movies to the best of their ability.

With Schneider in place, the feature animation department was no longer dissipating its energies. It was he who, with Roy Disney's support, guided the department to the point where it was ready to produce masterpieces like *The Little Mermaid* and *Beauty and the Beast*. And when feature animation became glamorous once more, and immensely profitable, it was Schneider who kept the department on an even keel, shielding it from understandable pressures to increase production at almost any cost and making sure that everyone felt part of its tremendous success.

All this was happening in California, but meanwhile an astonishing Disney project – partly live action but predicated on an acceptance of the universe created by animation – was under way in London.

Film rights to Gary K. Wolf's 1981 book *Who Censored Roger Rabbit?* had been purchased by the Studio's former management. Michael Eisner and Jeffrey Katzenberg looked over the property and were intrigued by the possibilities of a movie in which human actors and cartoon characters consorted together in a never-never land version of Los Angeles. It occurred to them that it was the kind of project that might interest director/producer Steven Spielberg.

Spielberg was fascinated by the idea but said that he would become involved only if he could be guaranteed that the interaction between live-action footage and animation would be seamless and completely naturalistic. Until then, moviemakers who had combined live and animated elements – in *Mary Poppins,* for example – had always shot the live-action elements with a locked-off camera (one anchored to the floor to prevent movement). This greatly simplified the task of combining the diverse elements, but it led to stilted filmmaking. Spielberg insisted that *Who Framed Roger Rabbit* (as the film was eventually called) would have to be made without sacrificing camera flexibility to the needs of animation. He also wanted to see cushions that sagged beneath the imaginary weight of cartoon figures and other instances of interactive naturalism that would make it believable that "toons" could visit our world and that humans could visit Toontown.

Animated characters had been combined with live actors before, but never as effectively as in *Who Framed Roger Rabbit,* 1988

Robert Zemeckis was selected to direct the proposed movie. In London, he discussed the project with the Canadian-born animation director Richard Williams – a legendary figure in the animation world – who was well known to and admired by the Disney animators. Williams had come to the attention of Zemeckis and Spielberg by way of fifteen minutes of animation he had produced, over a period of more than twenty years, for a movie titled *The Thief and the Cobbler*. At first, Williams expressed strong misgivings about *Roger Rabbit* but finally told Zemeckis that he felt the film could be made – if they threw the rule book out.

"We agreed that the key to making the combination work," says Williams, "would be interaction. We thought the cartoon characters should always be affecting their environment or getting tangled up with the live actors."

Williams told Zemeckis that he should just go ahead and shoot the movie the way he would shoot any movie, with fluid camera movements that did not take the animator's problems into account. It would be the animation crew's responsibility to make the cartoons fit into the live-action continuum.

The basic process was somewhat as follows. Scenes that involved both animated and live-action characters were storyboarded, just as for an animated movie. These storyboards were used as a guide for building sets and props and then for directing the live performers (who had to pretend that they were interacting with the cartoon characters). Photostat blowups were made of each frame of live action, and the animators matched their drawings to these photostats, in much the same way that they would normally match them to a layout. The resulting animation drawings could be integrated with the live action with the invaluable help of the optical-effects wizards at George Lucas's Industrial Light and Magic facility.

Not that it was quite that simple. The animation had to mesh precisely with the live action, otherwise it would have been totally unconvincing. It had to be integrated with physical effects and with complicated behavior on the part of the human performers. (Think of the scenes in which

Who Framed Roger Rabbit, 1988, is an astonishing tour de force in which an international team of animators, led by Richard Williams, invented new ways to combine animation with live action so that director Robert Zemeckis could use his actors as flexibly as he would in an all live-action film. In this scene, Roger takes a ride with Eddie Valiant (Bob Hoskins)

A larger than life presence in *Who Framed Roger Rabbit* is Roger's wife Jessica who proves to be more than a match for the characters played by Stubby Kaye (above) and Bob Hoskins

No more of a cartoon than some Hollywood
actresses of the 1940s and 1950s, Jessica is
pivotal in the artful balancing act that permits
animated and live action characters to interact.
As the Ink & Paint Club's resident chanteuse,
she leaves toons swooning and human customers
thoroughly confused

Overleaf: Traveling in their vintage
Black Maria, Judge Doom's weasel sidekicks
terrorize Toontown

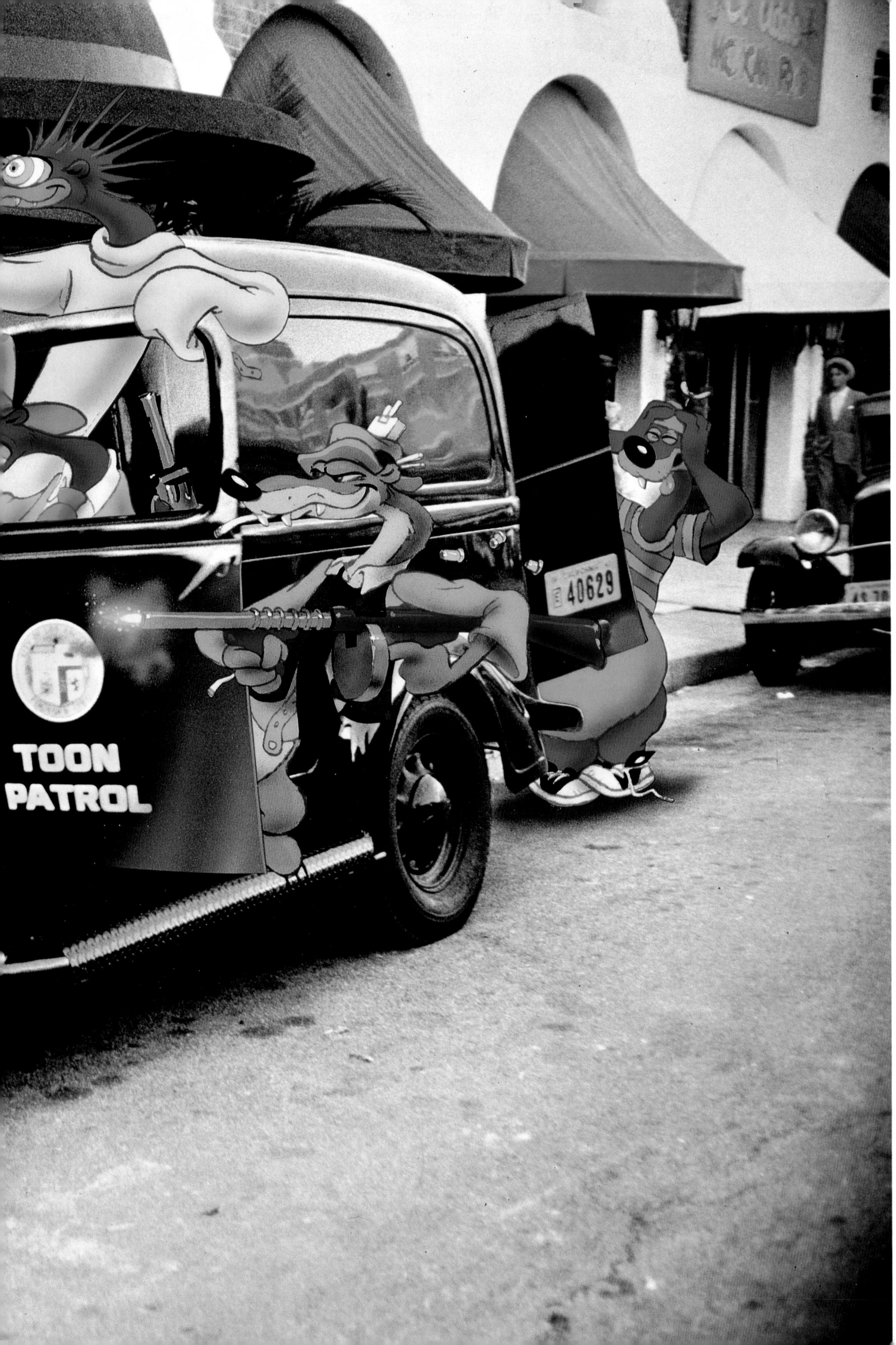
TOON
PATROL
40629

Who Framed Roger Rabbit is full of cartoon gags translated into live-action language, and vice versa

Roger and Eddie Valiant, played by Bob Hoskins, are handcuffed together.) Far from seeking out ways of making things easier for itself, Williams's animation team deliberately created technical problems, always with the idea of emphasizing the interaction between live action and animation. Almost every scene contains some virtuoso touch, and often those touches are used less to move the plot along than to persuade the audience to believe in the reality of this world where toons and humans coexist (if not always peaceably).

The scene for *Who Framed Roger Rabbit* is set by a one-reel cartoon titled *Somethin's Cookin'*, starring Roger and Baby Herman, which has been assigned a fictitious 1947 release date. It is the ultimate parody of the Bugs Bunny/Tweety & Sylvester/Tom & Jerry/Woody Woodpecker/ Popeye genre of cartoon short, a brilliant pastiche with more tasteless gags per second than a Friars' Club roast. From the moment it hits the screen, the audience knows that it is in the province of artists who know Mickey Mouse's white gloves – and Wile E. Coyote's paws – as well as they know the backs of their own hands.

The plot of the movie that follows this "Maroon Cartoon" is predicated on the fact that Roger believes that his wife Jessica (one of the sexiest cartoon characters ever) may be having an affair with Marvin Acme (a human played by Stubby Kaye), the gagman and real estate mogul who happens to own Toontown. This initial premise tells how tangled the two worlds are in this movie, and soon we learn that the all-too-human Eddie Valiant, the Chandleresque private eye called in to keep an eye on Jessica, has a grudge against toons because his brother was killed when a toon dropped a piano on his head.

Soon, Valiant and his allies – toons and otherwise – are pitted against Judge Doom (Christopher Lloyd) and his gang of toon thugs. Roger, it turns out, has been set up as the fall guy in Doom's plan to dissolve

Toontown with a toon-obliterating chemical called Dip. The evil judge – a very toonlike human – has already done away with the city's public transportation system (LA's beloved Red Cars), and now he wants to redevelop the site of Toontown as a commercial area that will take advantage of the route of a new freeway.

It's a story, in short, about big business attempting to raze the ghetto in order to generate more big business. This time, though, the ghetto dwellers are toons, and they come with a special set of values and physical abilities that sometimes works in their favor and sometimes works against them. In addition to Roger, Jessica, and Baby Herman, toons developed for the movie include Benny the Cab, Lena Hyena, Bongo the doorman, a spectacular octopus bartender, and the weasely members of Doom's Toon Patrol. All of these characters are splendidly realized and feel as if they belong in our collective memory of the cartoons of the Golden Age. This is just as well since they share the screen with an amazing array of genuine cartoon characters of that period, including – in bit parts and cameo roles – Daffy Duck, Daisy Duck, Donald Duck, Clarabelle Cow, Elmer Fudd, Goofy, Snow White, Speedy Gonzales, Betty Boop, Pinocchio, Foghorn Leghorn, Tinker Bell, Sylvester, Ferdinand the Bull, Bugs Bunny, Dumbo, Clara Cluck, Pluto, the Seven Dwarfs, José Carioca, Woody Woodpecker, Yosemite Sam, Bambi, and many others, not forgetting Mickey and Minnie.

Who Framed Roger Rabbit is an astonishing technical achievement. It is also an amazingly coherent and entertaining film, which enjoyed a great deal of well-deserved box-office success when it was released in 1988. Much of the credit should go to Zemeckis, to the screenplay by Jeffrey Price and Peter Seaman, and to the human performers, especially Bob Hoskins, who displayed an exceptional talent for being able to interact convincingly with cartoons. Still, it would be impossible to over-state the contribution of Richard Williams (who deservedly received an Academy Award for his work on the movie) and his animation crew. It was this team that made *Who Framed Roger Rabbit* the unique cinematic experience that it is.

Even if only a relatively small part of that team came from the Disney animation department – most of the animation was done in London – *Roger Rabbit* is still very much a Disney product. Although fiercely independent, Williams has been a lifelong admirer of the Disney school of animation, maintaining a close relationship over the years with men like Milt Kahl, Frank Thomas, Ollie Johnston, Art Babbitt, and Grim Natwick. This was his opportunity to make his own idiosyncratic contribution to the canon.

Its intrinsic merit apart, *Roger Rabbit* was very important for the future of Disney animation. It was a gigantic success, and it helped re-establish a bond, in the minds of moviegoers, between the Disney name and truly innovative animation. It could not have come along at a better time.

The new management team, meanwhile, was learning about animation and becoming enthusiastic about its future. It was even introducing certain innovations, such as placing an emphasis on the importance of having a screenplay.

In the early days of feature animation, the script had been something that had taken shape largely in Walt Disney's head, with the aid of storyboard artists who worked on the movie scene by scene but had little to say about the overall structure. Later, as Walt began to divide his time between animated features and other projects, the storyboard artists came more fully into their own. After Walt's death, plots evolved on storyboards as a kind of team effort that involved the director (usually Woolie Reitherman), the storyboard artists, and the principal character animators. A single writer – Larry Clemmons – was involved in the process (up to *The Fox and the Hound*), but he had been at the studio since the 1930s and thought like a storyboard artist.

Michael Eisner and Jeffrey Katzenberg came from a live-action background. They were familiar with storyboards as ways of planning, for example, expensive special-effects sequences, but not as a way of generating an entire film. They insisted on screenplays being produced along with the boards (even ahead of the boards), feeling that this would give them the means to come to terms with any given production.

Had they emphasized the screenplay as an *alternative* to storyboards, the results might have been disastrous. The action of an animated movie needs to be developed in primarily visual terms. In fact, the old storyboard methods were left untouched, and the screenplay was used as an adjunct to boards. This proved to be an entirely positive idea since it helped put the emphasis back on carefully thought-out storytelling.

Oliver & Company (1988), the animated feature that followed *The Great Mouse Detective*, was the first to give separate screenplay and story credits. In reality, the story artists and the writers worked together very closely, following a pattern that has little to do with the way live-action movies are scripted. Under the supervision of director George Scribner, more than twenty people contributed story ideas to *Oliver & Company*. At the end of their labors, the story was laid out in two forms – as a set of several dozen boards and as a much more compact screenplay. Each served its own purpose, yet each reinforced the value of the other.

The system was in its early days when *Oliver & Company* went into production, and, in fact, *Oliver* is not as fully realized, from a story point of view, as *The Great Mouse Detective* had been. Loosely based on Charles Dickens's *Oliver Twist*, the screenplay presents Oliver as an orphan kitten and Dodger and the other gang members as canines. Fagin and Sykes (*sic*) are human, though Sykes has animal alter egos in the form of a pair of vicious Dobermans. The setting has been changed from Victorian London to modern-day New York City.

Oliver & Company is notable for the large amount of computer-generated animation – by Michael Cedeno and Tina Price – used to bring to life such elements as cars, construction equipment, and the New York

With its mixture of human and canine protagonists, *Oliver & Company*, 1988, depended on the skills of character animators like Ruben Aquino (top), but the production also made a good deal of use of computer-generated animation, employed to create elements such as automobiles and urban landscapes

subway system. In and of itself, this computer animation is often brilliant, but at times it becomes intrusive and through overuse is allowed to interrupt the narrative flow. Later Disney features would use computer-generated imagery more discreetly and more effectively.

All in all, *Oliver & Company* is a lively movie, if a little awkward and overly cute at times. It contains some fine character animation by the likes of Glen Keane, Ruben Aquino, Mike Gabriel, and Mark Henn, and a mixed bunch of songs enthusiastically performed by a remarkable array of big-name vocalists, including Ruben Blades, Billy Joel, Huey Lewis, Ruth Pointer, and Bette Midler.

One of the *Oliver & Company* songs was written by Howard Ashman, best known at that time for his work on the long-running off-Broadway and Broadway hit *Little Shop of Horrors* (later turned into a movie directed by Frank Oz). Recruited for *Oliver* by Peter Schneider, who had worked for the company that managed *Little Shop of Horrors*, Ashman and his songwriting partner Alan Menken soon attracted the attention of Jeffrey Katzenberg.

"David Geffen was in the middle of producing *Little Shop of Horrors*," Katzenberg explains, "and when he heard we were using an Ashman song in *Oliver & Company*, he said to me, 'Howard and Alan are geniuses. They love Disney animation and I think you should meet them.'"

Katzenberg did meet them, was greatly impressed, and soon Ashman and Menken were asked to become involved with the Studio's next animated project, *The Little Mermaid*, based on the Hans Christian Andersen story, which was at an advanced stage of preparation with John Musker and Ron Clements slated as codirectors.

"We didn't know much about Howard," says Clements, "except that we liked *Little Shop*. Our first contact with him, I think, was a memo about Sebastian. Sebastian is a crab, and perhaps a little pompous. The way we had developed the story up to that point, Sebastian was probably going to be cast with an English accent. Howard's memo said 'How about making Sebastian a Rastafarian?'"

At first, the idea seemed mildly preposterous – even arbitrary – but in practice it made a great deal of sense because it gave the character a novel personality, and it permitted Ashman and Menken to introduce a couple of lively West Indian numbers into the movie. One of these – "Under the Sea" – went on to win an Academy Award.

Once they had met with Ashman, Musker and Clements were completely won over.

"He knew the Disney films," says Musker, "and he had an encyclopedic knowledge of American musicals. What's more, he showed us how what works for the musical can be made to work for the animated film. Walt understood that, of course – look at *Snow White* – but it was Howard more than anyone who taught it to our generation."

The outcome of all this was that Ashman became the film's co-producer, along with Musker, spending three weeks out of four in Glendale, working on his lyrics but also sitting in on story meetings and sweatbox sessions and contributing to the evolution of the movie in a score of ways.

The Little Mermaid, 1989, was the first Disney animated feature in almost thirty years to tackle a classic fairy tale. It was also the first film produced by the new generation of animation artists to capture fully the imagination of both audience and critics. In this sketch by Bruce Morris, Ariel – the heroine – is shown eluding a pursuing shark

This conceptual painting by Rowland B. Williams was one of many inspirational works produced to help establish the mood of *The Little Mermaid*

Musker and Clements, meanwhile – with the help of art directors Michael A. Peraza, Jr., and Donald A. Towns – imposed a distinctive look on the production that is especially effective in the undersea sequences. Inspiration came from a variety of sources, including pastels by Kay Nielsen, an artist who had contributed to the visual development of the *Night on Bald Mountain* episode of *Fantasia*. In the early forties, Nielsen had storyboarded ideas for two features based on Andersen stories, and these story concept pastels, which had been preserved in the Walt Disney Archives, provided a useful starting point.

Despite this nod to the past, however, Musker, Clements, and Ashman worked hard to make the characters contemporary, even in a period setting. Ariel (who was cast with the voice of Jodi Benson) was not the first spunky Disney heroine, but she was the first one who talked the language of today's teenagers and who expressed herself in ways that post-Beatles adolescents could identify with. Ursula (Pat Carroll), the principal villain of the piece, was portrayed with a self-aware campiness that would have been unthinkable in Disney films even a few years earlier. (The old features are full of campy characters, but – with the possible exception of Cruella De Vil – the campiness is never explicitly acknowledged, as it is with Ursula.)

Although characters like Ariel, Ursula, and Sebastian are treated in a distinctly contemporary manner, the movie plot stays reasonably close to Andersen's tale of the mermaid who falls in love with a human, though the screenplay provides the story with a happy ending that is far from the spirit of the original. Given the conventions of the Disney animated feature (or the conventions of the Broadway musical, for that matter), such a happy ending is acceptable. In this instance, it falls a little flat only because Eric, the human object of Ariel's affections, is boring and two dimensional compared with her. For that matter, the scenes aboard Eric's sailing vessel, and in his Ruritanian kingdom, don't measure up to those that take place beneath the waves.

Ariel rescues Eric

Despite its flaws, the movie never loses the audience, thanks to a wonderful theatricality that must be looked on as Ashman's gift to the evolving Disney animation renaissance (a gift eagerly accepted by Musker and Clements). *The Little Mermaid* unfolds like a great Broadway musical, with Ashman's lyrics and Menken's melodies moving the narrative along with wit and ease. That said, it is important to note that the Disney animation team, under the leadership of Musker and Clements, was able to rise to the occasion. For the most part, the character animation is excellent, and the movie represents an important stage in the resurgence of effects animation. The visual effects department, under the direction of Mark Dindal, was involved in a great majority of the scenes and was given several opportunities to shine, notably in the storm sequences.

Musker and Clements continued the efforts of the new generation of artists to use the whole arsenal of the animation department in the storytelling process. *The Little Mermaid* even involved a handful of multiplane shots.

"We didn't realize quite how expensive and time-consuming they were," says Musker. "And we found that the Studio's old multiplane rig was in poor shape and difficult to use. We ended up farming out most of the multiplane shots to an outside facility."

The effort to use every device available is clearly felt throughout the production, and it supports the fine animation, sound storytelling, and memorable songs in making a movie that deservedly enjoyed great popular and critical success when it was released in November of 1989. For the first time since the 1950s, film professionals and filmgoers alike were talking about a Disney animated feature as something that was more than just another entertaining continuation of the tradition that had begun with *Snow White and the Seven Dwarfs*. Like *Snow White, The Little*

Written by lyricist and producer Howard Ashman (left) and composer Alan Menken, the musical numbers for *The Little Mermaid* (overleaf) helped make the movie an instant animated classic. They would have crucial roles to play in the Disney animation renaissance

The Little Mermaid was marked by art direction reminiscent of Disney animation's first golden age, as exemplified (top) by this background painting by Donald Towns. Also featured were strong supporting characters such as Sebastian (center), and a larger-than-life villainess in the person of Ursula the sea witch

Mermaid has a real sense of magic about it. It reminded people that animation can do things that no other medium can do, and it gave notice that Disney had a new team of artists who understood how to tap into the old wizardry while bringing their own baby-boomer generation sensibility into play.

In one sense, though, *The Little Mermaid* was the last movie of an era – the last feature to be made by the principal Disney animation unit that depended upon hand-painted cels (as modified by the use of xerography that had been standard for almost three decades). The next film to come out of Glendale would employ a totally different system.

In the meantime, however, *DuckTales: The Movie* was in production in various corners of the globe, a movie that was storyboarded, laid out, and art directed in California but animated in France and England, while the cels were painted and photographed in China. (To differentiate it from the classic animated features, it would be released as a Disney Movietoon.)

A spinoff of the *DuckTales* television series, launched in 1987 (see chapter 14), which was inspired by the marvelous Scrooge McDuck comic books created for Disney by Carl Barks, *DuckTales: The Movie* (subtitled *Treasure of the Lost Lamp*) is an animated spoof on the *Raiders of the Lost Ark* type of movie – itself, of course, a spoof of the forties-era Saturday morning serial. The film is hardly a masterpiece, but it is a good deal better than might be gathered from reading the reviews that appeared when the film was released in the summer of 1990. The animation is more than adequate and the action moves along briskly. The production's chief weakness is that the structure of the story is rather sloppy, so that the movie feels like an overextended television episode rather than a true feature.

Far more interesting is *The Rescuers Down Under,* a 1990 sequel to the 1977 adaptation of Margery Sharp's Bianca stories, with Eva Gabor and Bob Newhart once again providing the voices for Miss Bianca and her friend Bernard. *The Rescuers Down Under* can be seen as an attempt to cash in on the popularity of Paul Hogan's *Crocodile Dundee* and things Australian in general. Whether or not this is so, *The Rescuers Down Under* is a modest but generally satisfying movie, though in overall concept it belongs to the middle-period style of Disney feature rather than to the more theatrical style of the era inaugurated by *The Little Mermaid*.

Set largely in the Australian outback, the story centers on a boy named Cody who is friends with the animals, notably Marahute, a giant golden eagle. Meanwhile, a poacher named Percival McLeach is trapping protected wild animals. When Cody stumbles into one of McLeach's traps, the poacher finds an eagle feather in the boy's possession. Thinking that Cody will lead him to the eagle, McLeach kidnaps the boy and makes it appear that Cody has been eaten by crocodiles. A mouse, saved by Cody, reports what has happened, and the news is conveyed to New York by way of the Rescue Aid Society's ham-operator telegraph system.

Two of the architects of Disney's animation revival are Peter Schneider (left), president of feature animation, and Roy E. Disney, Walt's nephew, who many insiders credit as being the savior of the animation department he has headed since 1984

One of the top animators of the younger generation is Andreas Deja, who has helped create some of the Studio's outstanding villains

The Rescuers Down Under, 1990, was conceived as a continuation of the adventures of Miss Bianca and Bernard. This skillfully made movie, which takes the altruistic mice to Australia, has not received the attention it deserves, perhaps because the story harks back to the middle-period kind of Disney feature, and the production as a whole is less rooted in musical theater than the studio's more recent successes.

In one important way The Rescuers Down Under looked forward rather than backward. This was the first film in which Disney's CAPS technology was employed. CAPS is a computerized production system that permits handmade animation drawings to be copied and colored electronically (eliminating the need for cels). It also allows different elements of an image to be combined in elaborate ways that formerly would have been almost impossible. CAPS does not generate animation, but it enables hand-drawn animated imagery to be manipulated in new ways, greatly enhancing production values. It can, for example, be used as a very sophisticated multiplane camera, as was the case in the restaurant scene, overleaf

That brings Bianca and Bernard to the rescue. They travel to Australia with the help of an albatross named Wilbur (the brother of Orville from the first *Rescuers* movie). Once there, they join forces with a resourceful kangaroo mouse named Jake, and McLeach's fate is sealed.

Directed by Hendel Butoy and Mike Gabriel and produced by Tom Schumacher, *The Rescuers Down Under* is notable for its strong character animation and imaginative staging of scenes. In the latter regard, the movie was greatly aided by the advent of the Studio's Academy Award–winning CAPS system.

CAPS is a sophisticated computer system dedicated to the task of managing and enhancing animation material. It is not used to generate animation: characters and effects are still drawn by hand, frame by frame. Rather, CAPS takes existing animation drawings and effects and backgrounds and combines them so that they can be seen in video form. It also provides the means to color the images electronically (only the backgrounds are colored with brush and paint). The CAPS system therefore replaces the old ink and paint department, and is operated by former members of that department who were retrained to work at computer workstations, bringing their years of expertise with them.

Enormously expensive, the CAPS system was fought for by Roy Disney and was justified economically because it would speed up production and save money in the postproduction phase. At the same time, it enabled the directors to plan far more complex shots and camera moves. With CAPS there was theoretically no limit to the number of planes or levels of animation that could be included in a single shot. Not only could the CAPS system replace the multiplane camera, it could do its work far more cheaply and with far greater efficiency.

Most significantly, CAPS eliminated cels since it generated finished imagery that could be transferred directly to film, frame by frame.

The use of CAPS in *The Rescuers Down Under* was somewhat tentative since the filmmakers were just beginning to familiarize themselves with the system and could only learn the full extent of its possibilities as they worked with it. Those possibilities are signaled, however, in sequences such as Cody's flight aboard Marahute. CAPS was an important new tool – an amazing electronic paintbrush – and with this system in place, the stage was fully set for the Disney animation renaissance.

11   A Second Flowering

By the turn of the decade, there were no longer any doubts about the new regime's devotion to the future of animation. Michael Eisner and Frank Wells were clearly aware of the value of the medium to the Studio, both for its own sake and as a way of generating secondary revenues (everything from books to games to clothing to new attractions in the Disney theme parks). Roy Disney was stalwart in his support of the feature animation department, which Peter Schneider continued to guide, and Jeffrey Katzenberg had become an enthusiastic, hands-on participant in the process of developing animation projects. It was in this context that Walt Disney's dream of producing one animated feature a year was revived.

The efficiency of the CAPS system made the realization of this dream plausible. In order to approach this goal, however, it was necessary to expand the staff. Talented animators, layout artists, and background painters were eagerly recruited, and by the time *The Rescuers Down Under* was released, in November of 1990, feature animation had spread into several buildings scattered around the same Glendale industrial park. In addition, there was now a branch of the feature animation department in Florida where animators and other artists worked in public view at the Disney-MGM Studios®, part of the Walt Disney World® Resort near Orlando (see chapter 15). Far from being just a sideshow, this unit has made significant contributions to all animated features since

1989, including the animation of major characters. The Florida unit is in fact a completely self-contained animation facility, which has been preparing to take on production of its own features.

Introduction of the CAPS system is not the only way in which execution has been streamlined. More effective use of manpower has also played a role. Topflight character animators are a rare commodity and in the past they were not necessarily used in the most efficient way. Often character animators would labor over drawings until they were almost perfect, so that cleanup artists had only to smooth a line here and erase a slip of the pencil there before the drawing was ready to go to ink and paint.

Today all that has changed. It has been recognized that the key character animators need only produce relatively rough drawings so long as someone else is available to turn these "ruffs" into CAPS-ready finished drawings. Today's cleanup artist does far more than polish existing drawings. He or she takes the character animator's "ruff" as a starting point and actually creates a new, highly finished drawing that retains the feel of the original. Key cleanup artists are also responsible for making sure that characters do not vary, in different scenes, from the demands of the model sheet. Clearly, this requires a special kind of talent – and an important one since it permits the principal character animators to work faster and to farm out more work to less experienced animators. (The cleanup keys can be relied on to iron out differences between the styles of one animator and another.)

Headed by Vera Lanpher, the cleanup department now numbers almost one hundred artists. It is their drawings – colored through the intervention of the CAPS system – that actually appear on-screen, and it is in large part due to them that Disney is now able to issue animated features with a frequency unmatched since the early forties.

The first movie to take full advantage of CAPS and the streamlining of the feature animation department was a retelling of *Beauty and the Beast* – a film that deserves to be judged by the high standards of the early Disney classics. In fact, *Beauty and the Beast* almost was one of those early classics. Walt Disney had broached the idea of tackling the subject back in the forties – "Probably before *Cinderella*," according to Ollie Johnston's recollections – but had abandoned it when modifying the fairy tale's bleak second half had proved uncommonly difficult. The idea was revived forty years later and almost abandoned once more.

There was a desire at the Studio to tackle another movie based on a classic fairy tale. *Beauty and the Beast* seemed like a good candidate, and, after other writers had made a couple of false starts, Linda Woolverton produced a screenplay that succeeded in providing the basis for a viable movie. Don Hahn – fresh from working with Richard Williams on *Who Framed Roger Rabbit* – was assigned to produce, and the original concept called for the British-based American artist Richard Purdum to direct. In the summer of 1989, Hahn took a party of animators and art directors to Europe, where they visited the Loire Valley in France for

Beauty and the Beast, 1991, proved to be a difficult subject to bring to the screen and much preliminary art was produced to help establish plot, mood, and characters. The concept drawing of the Beast carrying Belle through the snow (opposite top) was made by Glen Keane, who would be the principal animator of the Beast. An early version of the story (opposite center) called for a somewhat naturalistic approach and Andreas Deja drew a Gaston who was far more foppish than he later became. The panoramic study (opposite below) was used to help visualize an opening sequence for *Beauty and the Beast* which was eventually abandoned.

Conceptual art by Hans Bacher (right) helped inspire the look and atmosphere of the film. Like other aspects of *Beauty and the Beast,* the character and appearance of Belle (below) evolved a good deal during the conceptual phase. This drawing is by Glen Keane

As the project developed, the Beast under-
went radical changes, both physically and
psychologically, as can be gathered from early
concept drawings such as the examples
by Chris Sanders shown here, opposite top

Howard Ashman's story influence led to the
Beast's plight becoming pivotal to the story,
which is not the case with earlier tellings.
It was Ashman too who insisted on characters
like Cogsworth, Lumiere, and Mrs. Potts
being assigned major roles in order to prevent
total gloom from setting in. Lively musical
numbers featuring the castle's enchanted
objects (overleaf) were introduced into the continuity to provide relief from the somberness
of the central theme

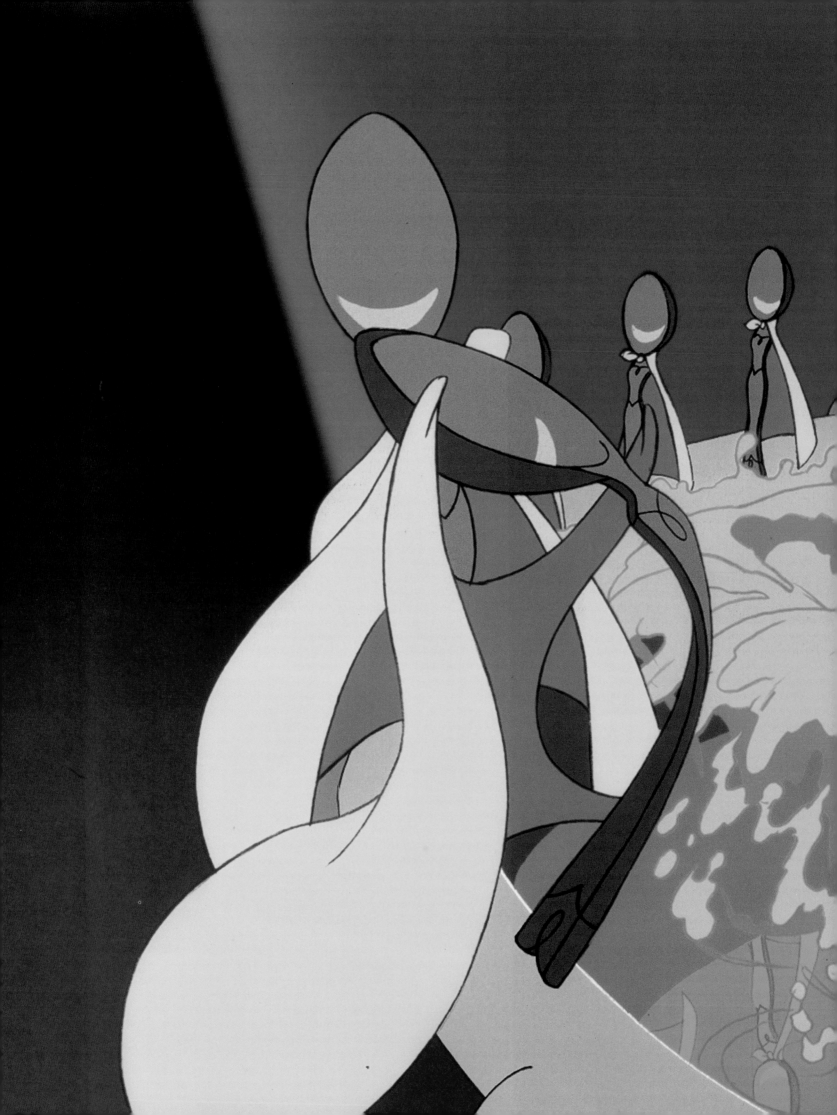

In *Beauty and the Beast,* the story builds relentlessly toward its powerful climax. Dramatic as it is, Belle's confrontation with hungry wolves is just one of several subclimaxes that help to heighten the tension. The Beast's inaccessible castle, below, is a symbol of his isolation

Gaston starts out as something of a comic
fool, vain and vapid, but before *Beauty and
the Beast* is over he proves to be among the
most evil of all Disney villains

The Bimbettes are crazy about Gaston, but
in this scene find themselves stuck with his
sidekick LeFou

Vera Lanpher (top) is head of the cleanup department. Brenda Chapman (center) has been a key member of the story team for several features, including *Beauty and the Beast* and *The Lion King*. At bottom, directors Gary Trousdale (seated) and Kirk Wise (right), along with producer Don Hahn (rear), headed the team that brought *Beauty and the Beast* to the screen

inspiration and then spent several weeks in London working with Purdum, who, along with his wife Jill, had storyboarded the projected movie.

The Purdums' vision of the tale owed a good deal to classic versions such as that of Madame le Prince de Beaumont, as seen through the eyes of French painters such as Watteau, Fragonard, and Boucher. The boards they had prepared were turned into a story reel which was screened for Jeffrey Katzenberg, who found the approach led to a denouement that was relentlessly grim. This was just as *The Little Mermaid* was being completed, and the very evident qualities of that movie prompted Katzenberg to invite Howard Ashman and Alan Menken to join the *Beauty and the Beast* team.

Ashman met with Katzenberg, Roy Disney, Peter Schneider, Don Hahn, the Purdums, and other key participants and proposed plot changes that led to Linda Woolverton's spending time with him in New York rewriting the script. Ashman's approach emphasized the Beast's story (the unfortunate creature tends to be schematic in most tellings and hardly an object of sympathy). He also worked hard to make Belle more three dimensional, a flesh-and-blood young woman capable of carrying the plot through her passion rather than just a vapid symbol of conventional virtue. Thirdly, Ashman did away with the unmitigated gloom that had plagued the second act by creating prominent roles for members of the castle's staff, who come to effusive life despite having been turned into objects. (This idea was present in the earlier version, but it was Ashman who insisted that characters like Cogsworth, Lumiere, and Mrs. Potts should have fully developed personalities.) Ashman also demanded a larger-than-life villain to be pitted against both Belle and the Beast.

And, naturally, there would be Ashman and Menken songs.

Richard Purdum participated in these revisions but felt the project was turning into something too far from his vision for him to remain with it in good faith. He resigned and was succeeded, as director, by Gary Trousdale and Kirk Wise, known for their strong story skills (though Wise had started his career as an animator). Ashman took the title of executive producer.

The elements of the story began to fall into place, but there were still many other things to settle. The Beast's appearance, for example, would be crucial to the success of the film.

Glen Keane began thinking about that during the preproduction trip to London. Crossing Regent's Park on his daily walk to work, his attention was caught by the wolves loping around their compound at the edge of the London Zoo. Their powerful presence haunted him as he began to visualize the Beast. Inside the zoo, he found Boris, a boisterous mandrill whose facial structure fascinated him. Later, in the Los Angeles Zoo, he sketched Caesar, a 600-pound gorilla who hurled himself against the bars, again and again, in an attempt to frighten the artist.

"I kept reminding myself," says Keane, "that that was how Belle would see the Beast – as this huge, terrifying creature."

Working with animator and sculptor Ruben Procopio, Keane began to combine the characteristics of various animals – gorillas, wolves,

mandrills, buffalo, wild boar – until he came up with the creature that eventually reached the screen, a beast whose emotions range from human sensitivity to brutish fury.

The Beast is a formidable creation, but Belle – as animated by a team of artists headed by James Baxter – is a worthy match for him. Her character is effectively spelled out during the opening musical number, at which time we see Belle going about her business in the village where she lives. Dark and faintly exotic-looking (story artist Chris Sanders contributed much to her final appearance), she is addicted to books but, though she enters into the romance of the tales she reads, we understand that she also has a solid, practical streak.

Almost immediately, we encounter Gaston, the villain of the piece, who at first comes across as an arrogant, macho bore (somewhat reminiscent of Brom Bones in *The Legend of Sleepy Hollow*, though with higher social aspirations) – an annoyance rather than a full-blown villain. This deception works well, since the audience is fooled into seeing him as something of a comic character; thus, the full force of his viciousness, revealed only at the movie's climax, comes as a complete surprise. Animated principally by Andreas Deja, Gaston has a unique place in the remarkable canon of Disney villains.

There are several other significant characters in the film, including LeFou (Gaston's clumsy sidekick), Maurice (Belle's inventor father), Mrs. Potts the housekeeper/teapot and her son/teacup Chip, Cogsworth the majordomo/clock, and Lumiere the butler/candelabra, all animated with skill and flair.

The miracle of *Beauty and the Beast* is that these satisfying characters are so effectively woven into the fabric of the story. Each has his or her proper weight within the narrative, and the comedy elements are used to counterbalance the tremendous force of emotion that emerges in the central relationship between Belle and the Beast. Everything seems to contribute to the momentousness of their encounters. Superb work by concept artists like Hans Bacher, by the layout department, the effects animators, the background painters, and especially the art director, Brian McEntee, helped turn the castle and the landscape that surrounds it into elements of the story as crucial as any of the characters. In *Beauty and the Beast,* the entire arsenal of animation techniques is used to drive the narrative.

Computer-generated imagery plays its role, notably in the ballroom scene when Belle and Beast dance through an enchanted environment that could not have been realized without the help of the computer. Meanwhile, the CAPS system permitted the use of camera setups of a complexity that could only have been dreamed of during Walt Disney's lifetime. Some of these setups might, in theory, have been possible before CAPS but they would have been prohibitively expensive to achieve. Others, such as many-layered multiplane shots, would have been physically impossible because of the limitations of conventional camera optics. In addition, CAPS supplied the means to orchestrate the color palette of the movie with a subtlety that had never been approached before.

The voice talent is outstanding, notably Paige O'Hara as Belle, Robby Benson as the Beast, Angela Lansbury as Mrs. Potts, David Ogden Stiers as Cogsworth, Jerry Orbach as Lumiere, and Richard White as Gaston. The songs (which take up almost a third of the running time of the movie) are superb, from the Oscar-winning title song to the memorable "Be Our Guest," as is Menken's score, which won another Academy Award.

All these elements help explain why the public flocked to *Beauty and the Beast,* making it the most commercially successful animated film ever to that point. Beyond the excellence of the components, however, the movie also carries an emotional punch that is astonishing for something that many people still refer to as a cartoon. It was this emotional power that helped pull in an adult audience to supplement the usual family viewers.

Beauty and the Beast appealed as much to dating couples as to kids. In all probability, this had something to do with the fact that the dating couples of the nineties have grown up with daily exposure to animation on television and are in no hurry to outgrow the medium. But that doesn't explain the fact that they came back to see this movie over and over again. The new generation of Disney artists had achieved their goal. They had produced a movie that could be matched against the classics, and they were rewarded with an Academy Award nomination in the category of Best Picture – the first time an animated film had been accorded this honor.

The Studio's next animated feature, *Aladdin,* would prove to be an even greater hit. Except for the element of commercial success, however,

James Baxter headed the crew that animated Belle

One of the greatest challenges of *Aladdin*, 1992, was visualizing the transformations of the Genie, a task that generated thousands of inspirational drawings and storyboard sketches. The upper example is by Eric Goldberg, the lower by Gary Trousdale

Aladdin and *Beauty and the Beast* have very little in common. If *Beauty* depends for its impact upon its ability to plumb emotional highs and lows, *Aladdin* is all witty invention, stylization, and surface flash. That this is so reflects the Studio's determination to avoid the danger of repeating itself and to demonstrate that the new generation of artists is not wholly dependent on the example of its predecessors.

Aladdin evolved as the third directorial outing of John Musker and Ron Clements, who also produced and were the supervising writers. Howard Ashman and Alan Menken were involved once again and wrote six songs for the film (three were used in the final cut) before Ashman, who had been ill for some time, succumbed to AIDS. After his death, Tim Rice – lyricist of *Jesus Christ Superstar* and *Evita* – was brought in to write the remaining songs with Menken.

The basic story of Aladdin and his magic lamp is well known. As with all of their retellings of traditional tales, however, the Disney team looked for ways of making it applicable to a contemporary audience. Aladdin is a Robin Hood–like thief who, in the movie, develops a distinctly twentieth-century conscience. His love interest, the Princess Jasmine, is a spirited young woman with a mind of her own. Finally, it is she who will choose to marry Aladdin, rather than vice versa, and then only when he comes to terms with his problems and admits to his humble beginnings instead of trying to pass himself off as a prince.

In the end, though, conventional narrative is probably less important to *Aladdin* than to any other major Disney animated feature, with the obvious exception of *Fantasia*. Above all, *Aladdin* is a feast for the eyes leavened with wild flights of comedy and imagination.

Much of the look of *Aladdin* – especially in the area of character design – can be attributed to the arrival at the Studio of Eric Goldberg. Like Richard Williams and Richard Purdum, Goldberg had been born in the New World but had achieved success in London, where he headed Pizazz Pictures, a studio that made some of the cleverest animated com-

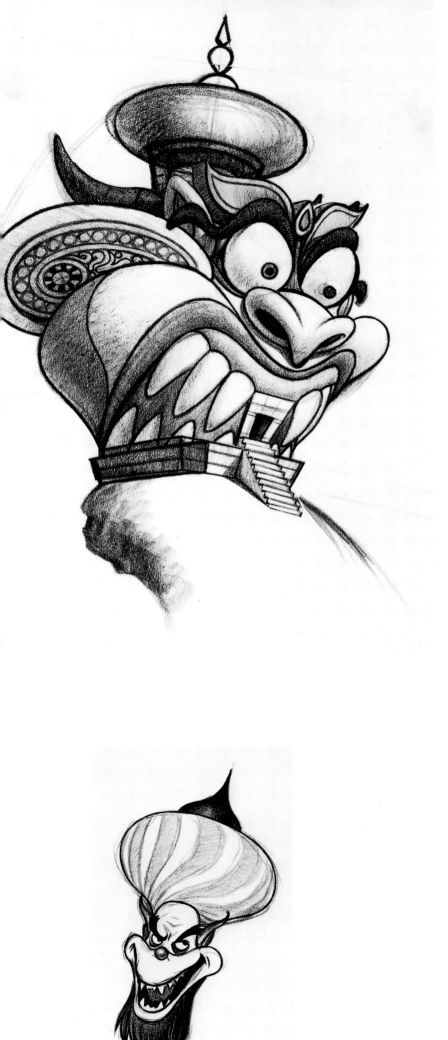

Few animated films have ever explored the grotesque for its own sake as thoroughly as *Aladdin*. These drawings by Richard Vander Wende are from the film's pre-production phase and give some suggestion of the kind of ideas that were being hatched

mercials of the 1980s. Musker and Clements were well aware of Goldberg's talents and were delighted to welcome him to their team.

Goldberg's principal animating assignment was the Genie, but his influence can be felt throughout the movie. Production designer Richard Vander Wende and art director Bill Perkins were working from the supposition that the curvilinear flow of Islamic calligraphy and the graphic poetry of Persian miniatures should be integral to the look of the film. Goldberg took this as a starting point, then turned to one of his heros – the caricaturist Al Hirschfeld – for further inspiration. Hirschfeld's line has the same kind of whiplash expressiveness that can be found in Islamic calligraphy, so that his style of drawing could be incorporated into the texture of the movie without causing any stylistic dislocation.

In the case of the Genie, Goldberg modeled him in part on a Hirschfeld caricature of Maurice Chevalier. (Coincidentally, Chevalier had been one of the inspirations for Lumiere in *Beauty and the Beast*.) Goldberg designed the Genie as a character who is defined by his outline. This may be contrasted with Glen Keane's design of the Beast, which has mass and solidity. For the Beast, that was a necessity since the audience must sense his weight and power. For the Genie, the opposite is needed, as the character is lighter than air and can transform himself into anything from a game show host to a bodybuilder, and it is the infinitely flexible outline that makes this possible. Without Goldberg's mastery of this style it would have been impossible for him to keep up with the verbal and mental acrobatics of Robin Williams, who provided the character's voice.

This emphasis on outline extended to other characters as well. Jasmine, for example, has a basic hourglass figure that registers even if she is seen in silhouette in the far distance.

Goldberg may have been chiefly influenced by Hirschfeld, but he is also a student of Disney animation and an admirer, in particular, of Fred Moore's work on characters like the Seven Dwarfs. This helped ensure that there would be a sense of continuity with Disney tradition, even as the animators moved into fresh territory.

The strongest character in the movie, after the Genie, is Jafar the evil vizier (the voice of Jonathan Freeman), animated principally by Andreas Deja. This was Deja's second villain in a row, following Gaston, but here the challenge was very different. Gaston is rather naturalistic. His jaw and muscles may be exaggerated, but – like the Beast – he is a solid character with weight and mass. Jafar, on the other hand, is strictly two dimensional (from a graphic point of view). With his broad shoulders, his elastic mouth, his haughty eyebrows, and his expressive hieroglyph of beard, Jafar is an invitation to unbridled linear invention, and Deja made the most of it.

Aladdin himself is a slightly annoying character, though the problem has nothing to do with the way he is drawn. With Glen Keane as the directing animator, he is brought to life with enormous skill. The problem has more to do with the conception of the character. The directors perhaps tried *too* hard to make him contemporary, so that he always

Aladdin was an opportunity for Disney concept artists to exercise their imaginations and their taste for the exotic. Right: a study by Richard Vander Wende. Below: two more by Hans Bacher

Color models for each scene are prepared with the aid of Disney's Academy Award-winning CAPS digital production system. From a model such as this, generated in the computer, each frame in the scene can be electronically colored by a skilled craftsperson. The finished images are scanned directly from the CAPS system onto film stock, thus eliminating the need for cels

Like Ariel and Belle before her, Jasmine is one of Disney's spunky new breed of heroines, a young woman with a mind of her own and a bottomless supply of willpower

Among the notable comic characters in *Aladdin* is the hero's pet monkey, Abu, opposite

Robin Williams provided the voice for the Genie and his wildly improvisational sense of humor. Another inspiration was a drawing of Maurice Chevalier by the caricaturist Al Hirschfeld, whose highly linear, calligraphic style is felt as a strong influence throughout the movie.

Animated by a team led by Andreas Deja,
Jafar is a most demonic villain, a formidable
adversary for Aladdin and Jasmine, and for
the befuddled Sultan

Aladdin was produced and directed by
John Musker (opposite bottom, seated) and
Ron Clements (standing), who made a
brief appearance in the film itself (above),
caricatured as fellaheen on the streets of
Agrabah. Eric Goldberg (opposite top) led
the team that animated the genie and
was to a large extent responsible for styling
Aladdin's cast of characters

seems out of step with the rest of the cast. Aladdin's voice, supplied by Scott Weinger, is also jarringly American in the Middle Eastern context of the movie.

Jasmine is a feisty heroine, and there are many well-realized secondary characters, including Abu, Aladdin's monkey; Rajah, Jasmine's pet tiger; and Iago, Jafar's parrot sidekick, while Randy Cartwright's unit had fun with the flying carpet.

The entire look of the film is fantastic, the Arabian Nights atmosphere having been developed with the aid of more than 1,800 photographs taken by layout supervisor Rasoul Azadani in his hometown, Esfahān, Iran. Along with concept artist Hans Bacher, Azadani was one of the key players in the visualization of *Aladdin*, heading the team that stages the movie and plans the camera moves. Many of the scenes were planned by Azadani himself, taking shape as sketches in workbooks which serve as "bibles" for other artists producing more detailed layouts. Other scenes were developed in sketches by artistic coordinator Dan Hansen.

One of the most remarkable things about *Aladdin* is the way it was choreographed in terms of color. *Beauty and the Beast* had taken this idea quite far. For *Aladdin*, the art director and production designer went even farther, so that no color was used without having some story significance. For example, blue would be used for sky and water, of course, but beyond that it would stand for the good, the positive, the idealistic. Red would stand for evil and the hellish powers of destruction. Not surprisingly, green would represent the earthly paradise while various yellows designated everything from greed (gold) to earthiness (ocher). Richard Vander Wende thought this all through in great detail and even produced a "color script" of the entire movie in which sequences were broken down into schematic representations of their color components, shot by shot.

Like *Beauty and the Beast*, Aladdin contains spectacular backgrounds and astonishing examples of the effects animator's art. The songs are perhaps less important than they were in *Beauty and the Beast* but they do all that is asked of them, and Menken's Academy Award–winning score is first-rate.

Aladdin is full of plums, but in the end what makes the movie unforgettable is the virtuoso collaboration between Robin Williams and Eric Goldberg's animation team in creating the Genie. Williams is famous in his stage performances for his ability to perform stream-of-consciousness ad libs in which his mind turns on a dime then shoots off in any number of directions, each of which provides him with the excuse to invade and inhabit a menagerie of characters – famous, infamous, anonymous, and androgynous. Williams reproduced this routine in the recording studio, improvising around gags devised by story artists and supplying touches of his own. Working to his voice track, the animators succeeded brilliantly in capturing Williams's chameleon persona on film, permitting the Genie to impersonate a dragon, a slot machine, Jack Nicholson, and dozens of other entities.

Aladdin captured the enchanted atmosphere of the Arabian Nights, and it did enchanted business for The Walt Disney Company, like its predecessor breaking all records for an animated film and becoming one of the all-time top money earners among all categories of film.

While *Aladdin* was still in production, another team of artists was preparing *The Lion King* for the moment when the best character animators and other key artists would become available. As with *Beauty and the Beast,* there was a false start in the development stage, but by the end of 1991 things were beginning to take shape.

Tom Schumacher was the original producer, but toward the end of 1991 he was promoted to a newly created position as head of feature animation development and handed over the reins of *The Lion King* to Don Hahn, though Schumacher remained with the project as executive producer. A new directorial duo was created by pairing Roger Allers, story chief for *Beauty and the Beast,* with Rob Minkoff, a gifted animator and story artist who most recently had been working on an aborted Roger Rabbit project. The first thing Allers and Minkoff did, upon being teamed, was to put together a brain trust. For two days, Allers, Minkoff, Hahn, and story head Brenda Chapman shut themselves in a room with *Beauty and the Beast* directors Gary Trousdale and Kirk Wise (co-opted to lend their talent and experience before moving on to a new project of their own). At the end of the two days, many of the plot problems that had been stalling the project were solved.

If *Aladdin* is quite different from *Beauty and the Beast, The Lion King* is distinctively different from both of them. The first Disney animated feature ever to be based on a completely original story, *The Lion King* is also the first since *Bambi* to present naturalistic animals in an environment that closely approximates their true habitat. No humans are found in this world, not even the invisible hunters who intrude into Bambi's universe by way of gunshots and carelessly tended campfires.

The Lion King differs from *Bambi* in another key respect. The story of Simba the lion and his adventures in the Pride Lands is a traditional Aesopian fable, so that – for all the surface naturalism – the idea of animals talking to one another and otherwise violating the laws of nature is less disturbing than in the earlier film.

The Lion King presents the rites of passage of Simba, who, at the beginning of the film, is the newborn heir apparent to the kingdom of the Pride Lands, wisely ruled by his father, Mufasa. In early sections of the movie, Simba is shown learning the vital lessons of life from Mufasa. With his best friend Nala, Simba also has an unpleasant encounter, in an elephant graveyard, with a trio of sadistic hyenas. This leads to a final soul-searching session between Simba and Mufasa. Shortly afterward, Mufasa is killed while trying to save Simba during a stampede engineered by Mufasa's evil brother Scar and carried out with the help of his hyena allies.

Finding Simba terrified but unharmed beside his father's body, Scar persuades the cub that he was responsible for Mufasa's death. Guiltily, Simba follows Scar's advice and runs away, certain that he can never go back to the pride. With Simba out of the picture, Scar heads for Pride

ROUGH MODEL SHEET
YOUNG SIMBA
PRODUCTION 0885
"King of the Jungle" 1/13/92

Made for *The Lion King,* 1994, this model sheet for young Simba, drawn by Jean Gillmore, is a good example of the way in which the new generation of Disney artists has learned how to blend humor with naturalism.

Rock, where he tells the assembled lionesses that both Mufasa and Simba are dead. With mock sorrow, Scar assumes reign of the Pride Lands and introduces the horrified lionesses to his army of hyena mercenaries.

Simba, meanwhile, almost perishes in the desert but is saved by an unlikely duo, a meerkat named Timon and a warthog called Pumbaa. Simba joins this pair of outcasts in a jungle paradise which becomes his home as he grows to adulthood. Along the way he absorbs Timon's and Pumbaa's philosophy of life – "Hakuna Matata" – which, they teach him, means no responsibilities, no cares. There comes a time, though, when this point of view no longer satisfies Simba, and he begins to hanker for something more, without knowing quite what. Soon after, Nala appears on the scene, helping to precipitate Simba's return to the Pride Lands and a final showdown with Scar.

The story has a simple arc to it, yet it provides plenty of opportunity for character development and rich detail. The film depends on a strong depiction of the father-son relationship combined with a graphic presentation of the notion that everyone must take responsibility for his or her own life. As usual, all this is backed up by lively comic relief. This may be the first Disney animated film to be written from scratch, but it has

The concept studies by Hans Bacher, opposite, show how, at the pre-production stage, *Lion King* artists were already thinking about the way that animals are seen in wildlife documentaries, in which the telephoto lens sometimes causes dramatic optical effects. Throughout *The Lion King*, the African landscape is used to establish both atmosphere and authenticity, as in this image of Rafiki's tree, right

Overleaf: Rafiki holds up Simba's heir for the approval of the denizens of the Pride Lands. A great moment from *The Lion King* – or so it seems. In fact this image does not appear in the movie. It was created for publicity purposes by taking advantage of the CAPS computerized production system to combine elements from different parts of the movie. Simba and Nala have been plucked from a frame at the end of the movie, Rafiki and the cub from a frame near the beginning. Simba, therefore, appears twice – as an adult and as an infant

every bit as much of a mythic feel to it as any of those derived from classic fairy stories.

Like *Beauty and the Beast* and *Aladdin, The Lion King* is a visually exciting movie. The spectacular settings owe much to the concept art prepared by Hans Bacher and the preliminary design work of the layout unit supervised by Dan St. Pierre. The same layout artists did much to give passages of the film the look of a wildlife documentary (typically shot with telephoto or zoom lenses) while maintaining a slightly stylized look that derives in part from African art. Doug Ball's background crew helped give the movie its epic look, also creating a sense of the heat of the savannas. The astonishing wildebeest stampede was achieved by computer animation artists working under Scott Johnston. As for the effects department, headed by Scott Santoro, they had a field day once again, creating notable effects for the opening Circle of Life sequence, the elephant graveyard, the appearance of Mufasa's ghost, and the climactic storm.

It was Allers and Minkoff who determined the overall look of the film, but their ideas were convincingly implemented by art director Andy Gaskill, who was also responsible for the staging of many of the key scenes. (He was promoted to this position because of his highly cinematic storyboarding of the complex opening sequence.) Certain scenes – such as Simba's Busby Berkeleyish musical number, "I Can't Wait to Be King," and the appearance of Mufasa's ghost – were conceived and supervised by production designer Chris Sanders, who also contributed many ideas and visual concepts to the development of the movie as a whole. Another important member of the crew was Randy Fullmer, a former effects supervisor who for this project took on the role of artistic coordinator – a recently created position that has been necessitated by the sheer complexity of animation production today. It is the artistic coordinator's job (along with that of the animation checkers) to ensure that the art coming from the different departments will mesh together seamlessly when they reach the CAPS system. There they are first handled by scene planner Ann Tucker, whose department serves as a bridge between the

The principal villain of *The Lion King* is Scar
(opposite bottom), a sardonic egotist skillfully
matched to the voice of Jeremy Irons by a
team of animators led by Andreas Deja. Scar's
allies are the lions' traditional enemies, the
hyenas. As a class (above) they are portrayed as
goose-stepping fascists. The three principal
hyenas (opposite top), however, are anarchistic
and manic

hand-drawn animation world and the computer-driven compositing and postproduction zone.

A problem that faced the character animators working on *The Lion King* was a need to work virtually without props (Rafiki's cane is an exception). Props help animators by providing opportunities for "business" and helping define character. (Think of Jiminy Cricket's umbrella or Cruella De Vil's cigarette holder.) It would have been unthinkable, however, to give the king of beasts a crown or have Scar wear dark glasses. The animators were required to aim for convincing naturalism, in keeping with the setting, while still giving the animals some anthropomorphic characteristics. After all, they do speak dialogue and even sing.

As so often in Disney's animated features, the villain comes close to stealing the show. Wittily animated by a team headed by Andreas Deja (his third prime villain in as many films) and greatly benefiting from the sardonic voice inflections provided by Jeremy Irons, Scar is an unforgettable piece of work in more than one sense. The animation of the other characters is up to the same standard, and special note should be made of the work of Mark Henn, Ruben Aquino, Tony Fucile, and James Baxter (who makes a memorable character out of Rafiki). The outstanding comedy figures Timon and Pumbaa were animated by teams led by Mike Surrey and Tony Bancroft, respectively, and brought to life by the voice talents of Nathan Lane and Ernie Sabella.

One of the most spectacular sequences in *The Lion King* is the wildebeest stampede. The animation was computer generated by a team led by Scott Johnston (above), members of which employed their highly specialized skills to capture the spirit of the cataclysmic event that, much earlier, had been suggested in concept paintings such as the one by Hans Bacher, top

328

Nathan Lane and Ernie Sabella recording
the voices of Timon and Pumbaa

Timon the meerkat and Pumbaa the
warthog are *The Lion King*'s outstanding
comedy characters.

As *The Lion King* approaches its climax,
Simba is shaken from his complacency by an
encounter with his father's spirit which
begins as he contemplates his own reflection
in a pool (above). Returning to Pride Rock,
he finally resolves to confront Scar as the
surrounding landscape burns (opposite top).
Bringing all his cunning into play, Scar almost
manages to win the day, literally pushing
Simba to the edge (opposite bottom), but in
the end justice prevails

The rest of the voice talent is equally strong. Along with Jeremy Irons, it includes Matthew Broderick (as adult Simba), James Earl Jones (Mufasa), Robert Guillaume (Rafiki), and Whoopi Goldberg and Cheech Marin as two of the principal hyenas. There are distinctively flavored musical numbers from the team of Elton John and Tim Rice, and the powerful score, by Hans Zimmer, evokes Africa from the opening moments of the film.

With its immediate predecessors having been received so enthusiastically, expectations for *The Lion King* were positively intimidating. Anticipation began to mount months before the June, 1994 release date when a four-minute promotional clip from the movie was shown in theaters around America. By early that spring, *The Lion King* was being touted as an almost surefire summer blockbuster.

Nothing is surefire, but in this case the film outperformed the most optimistic projections and quickly displaced *Aladdin* as the all-time box-office champion for animated films. By July of 1994, *Daily Variety* – an industry magazine – was predicting that *The Lion King* would be the most profitable movie of all time, animated or live action.

It would also be the last animated feature to be released during Jeffrey Katzenberg's extremely successful tenure as chairman of Walt Disney Studios. Shortly after the film passed the $250 million mark in domestic rentals – and ten years after he joined the Disney team – Katzenberg left the Studio, apparently unhappy at not being appointed president of The Walt Disney Company in the wake of Frank Wells's tragic death in a helicopter accident earlier in 1994.

Katzenberg's departure created a situation in which some of his responsibilities were divided between Joe Roth, a former chief of Fox's movie division, who was appointed chairman of Walt Disney Motion Pictures, and Richard Frank, who was made chairman of the television and telecommunications division (which he had been instrumental in building into an enormously profitable part of the Disney empire). Sanford Litvack, the company's general counsel, was promoted to executive vice president and chief of corporate staff, taking on many of Frank Wells's former responsibilities.

Meanwhile, Roy Disney remained the champion of animation while continuing to exert considerable influence on overall corporate policy from his position as vice chairman of The Walt Disney Company. A strong sense of continuity in feature animation was ensured by Peter Schneider's ongoing role as a very active and effective department head and by the existence of an extraordinarily able creative team of young veterans. In addition, Michael Eisner announced his intention of becoming more directly involved with the day-to-day operations of the department.

Changes of leadership notwithstanding, Disney animation was riding high, driven once again by the kind of inexplicable momentum – a magical conspiracy between artists and audience – that had first been generated more than six decades earlier with the debut of Mickey Mouse.

Rob Minkoff (left) and Roger Allers directed *The Lion King*

12   The Tradition Continues

The magical conspiracy between artists and audience depends upon a number of factors, one of which is surprise. It would be relatively easy for Disney's feature animation team to produce variants on films like *Aladdin* and *The Lion King* well into the twenty-first century. That strategy might even succeed for a while, but before long a certain ennui would set in, on the part of artists and audience alike.

That there is no probability of this happening is amply illustrated by the Studio's most recent feature, *Pocahontas*.

This production is based upon the traditional story of the relationship between Pocahontas, a young Native American woman, and John Smith, a swashbuckling adventurer who was a member of a 1607 British expedition to Virginia. Pocahontas and John Smith were historical characters who did in fact meet in the American wilderness all those years ago. Over the centuries, the tale of their encounter has become woven into the fabric of American folklore and has achieved the status of legend. The Disney retelling of the story draws on the folklore and adds to the legend by emphasizing the perspective of the Native American characters, using the Studio's animation expertise as a way of presenting their worldview.

The movie begins in seventeenth century London where the proud ship *Susan Constant* is readied to set sail for America. Most of those who will embark on this voyage are honest British yeomen looking for a better life, but their leader, John Ratcliffe, is a haughty and rapacious

blackguard who sees the New World only in terms of the promise of riches. Among those who have signed on with the expedition is Captain John Smith, who already enjoys a reputation as a formidable Indian fighter.

After a perilous Atlantic crossing, the *Susan Constant* reaches Virginia safely. Pocahontas – daughter of Powhatan, the local Indian leader – spies the ship, and soon she spots John Smith, too. Like her, he has an adventurous and inquisitive nature and inevitably their paths cross. While Ratcliffe urges his men to tear up the wilderness in search of mineral wealth, Pocahontas and Smith get to know each other and soon Smith begins to understand the Indians' sacred respect for nature.

There are complications ahead, however. Pocahontas is already betrothed to Kocoum, a brave but overly serious young warrior who eventually is killed by Smith's friend Thomas. Ratcliffe meanwhile is still hungry for Indian gold. Smith is captured by Powhatan and sentenced to death as Kocoum's murderer. Only Pocahontas can save Smith's life.

Produced by James Pentecost and directed by Mike Gabriel and Eric Goldberg, the Disney version of the tale reinvents the legend once more, providing it with a sense of freshness and a modern perspective on the clash of cultures. The story is told within a visual context of stylized realism that is splendidly effective.

The basic idea for the movie came from Mike Gabriel, who in 1990 had recently finished directing *The Rescuers Down Under* and was looking for a new challenge.

"I was interested in doing something that involved Native Americans," he says. "I began by looking at the most familiar stories and almost

Pocahontas is notable for historically accurate settings, as can be judged from this concept painting of a Native American long-house by Barry Atkinson

Right: Captain John Smith, seen here in an
early concept drawing by John Pomeroy, is
significantly different from other handsome
Disney heroes, being more fully rounded as a
character and decidedly less bland. Below:
Pocahontas observes the departure of the settlers' ship. Storyboard art by Glen Keane.
Bottom: Upon landing in the New World, the
European settlers immediately transform their
ship into a fortress. Panoramic background
painting by Allison Belliveau-Proulx

Below: Pre-production art for *Pocahontas* evokes both the Arcadian world of the American wilderness (concept painting by Natalie Franscioni-Karp) and the dangers of the Atlantic crossing (effects development art by John Emerson and Chris Jenkins)

Digging for gold, above, Ratcliffe and his men ravish Virginia's forests. Ratcliffe, seen opposite top in a storyboard drawing by Duncan Marjoribanks, is a caricature of the colonizer as blatent exploiter

Overleaf: Pocahontas tracks John Smith as he explores her world

immediately the Pocahontas story jumped out at me. It seemed to have all the elements that would make a great Disney film.

With a small team, Gabriel began to develop the idea. When *Aladdin* was completed, Goldberg joined him as co-director, intrigued by the potential of a movie in which a strong heroine or hero would have to carry the story.

"I don't think Disney has ever done anything quite like this before," Goldberg says. "Usually there's a clear-cut villain, and resisting his evil plan is what the film is all about. And usually the comic characters pick up a lot of the slack. We have comic characters, but they're secondary, and our villain, Ratcliffe, is not out-and-out *evil*. He's just a regular, unpleasant, greedy guy who sees the colonies as nothing but an opportunity to make a fast buck. In the end, it's the relationship between Pocahontas and John Smith that has to carry the film. You've got to believe in that relationship or you've got nothing, and that's what makes this picture different. There's never been a Disney animated feature in which the heroine and hero were asked to carry the whole thing."

"This is a film," says producer Pentecost, "in which you see the clash between two cultures, and we've tried to present that in very graphic ways. The landscape itself becomes a key element in the story. When it's seen from the point of view of the Europeans, it's a mysterious new world – both wonderful and scary – a wilderness full of unfamiliar plants and creatures. Seen from the viewpoint of the Indians, it's a completely

The relationship between Pocahontas and
John Smith is presented with a degree of subtlety
that is not common in animated films, as it
is tempered by their need to come to terms with
sharp cultural differences

different place in which the trees and animals are not only familiar but have assigned powers within the mythology by which the tribe lives."

Among the artists who helped establish this world was Glen Keane. After his work on *Beauty and the Beast* and *Aladdin,* Keane joined the *Pocahontas* crew at a very early stage and made key contributions not only to the development of the leading characters but also to the evolution of the world in which they act out their destinies.

Keane's primary contribution to the film, however, has probably been the inspiration and insight he has brought to the character of Pocahontas. While it's true, as Goldberg says, that the relationship between Pocahontas and John Smith must carry the movie, it is Pocahontas who is the key to that relationship. If she were not so captivating and, ultimately, so ready to sacrifice herself, the essential spark would be missing.

Keane designed the character from scratch, thinking about every detail, from the way she moved through the wilderness to the way her hair flowed in the breeze as she ran. Mostly, though, he pondered the way she would think and feel in any given situation, and how this would be reflected in her movements and facial expressions. What were the things, he asked himself, that would define the personality of a seventeenth-century Native American girl? Some of the answers to this came from research. Pocahontas is not a conventional Indian princess, like Tiger Lily in Disney's version of *Peter Pan.* When it came to the appearance of indigenous Virginians, Keane and other Disney artists drew their inspiration from authentic sources, such as the drawings and watercolors of explorer-artists like Jacques Le Moyne de Morgues and John White, who accompanied early expeditions. Correct appearance is only part of the story, and what Keane was equally involved with was the inner life of his character.

The importance of the Pocahontas character can be gauged from the fact that Keane found himself heading a team of no fewer than fifteen character animators devoted to bringing her to the screen – a team that included outstanding talents such as Mark Henn, Pres Romanillos, and

Designed by Glen Keane, Pocahontas was a demanding character to animate, needing to be conceived in broad enough strokes to command the screen, yet to be capable of displaying considerable delicacy of emotion.

Hearing that John Smith has been taken captive, the settlers swear vengeance

Randy Haycock. Whoever has done the animating, however, it is very much Keane's vision of Pocahontas that dominates the screen.

Featuring the voice talent of Mel Gibson and animated by a team headed by John Pomeroy, John Smith is also a strong character. Coming from a European background, he is a less original concept than Pocahontas, but the artists have avoided the pitfalls that might have made him a conventional two-dimensional comic-book hero; thus, he provides the heroine with the kind of foil she needs to be fully effective.

If Disney animated features have had a major weakness, it has been in the portrayal of two-legged heroes, most of whom have approximated to the bland Prince Charming stereotype. (Even the Beast becomes one of these royal bores when released from his curse.) John Smith is handsome enough to be a Prince Charming, but he is not bland and he is not stereotypical. He is, in fact, the most successful leading man Disney animators have so far created, and this bodes well for the future since believable heroes would permit a considerable extension of dramatic possibilities to the animation crews.

Other significant characters are Ratcliffe, the gold-hungry Governor (animated by a team headed by Duncan Marjoribanks), and Powhatan (strikingly realized by a team led by Ruben Aquino).

Stylistically, the film draws somewhat on the American tradition of illustration. The way these influences, and others (especially the look

The appearance and behavior of the Native American characters in *Pocahontas* are the result of extensive research. Various accounts of the Pocahontas story describe John Smith's brush with death by cudgel

Ratcliffe has appropriately comic sidekicks in the form of the charming Wiggins (right) and the spoiled pug Percy

of John White's seventeenth-century watercolors), were integrated into the look of the film was supervised by art director Michael Giaimo and artistic coordinator Dan Hansen. Once again, the layout department – under the leadership of Rasoul Azadani – and the background artists – headed by Cristy Maltese – made strong contributions to the film.

With songs by Alan Menken and Stephen Schwartz, *Pocahontas* reaches back to the musical approach established for earlier films by Howard Ashman and Menken. If *The Lion King* dipped into a modern pop style – thanks to the contribution of Elton John – the Menken and Schwartz songs, and the Menken score, have much more to do with the Broadway musical tradition.

Perhaps the most notable thing about *Pocahontas* is the fact that it advances the art of feature animation further into the area of movie-making for adults. It is still designed to appeal to a family audience, and there is still comic relief from characters like Meeko, Flit, and Percy but the relationship between the hero and heroine is portrayed in much the way it might be in a live-action film.

1995 also saw the release of a very different kind of animated feature – *A Goofy Movie*. The second theatrical production from the television animation team, this film is considerably more successful than its predecessor, *DuckTales: the Movie*. Directed by Kevin Lima and produced by Dan Rounds, *A Goofy Movie* blends the brashness and visual inventiveness of the old Disney short cartoons with MTV-generation hipness and – no mean feat – a large dose of tenderness.

In this movie, as in the *Goof Troop* television series (see chapter 14), Goofy is a single dad bringing up – in his own bumbling way – a son called Max. Max is a spunky teenager who finds his mambo-loving father out of touch with rock era reality. To impress Roxanne, the girl he yearns for, Max disrupts a school assembly with a performance that gets

A Goofy Movie, 1995, is a feature-length production that successfully captures the spirit of the classic Disney shorts of the thirties and forties

him into deep trouble with the principal, who warns Goofy that Max is hanging out with the wrong crowd and is likely to end up in the electric chair. Visualizing Max as a latent gang member, Goofy decides to take his son on a long fishing trip to straighten him out. Max – who was looking forward to his first date with Roxanne – is anything but delighted. The trip is a disaster until Max and Goofy begin to see each other's point of view and join forces to keep an outlandish promise Max has recklessly made to Roxanne.

The high-school scenes are lively and fun – like an animated version of *Grease* – and the ill-fated trip is peppered with good visual gags, some of them apparently adapted from 1930s cartoons such as *Mickey's Trailer*. For the most part the animation is sound and the production values are more than adequate to the task in hand. Best of all, the story line has been well constructed so that *A Goofy Movie* turns out to be a true feature film – much more than just an inflated television special.

Turning back to the feature animation division, the more mature values seen in *Pocahontas* are also to be found in *The Hunchback of Notre Dame,* which is in production at the time of writing.

Hunchback is a retelling of Victor Hugo's famous novel *Notre-Dame de Paris,* first published in 1831 and best known to Americans through two live-action films based on the Hugo story: one, featuring the great Lon Chaney, made in the silent era, the other, starring the equally magnificent Charles Laughton, released by RKO in 1939. A lesser but not uninteresting French-produced theatrical film version, with Anthony Quinn as Quasimodo, appeared in 1957.

The Disney production team, led by producer Don Hahn and directors Gary Trousdale and Kirk Wise, made an early decision to stay away from these live-action versions – fine as they are – and take Hugo's original as their starting place. This brought with it certain problems (the novel has literally hundreds of individuated characters) but also certain rewards. Chaney and Laughton had both played Quasimodo, the hunchback in the bell tower, as middle-aged. The Disney team was delighted to discover that Hugo's Quasimodo is actually a very young man. By presenting him that way – as a troubled adolescent fascinated by a world he could only experience from a distance – the Disney artists felt they could surprise audiences with a vision of the hunchback that would be fresh to most viewers.

As the directors and the story team (led by Will Finn) struggled to simplify Hugo's sprawling tale into something manageable, other artists began to try to visualize the Paris of the novel and especially the soaring yet confining world of the cathedral church of Notre Dame, with its great stained-glass windows and its grotesque gargoyles.

The story is set at the end of the Middle Ages, when putrid slums with open drains crowded around the cathedral, and around the magnificent homes of the wealthy. Concept artists, and layout artists under Dave Goetz and Ed Ghertner, began to research this world, studying photographs, as well as the works of many artists, including those of Victor Hugo

Scheduled for release in 1996, *The Hunchback of Notre Dame* conjures up the teeming streets and underworld of medieval Paris. On this page, a storyboard sketch by Paul and Gäetan Brizzi (left), and pre-production paintings by Don Moore (below) and Rowland Wilson (bottom), the former based on a drawing by Marek Buchwald

himself, Hugo being a gifted draftsman who created his own gothic visions of medieval Paris. As the research yielded solid results, they began to set down on paper a very concrete image of the city that would appear on screen. The square in front of the cathedral, for example, was established in great detail so that, long before animation began, every shop, every tavern, every home, every warehouse facing onto the square was delineated with as much detail as the facade of the cathedral itself.

The interiors of the cathedral were also explored. In certain scenes, actual interiors would have to be reproduced on screen much as they appear in reality. This would be appropriate to the scenes in which the gypsy girl Esmeralda first seeks asylum in the cathedral. More complex a challenge would be Quasimodo's world within the bell tower. This had to be a magical miniuniverse in which the agile hunchback is completely at home but which anyone else would find bizarre in the extreme. While the bells chime, Quasimodo can swing from beam to beam, dodging the whirring flywheels and escapements as he goes casually about his business in a manner that would spell certain death to anyone else.

Storyboard sketch by Paul and Gäetan Brizzi

Quasimodo is happy among the bells, but he looks down from the tower, at the city from which he has been banished, with infinite sadness. It is his desire to join the crowds that brings him into contact with Esmeralda and embroils him in her complex relationship with Phoebus, the handsome knight home from the wars. It is this desire, too, that brings him into conflict with Frollo, his guardian.

The Disney team has brought its own twist to the Quasimodo story, but it would be unfair to reveal the outcome. As a work in progress, it promises to be another landmark in the evolution of the animated feature. Significantly, and appropriately, about 10 percent of the animation will be handled by Disney's Paris plant under the supervision of co-producer Roy Conli, freeing up the Florida animation unit to work full-time on its own productions.

The first of these Florida productions is scheduled to be *The Legend of Mulan,* a retelling of an ancient Chinese story about a young woman who dresses as a man and becomes a great warrior. Disney has actively recruited Chinese artists to work on this film, which will feature backgrounds and other elements that reflect the spirit of traditional Chinese art.

The next California production, after *Hunchback,* will be *Hercules,* a comedic romp through Ancient Greece being developed by John Musker and Ron Clements, with music by Alan Menken and lyrics by David Zippel. Perhaps the most intriguing of all promised animated releases, however, is *Fantasia Continued.*

A project in which Roy Disney has taken a special interest, this will be a mix of elements from the original *Fantasia* and new segments featuring both traditional animation and computer-generated imagery. One segment already in production is a version of Sir Edward Elgar's "Pomp and Circumstance Overture," featuring Donald Duck. Another is a lyrical episode involving whales who take to the air following a solar disturbance, the action presented in the form of computer-assisted animation and set to the score of Ottorino Respighi's *The Pines of Rome.*

As is the case in the Victor Hugo novel on which it is based, much of the power of *The Hunchback of Notre Dame* derives from its strong sense of place, and its use of architecture as a way of symbolically describing different aspects of the human condition. Top: Pre-production painting by Lisa Keene, based on a drawing by Darek Gogol. Center: Pre-production painting by Fred Warter, based on a drawing by Darek Gogol. Bottom: Pre-production art by Dave Goetz, Kathy Altieri, and Fred Warter

Above: Quasimodo in his bell tower. Visual development art by Tom Shannon. Below: Pre-production art by Dave Goetz. Opposite: Medieval Paris. Pre-production art by Dave Goetz and Lisa Keene

Due in the near future, *Hercules* (above) explores the world of Classical mythology with wit and imagination. This concept art is the work of layout artist Bruce Zick and painter Mark Humphries. *Fantasia Continued* (left) will blend new episodes with favorites from the 1940 release. Illustration by Bill Perkins

Opposite: Deriving from a traditional Chinese story, *The Legend of Mulan* is scheduled to be the first feature to be produced entirely by Disney's Florida animation unit. This pre-production painting is by Sai Ping Lok, based on layout art by Gay Lawrence and Valerio Ventura

In January 1985, after more than half a century of glory, Disney's proud animation department found itself struggling for survival, banished from the Burbank lot it had once paid for, and relocated to an industrial park in Glendale. Disney animation proved to have resilience, and five years later it released its first major hit of the new era, *The Little Mermaid*. The next five years produced more triumphs, each eclipsing the last, and at the end of 1994 the feature animation department began to move into a spectacular new building adjacent to the Burbank lot, built on property Walt Disney had once considered using for his first theme park.

Planned in the early days of the renaissance, the new animation building was designed to accommodate close to 700 and support personnel. The problem was that by 1994 the California animation staff (not counting Florida or Paris) had grown to more than 1,000. Despite the five-story-high sorcerer's hat outside the new building, there was no way that all the extra people could magically be squeezed in.

This astonishing growth was an expression of an extraordinary phenomenon. The Walt Disney Company had grown tenfold in earnings during Michael Eisner's tenure as chairman, and, against all the odds, animation had become the engine that was driving the machine once more.

"Walt and my father built this company around animation," says Roy Disney. "Today we do many different things, but animation is still central and I believe it's what gives us our special place in the industry. It's not just that it provides characters for the parks, or that it generates merchandising revenue. All that's important, but even more important is the fact that it affects the way we think about everything we do. It's our animated features that set the standards for the other things, and maintaining those standards pays off in practical ways that enable us to go out and make more animated features."

III Live-Action Films

13   Muskets and Mouseketeers

Walt Disney's greatest contribution to the motion-picture industry was the genius he brought to the art of animation. After World War II, however, his studio became well known for its live-action movies and also for its television shows. The live-action movies ranged from low-budget nature films to lavish productions like *20,000 Leagues Under the Sea*. The one thing they all had in common, during Disney's lifetime, was that they were carefully tailored for family audiences in the most traditional sense of the term.

Although the Alice Comedies had included live-action material, *The Reluctant Dragon*, released in 1941, was a major departure for Disney. At one level, it is a documentary about Disney animation – complete with cartoon inserts – but it is much more than that because of a linking live-action narrative which sees the comic writer and actor Robert Benchley set loose on the Burbank lot, with predictably amusing consequences. Unpretentious and charming, *The Reluctant Dragon* presents an interesting, if somewhat fictionalized, picture of the Disney Studio during its Golden Age.

A little later, in the mid-forties, segments of live-action footage found their way into package films such as *The Three Caballeros* and *Fun and Fancy Free*, but the real breakthrough had come with *Song of the South* (1946), in which a full complement of professional actors was used to tell an entirely fictional story. The three cartoon segments helped sell the movie – as did scenes that combined live action and animation – but the success of the movie depended chiefly on strong performances (notably by James Baskett as Uncle Remus), crisp direction, and the cinematography of Gregg Toland, best known for his work on *Citizen Kane*.

A little more than two years later, Disney released *So Dear to My Heart*, which, like *Song of the South*, was a costume drama starring Bobby Driscoll and Luana Patten and set in rural America. A minimal amount of animation was employed, but to all intents and purposes this was an entirely live action film.

The next phase in the development of Disney live-action production came about largely as the result of a historical accident. Because of postwar monetary restrictions, a sizable amount of Disney capital was frozen in the United Kingdom. This money could not be taken out of the British Isles, but it could be used there, and, on the advice of his brother Roy, Walt Disney decided to utilize these funds to make live-action films in Britain. The fruits of this venture – *Treasure Island, The Story of Robin Hood and His Merrie Men, The Sword and the Rose,* and *Rob Roy, the Highland Rogue* – were released between 1950 and 1954.

These are well-told, satisfying adventure stories full of muskets and longbows and appropriate period detail. *Treasure Island* is a minor masterpiece of the genre, a faithful rendition of Robert Louis Stevenson's classic novel, highlighted by Robert Newton's mesmerizing performance as Long John Silver. With his wooden leg and almost mechanical mannerisms, Long John resembles one of Disney's great animated villains, both menacing and funny. As played by Newton, he is also very human.

The other British costume dramas featured fine performers such as Richard Todd, Jack Hawkins, James Robertson Justice, and Glynis Johns, introducing Disney to the reservoir of acting talent available in London, one he would draw upon often for future projects. Beyond that, the movies made imaginative use of the natural beauties of the British landscape. Disney himself was very much in charge of these productions, spending extended periods each year in the United Kingdom.

Modest as these movies were, they did a good deal to restore the Studio's fortunes and must have made Disney increasingly aware of the part that live action would have to play in his future plans. By the early 1950s, he was fully committed. Animation would continue, but the Studio's facilities would be modified and expanded to accommodate other kinds of production.

The Disney Studio had one great advantage over its competitors. Because of its background in animation, it was equipped to deal with unconventional ideas. Of necessity, Walt Disney had become unusually resourceful as a filmmaker, unbound by convention when it came to imagining what might make a commercial movie. Ideas that would have been thrown out at other studios were actively sought by Disney.

At some point soon after the war, he began to think about making a film about America's last frontier – Alaska. Instead of hiring a writer to script an epic, he got in touch with Al and Elma Milotte, who ran a

In *The Reluctant Dragon*, 1941, Robert Benchley finds himself on the loose on Disney's Burbank lot. In the bottom picture, Benchley is seen with Clarence Nash and Florence Gill, the voices of Donald Duck and Clara Cluck

Although it includes fine segments of animation, *Song of the South,* 1946, is primarily a live-action film highlighted by James Baskett's outstanding portrayal of Uncle Remus

Starring Robert Newton and Bobby Driscoll,
Treasure Island, 1950, was the first of a series
of costume dramas filmed in the British Isles

camera store in Alaska. The Milottes were nature buffs and had some experience with 16mm cinematography. Disney asked them to film glimpses of Alaskan life that might suggest possible lines of development. After sending back footage on a variety of topics, from salmon fishing to gold mining, Al Milotte wrote to ask if Disney would be interested in material about the tens of thousands of fur seals who inhabited the Pribilof Islands – bleak rocks in the Bering Sea. Disney wired his approval, and soon reels of seal footage began to arrive at the studio. According to James Algar, one of those entrusted with shaping the material, it was difficult at first to make sense of the footage they were screening. But Disney saw something that held his interest. The seals were acting out a primitive rite that had been repeated for thousands of years. The problem was to present this rite in dramatic terms that would be readily understood by a theater audience. The Disney staff began to research the subject and to put together the story of the seals' life cycle. The film sent by the Milottes was tailored to fit this story, and the result was a twenty-seven-minute picture titled *Seal Island,* released in 1949.

At first, *Seal Island* attracted little attention, but after it won an Academy Award for best short subject of that year, it received wide distribution. Its success led to Disney launching a whole series of nature documentaries which he called True-Life Adventures. Most ran between twenty and thirty minutes, but six feature-length movies were also produced – *The Living Desert, The Vanishing Prairie, The African Lion, Secrets of Life, White Wilderness,* and *Jungle Cat.*

The Milottes were involved in several of these productions, but many other cameramen also contributed to the True-Life Adventures – most of them trained naturalists. The same basic formula was used for all these films. Location or laboratory footage was shot and then sent to Hollywood to be edited into usable form by a team headed by James Algar, Winston Hibler, and Ben Sharpsteen. Trained in the animation side of the business, they tended to look – sometimes too assiduously – for the humor in any given subject and were not above tinkering with their raw material, in the cutting room, to bring out its gag potential. Anthropomorphism was also emphasized – probably a necessary technique for selling the idea of nature documentaries to the public at a time when they were a complete novelty and considered decidedly uncommercial.

Some of the later True-Life Adventures, such as *The African Lion,* were more objective, less influenced by "animation thinking." And even the corniest of these movies was full of wonderful cinematography. Disney gave naturalists the time and equipment they needed, and they repaid him with footage of a quality that had never been seen before. For all their defects, the True-Life Adventures pioneered a genre which was to become a staple of television programming in the form of shows like the *National Geographic* specials.

Spin-offs from the True-Life Adventures included the People and Places documentary series and, more significantly, the many Disney films – such as *Nikki, Wild Dog of the North* and *The Legend of Lobo* – that blended documentary animal footage with staged footage (sometimes involving

Seal Island (top) was the first of Disney's True-Life Adventures, a pioneering series of wildlife films that also included *The African Lion* (center) and *The Living Desert*

Al and Elma Milotte shot the footage used to produce *Seal Island* and *The African Lion*

human actors) in order to create a dramatic story. Other studios had used this technique for series such as *Lassie* and *Rin-Tin-Tin* that featured canine stars, but Disney producers often employed nondomestic animals including bears, coyotes, and even wolves and wolverines, in this way.

Movies of that genre demand great patience on the part of both animal handlers and cameramen, and producers like Algar, Hibler, Harry Tytle, Ken Peterson, and Roy E. Disney developed remarkable expertise in this field.

As far back as the 1930s, Walt Disney had been aware of the potential importance of television – Mickey Mouse cartoons were used in early tests of transmitting equipment – and Disney was careful to retain television rights to all of his films. In the late 1940s, when other studios were trying to make quick money by selling the home-screen rights to their film libraries, Disney resisted the temptation.

Given this foresight, one might have expected Disney to be eager to involve the Studio in television production, but that was not the case. As the television boom gathered momentum, he turned down series opportunities (but did produce Christmas specials in 1950 and 1951). Finally, in 1954, he agreed to develop a series for the American Broadcasting Company. This had little to do with enthusiasm for television but a great deal to do with the fact that ABC was prepared to make a sizable investment in Disney's proposed theme park in return for Disney lending his prestige to the network. Appropriately, the new series was titled *Disneyland*.

Now it became apparent that Disney had been very smart to hold on to the television rights to his library of back products. Major features like *Bambi* could be reissued theatrically while lesser productions, including shorts, could be recycled as part of the television series. Still, a good deal of new material would be needed, and one of the first ideas slated for

Buddy Ebsen (left) and Fess Parker starred in
Davy Crockett, Disney's first television hit

production was *Davy Crockett*, scheduled as a three-parter starring Fess
Parker and Buddy Ebsen. According to Bill Walsh, the series producer,
the subject was picked by sheer dumb luck: "At that time [Davy Crockett]
was considered just one more frontiersman."

When the three episodes were edited, they ran a little short, and Disney
suggested that they fill in the needed time with a montage of evocative
drawings. The drawings were just fine but a little dull, so Disney suggested
a song to go with them. Tom Blackburn, who had written the script,
and George Bruns, who composed the score, went off for about twenty
minutes and came back with a song that began "Born on a mountaintop
in Tennessee. . . ." Walsh thought it sounded pretty awful, but there
was no time for anything else.

The song was, of course, "The Ballad of Davy Crockett," and it became
a smash hit on both sides of the Atlantic. The three *Davy Crockett* shows
were equally successful, creating a craze for coonskin hats and providing
ABC television with an enormous boost. (Later, *Davy Crockett* was recut
and released as a feature film.)

The *Disneyland* series itself went from strength to strength. Later its
name was changed several times (to *Walt Disney Presents*, then *Walt
Disney's Wonderful World of Color*, then *The Wonderful World of Disney*,
then *Disney's Wonderful World*, and finally *Walt Disney*); its time slot
moved from Wednesday to Friday to Sunday, and the show even changed
networks, in 1961, from ABC to NBC, and in 1981 from NBC to CBS;
but these changes had no effect on the fact that the sixty-minute weekly
format Disney developed in 1954 remained successful for twenty-nine
seasons.

Another hugely popular Disney show, *The Mickey Mouse Club*, was
launched on ABC in 1955, running each weekday afternoon until 1959.

Again, Bill Walsh was entrusted with getting the series off the ground, and his first task was to find the right kind of young performers.

"I remember Walt saying, 'Don't get me those kids with the tightly curled hairdos – tap dancers – get me children who look like they're having fun. Then later we can teach them to tap dance or sing or whatever.' He suggested that if we went to ordinary schools and watched the kids at recess, pretty soon we'd find there'd be one we would watch – whether he was doing anything or not. . . . And that would be the kid we wanted for the show. So we used this technique and we found Annette and Darlene and Cubby and the bunch."

The show developed a pleasant, informal format with which children could identify. The talents of the Mouseketeers were combined with old Disney cartoons and many other kinds of material. Dramatic serials, such as "Spin and Marty," became a popular feature of the program.

All of the Mouseketeers became popular, but from the beginning it was Annette Funicello who attracted the most fan mail. Walsh and the other producers tried to maintain an ensemble feel, but gradually Annette's inescapable popularity caused more and more of the show to be keyed to her. The show was still receiving excellent ratings when it ended, but it had become very expensive to produce and Walt Disney was feuding with ABC over the number of commercials the network wanted to insert into the program. Annette was also beginning to outgrow her role. For these combined reasons, it was decided to take the show off the air. (*The Mickey Mouse Club* format was revived in 1977 and 1989.)

Annette moved on to film stardom outside the Disney Studio orbit, but she was still under the guidance of Walt Disney, who continued to own her contract.

In 1954, the year in which the *Disneyland* series was launched, the Studio released 20,000 *Leagues Under the Sea,* easily its most ambitious live-action picture to that point – a big-budget movie using major Hollywood stars (Kirk Douglas, James Mason, Paul Lukas, and Peter Lorre) and state-of-the-art special effects.

The film 20,000 *Leagues* came into being as a by-product of the True-Life Adventures. Bill Walsh and Card Walker had raised the possibility of making an undersea film for the nature series, and this triggered the idea of bringing Jules Verne's classic to the screen. Disney was not enthusiastic at first but eventually bought the rights to the property from MGM and called in Earl Feldman and Richard Fleischer – known for their imaginative B movies – to write and direct the film.

The project demanded elaborate sets and a great deal of trick photography. Much of the action was shot in a large water tank on one of the Disney soundstages; other scenes were filmed in an outdoor tank at the Fox lot, and location work was done in Jamaica and off San Diego. One high spot of the action is a violent fight between the crew of the submarine *Nautilus* and a giant squid – a sequence that called for all the ingenuity the Studio could muster. The first version, shot at tremendous expense, did not satisfy Disney. The squid did not look real enough and the action

The Mickey Mouse Club featured the Mouseketeers, a group of children with no previous show-business experience. Although no one performer was designated as the show's star, Annette Funicello emerged as a great audience favorite and went on to a career in movies

20,000 Leagues Under the Sea, 1954, was a
big-budget adventure film with an all-star
cast that included James Mason (top), Kirk
Douglas, Peter Lorre, and Paul Lukas

Hayley Mills, second from left, starred in several Disney films, including *Pollyanna,* 1960

was filmed against a pink sky, which provided quite the wrong atmosphere. A new squid was prepared and the sequence reshot, this time during a simulated storm.

James Mason is splendid as the heroically demented Captain Nemo, and Kirk Douglas has fine moments as the stalwart whaler Ned Land. The contrast between these two characters is a little overstated, but *20,000 Leagues Under the Sea* grips our imagination because it is convincing as a battle of ideas and emotions.

Released in 1960, *Swiss Family Robinson* is another big-budget movie taken from a classic adventure story. With John Mills in the lead role, we see how a shipwrecked family learns to cope with life on a tropical island, how they bring European ingenuity to bear on their unfamiliar environment, and how they deal with a band of pirates that invades the island. The production offers some excellent scenic photography, but in the end, the movie lacks the dramatic tension of the best Disney adventure films.

The Shaggy Dog, released in 1959, was the first of the Studio's zany comedies. It starred Fred MacMurray, who had been seen in many of the screwball comedies of the thirties and early forties. *The Shaggy Dog* was to some extent an update of that kind of film, though aimed chiefly at the juvenile market. It was a box-office success and was followed by other similar vehicles tailored to MacMurray's talents, notably *The Absent-Minded Professor,* 1961, and *Son of Flubber,* 1963. The young British actress Hayley Mills also starred in several Disney films during this period, including costume pieces such as *Pollyanna* and contemporary comedies like *The Parent Trap.*

In 1964, Disney released *Mary Poppins,* a film which became one of the greatest hits in the history of the motion-picture industry to that date.

Adapted from P. L. Travers's children's stories, the movie provided Julie Andrews with a spectacular screen debut and smashed box-office records at home and abroad.

Walt Disney had been aware of Travers's remarkable nanny for many years and had made several attempts to obtain the rights to the Poppins stories, probably intending to adapt them for an animated feature. The author resisted his overtures until he visited her in London and persuaded her that the time was ripe to bring her world to the screen. (By then, several other studios were bidding for the rights, and Rodgers and Hammerstein were interested in turning the stories into a musical.)

Back in Burbank, Bill Walsh – who would coproduce the movie – and Don DaGradi began to work on a script that would weave fragments from the original stories into a continuous narrative. The brothers Richard M. and Robert B. Sherman were called in to write music and lyrics.

Next came the crucial matter of casting an actress to play Mary Poppins herself. Mary Martin and Bette Davis were considered front-runners, but Disney had seen Julie Andrews on stage in *Camelot* and was taken with her. He especially liked the way she whistled. The part of Mary's friend Bert went to Dick Van Dyke, whose television show was at the peak of its popularity and who was the only American principal in the cast. The children who become Mary's charges were played by Matthew Garber and Karen Dotrice, both of whom had earlier Disney experience. Glynis Johns, another Disney veteran, was cast as their mother and David Tomlinson as their father. Yet another Briton, Robert Stevenson, was assigned to direct.

Mary Poppins lacks the ethereal charm of Travers's stories, but it has its own virtues. In providing the movie with a coherent structure, Walsh and DaGradi transformed those stories into something more robust than the original. But then again, Julie Andrews is a far more glamorous and youthful version of Mary Poppins than the one we meet on the printed page. She brings a charm and spark of her own, and her singing voice and

Released in 1964, *Mary Poppins* combined live action with interludes of animation and became the biggest commercial success that the Studio would enjoy during Walt Disney's lifetime

An airborne tea party that ends in hysterical laughter is one of many special effects sequences that contribute to the magic of *Mary Poppins*

dancing ability – matched to memorable songs – are great assets. In the end, though, the key to her performance is her ability to seem prim and proper yet be perpetually on the verge of some kind of marvelous insanity.

Dick Van Dyke's attempt at a cockney accent leaves much to be desired, but the rest of the cast is excellent, and Edwardian London is evoked with a good deal of feeling for atmosphere, clever use being made both of remarkable special effects and of simple sets that would not seem out of place on the stage of a Broadway theater. Throughout the film, the real and the imaginary are combined in inventive and believable ways, though the scenes that combine live action with animation now seem stiff and dated in the wake of *Who Framed Roger Rabbit*.

In the production of *Mary Poppins*, all of the Studio's resources were pooled to produce a motion picture that probably could not have been made anywhere else.

The greatest of those resources, Walt Disney himself, would soon be gone, but the kind of live-action family films he had espoused continued to be produced at the Studio. *The Love Bug*, 1969 – developed, written, and produced by Bill Walsh – inaugurated a series of movies about Herbie, a Volkswagen with a mind of its own. *Bedknobs and Broomsticks*, 1971, was a lively fantasy adventure featuring Angela Lansbury, and *Freaky Friday*, 1976, was the best of a number of Disney films that starred future Academy Award–winner Jodie Foster.

Walt Disney picked Julie Andrews to
play Mary Poppins in part because he was
impressed by her whistling ability

David Warner was one of the stars of *Tron*,
1982, which made use of electronic effects to
place human protagonists inside a video game

The Love Bug, 1965, was the first of several
successful comedies conceived by producer Bill
Walsh and built around Herbie, a Volkswagen
with a mind of its own

In 1979, there was an attempt to cash in on the science-fiction movie
craze by producing a space-opera version of 20,000 *Leagues Under the
Sea* titled *The Black Hole*. It was strong on special effects but weak on
story and fared miserably at the box office. Another disappointment was
the video-game fantasy *Tron*, which made spectacular use of computer-
generated imagery but failed to generate any empathy between protagonists
and audience.

Tron was made during the brief tenure of Tom Wilhite – former
head of the Disney publicity department – as vice president of creative
development. Along with *Tron*, Wilhite was largely responsible for some
interesting movies, such as *The Last Flight of Noah's Ark* and *The Devil
and Max Devlin* (both starring Elliott Gould) and the powerful rite of
passage drama *Tex* (starring Matt Dillon).

The problem was that the family film market was proving demograph-
ically less profitable than the young adult audience, and, despite strong
efforts like *Tex*, the Studio had a problem expanding its live-action
production in a direction that would appeal to those young adults. As
noted in chapter 10, testing showed that the Disney name was actually
off-putting to young adults since they associated it with the world of
childhood from which they were trying to graduate.

With this in mind, Ron Miller, then head of production, decided in
the early eighties to begin issuing a new and more adult-oriented line
of films for which a different brand name – Touchstone – was eventually

Splash!, 1984, was the first Disney feature to be aimed at a sophisticated adult audience

adopted. With Wilhite in charge of this program, the first Touchstone movie was *Splash!,* starring Tom Hanks and Daryl Hannah and directed by Ron Howard. It was released in 1984 with much fanfare and enjoyed considerable critical and commercial success.

Clearly, Touchstone was a good idea, but it came too late to help save the Studio from being plunged into a state of turmoil later that year. Touchstone would come fully into its own only after the team led by Michael Eisner, Frank Wells, and Roy Disney took control of the Studio and began to restructure the entire production program.

14 Expanded Horizons

One of the first films to go into production after Michael Eisner and Frank Wells took control of the Studio was *Down and Out in Beverly Hills* (1986). A very adult (and very funny) comedy written and directed by Paul Mazursky, starring Bette Midler, Richard Dreyfuss, and Nick Nolte, it was a signal that the Studio, sparked by production chief Jeffrey Katzenberg, was ready to make good on its promise to expand into markets where Disney had seldom, if ever, ventured before.

One of Katzenberg's strategies was to inaugurate a series of high-concept comedies that depended on clever scripts peppered with adult humor, precisely the kind of thing he and Eisner were known for during their Paramount years. Typical of their Paramount successes was *Beverly Hills Cop,* in which a brash black detective from the Detroit slums is set loose in the gilded ghetto. Now, at Disney, came *Down and Out in Beverly Hills,* in which a homeless man is set loose in the same gilded ghetto. This was a formula that Katzenberg understood as well as anyone in Hollywood and he implemented it with enthusiasm.

Still, while Eisner's mandate to Katzenberg included broadening the Studio's approach to production, so that Disney could have a full range of pictures and compete head-to-head with companies like Paramount and Columbia, it also included a directive to find a way to make "real Disney movies" again. George Lucas knew how to make "real Disney movies." Steven Spielberg knew how to make "real Disney movies." It

was time for the Walt Disney Company to rediscover the secret, in live action as well as in animation.

(In fact, except for a nod in the direction of *20,000 Leagues Under the Sea*, Lucas and Spielberg did not make the kind of movies that Walt Disney had actually made. Rather – as both have made clear in interviews – they made the kind of movies they believed he might have made had he launched his career in the 1970s. What they learned from Disney was a basic attitude to filmmaking rather than a formula.)

Team Disney (as the new executive group was titled) soon had a hit that Walt Disney would surely have approved of in the form of *Flight of the Navigator* (1986), a well-conceived, youth-oriented science-fiction film directed by Randal Kleiser, who is perhaps best known for *Grease* (produced at Paramount during the Eisner period). *Flight of the Navigator* proved that Katzenberg had a feel for family-oriented fantasy. At the same time, though, he was quick to point out in interviews that it would be a waste of time to guess what Walt Disney might do if he were still alive, and so Katzenberg actively pursued other kinds of projects tailored for today's youth audience. Just such a project was *Ernest Goes to Camp*, a decidedly juvenile comedy built around the character of gawky Ernest P. Worrell (Jim Varney), a handyman with so many screws loose he is in desperate need of his own services. Released in 1987, *Ernest Goes to Camp* launched a successful series of movies built around the Ernest character.

Released the following month, *Benji the Hunted* revived a favorite Disney genre of the fifties and sixties, the fiction film that blends staged and documentary wildlife footage into a rousing entertainment with ethics that have more to do with man's view of the world than with the laws of nature.

Soon after, in November of 1987, came *Three Men and a Baby*, a movie that, though not modeled on Disney films of the past, can certainly

As Ernest P. Worrell, Jim Varney has starred in a series of slapstick comedies

374

Directed by Paul Mazursky, *Down and Out in Beverly Hills,* 1986, signaled a move toward more adult-oriented films instigated by new Disney chairman Michael Eisner and his studio head Jeffrey Katzenberg

Overleaf: Under the policies inaugurated by Michael Eisner and Jeffrey Katzenberg, Disney greatly expanded its live-action production program, attracting major stars in the process. *Ruthless People,* 1986 (left), capitalized on the talents of Bette Midler (top), Danny DeVito and Judge Reinhold (inside the clown costume). The slate of films released during Katzenberg's decade as Studio head included comedies such as the Whoopi Goldberg vehicle *Sister Act,* 1992 (right bottom), and ambitious productions such as *Dead Poets Society,* 1989 (right top), in which Robin Williams gave one of his most affecting performances

SEE WHAT HAPPENS WHEN A DIRTY BUM MEETS THE FILTHY RICH.

DOWN AND OUT IN BEVERLY HILLS

A PAUL MAZURSKY FILM

NICK NOLTE · BETTE MIDLER · RICHARD DREYFUSS

TOUCHSTONE FILMS presents in association with SILVER SCREEN PARTNERS II A PAUL MAZURSKY FILM
Starring NICK NOLTE BETTE MIDLER RICHARD DREYFUSS
"DOWN AND OUT IN BEVERLY HILLS" Co-Produced by PATO GUZMAN Based upon the play "BOUDU SAUVÉ DES EAUX" by RENÉ FAUCHOIS
Screenplay by PAUL MAZURSKY & LEON CAPETANOS Produced and Directed by PAUL MAZURSKY

Released in 1990, *Dick Tracy* was an
imaginative exploration of pop culture directed
by Warren Beatty, who also starred

A variation on the Pygmalion theme in which the heroine is a Hollywood hooker rather than a cockney flower girl, *Pretty Woman* was one of the major hits of 1990. Here the camera sets up to shoot the movie's star, Julia Roberts

be thought of as one Walt Disney might have enjoyed. This story (adapted from a French film) of three bachelors bringing up a baby starred Tom Selleck, Steve Guttenberg, and Ted Danson.

Who Framed Roger Rabbit (see chapter 10) proved that Eisner and Katzenberg were serious about making the kind of movies that would recapture the old magic. At the same time, the Studio continued to produce more "mature" films – movies that generally received PG or R ratings – often with considerable success. *Down and Out in Beverly Hills* was followed by other Bette Midler vehicles, including the hilarious *Ruthless People* (1986), *Outrageous Fortune* (1987), *Beaches* (1989), and *Scenes from a Mall* (1991), the latter costarring Woody Allen. Danny DeVito, one of the stars of *Ruthless People,* also headlined, along with Richard Dreyfuss, in director Barry Levinson's *Tin Men* (1987), while Robin Williams lent his unique talents to a couple of best Disney movies of the eighties, the blatantly anarchistic *Good Morning, Vietnam* (1988), also directed by Levinson, and the more subtly subversive *Dead Poets Society* (1989).

Other important mainstream pictures of the period were *The Color of Money* (a 1986 sequel to the fifties classic *The Hustler,* directed by Martin Scorsese and starring Paul Newman and Tom Cruise), *New York Stories* (1989), and *Pretty Woman* (1990). A huge commercial success, the latter was a far cry from the traditional Disney movie, the plot being built around the redemption of a street prostitute (Julia Roberts) through the intervention of monied refinement as supplied by a classic yuppie-era overachiever (Richard Gere).

That same year, the Studio released *Dick Tracy,* a big-budget spectacular directed by and starring Warren Beatty, with a supporting cast that included Dustin Hoffman, Al Pacino, and Madonna. The movie was stylish, using sets and props that featured only seven colors, the art direction reproducing the feel of a Sunday comic strip very effectively. Perhaps too effectively since, striking as it is in its performances (especially

Honey, I Shrunk the Kids, 1989, was a successful return to the kind of special effects comedy the Studio had exploited effectively in the sixties and seventies

Pacino's) and its production values, *Dick Tracy* never quite transcends its print model to bring the screen to life.

Year by year, Disney's share (as represented by Buena Vista, its distribution arm) of the feature-film market was growing, as were profits. Known in the industry for keeping tight control on budgets and production schedules, Katzenberg turned the Studio into an efficient moviemaking machine. At the same time, though, he was not afraid to call on the best available talent, as can be seen from the names mentioned above. Just to consider one category, notable directors to work for Disney during the first five years of Katzenberg's tenure included Mazursky, Levinson, Scorsese, Beatty, Kleiser, Peter Weir, Garry Marshall, and Robert Zemeckis.

Most of the more adult movies were being released by Touchstone, though by 1990 another new production division, Hollywood Pictures, had also been introduced, its first release being the horror movie *Arachnophobia*. The Walt Disney label was now reserved for animated features and family-oriented pictures like *Honey, I Shrunk the Kids* (1989), a well-received Rick Moranis vehicle that was decidedly reminiscent of such earlier Disney special-effects releases as *The Absent-Minded Professor. Honey, I Blew Up the Kid* was a 1992 sequel.

At the same time, Touchstone and Hollywood were enjoying some success in reaching the teenage audience – the group that had in the recent past proved most immune to the Disney name. Touchstone, for example, released *Adventures in Babysitting* (1987), which presented an adolescent baby-sitter and her young charges at large on the seamier side of Chicago. Hollywood Pictures followed *Arachnophobia* with films like *The Hand That Rocks the Cradle,* a 1992 chiller about a psychotic nanny, and *Encino Man,* also 1992, which tells the story of a cryogenically preserved caveman who, after learning a few syllables of Valleytalk, becomes the most popular dude in the San Fernando Valley.

More in the earlier Disney tradition was *The Rocketeer* (1991), a fantasy thriller set largely in the Hollywood of the thirties, centered on a

Tim Burton's *The Nightmare Before Christmas*, 1993, added stop-motion animation to the Disney repertoire

Tim Burton with some of the characters created for *The Nightmare Before Christmas*

secret rocket motor and featuring everything from Nazi spies to a scenery-chewing matinee idol.

Films with a broader appeal have included *Sister Act* (1992) and *Sister Act 2: Back in the Habit* (1994), popular hits for Whoopi Goldberg, as well as a remake of the old MGM favorite *Father of the Bride* (1991), with Steve Martin and Diane Keaton, and *Billy Bathgate* (1991), based on the novel by E. L. Doctorow. Directed by Robert Benton, the latter film explored the criminal underworld of the Depression era with imagination and honesty and provided interesting acting opportunities for a fine cast that included Dustin Hoffman, Nicole Kidman, and Bruce Willis.

Another area that has been extensively explored, especially since the 1992 success of *The Mighty Ducks,* about the vicissitudes of a kids' ice hockey team, is the youth-oriented sports comedy, a genre that has produced several modest hits for Disney, such as *Cool Runnings* (1993) and *Angels in the Outfield* (1994). There were two sequels to *The Mighty Ducks.* One of them – D2: *The Mighty Ducks,* a 1994 film – performed respectably at the box office. The other – the Anaheim Mighty Ducks, a Disney-owned National Hockey League team – did stellar business when it made its league debut in 1993.

The year 1993 also saw the release of *The Nightmare Before Christmas,* a stop-motion animated musical feature produced by Tim Burton, who, before his successes with movies such as *Beetlejuice* and *Batman,* had been an artist in the Disney animation department. *The Nightmare Before Christmas* features flexible, puppetlike figures who are animated by hand and filmed one frame at a time, and tells the story of Jack Skellington of Halloweentown and his misguided efforts to supplant Santa Claus.

It will be noted that one genre of film has been conspicuously absent from Disney's lineup since the new management team took over, as it was before: at Disney, gratuitous violence is still shunned.

"I have never done that kind of picture," says Michael Eisner. "I didn't do them at Paramount, and I don't do them here. I'm just not interested. I have nothing against action movies – if we're talking about pictures like *Raiders of the Lost Ark* – but I've never done the kind of films in which someone's head is sliced off every couple of minutes. There's a theory that you have to do that kind of thing to reach an international audience, but it's not true. *Dead Poets Society* was a big international hit and that was about language."

The Studio's commitment to quality, along with a desire to be in a position to release more than thirty movies a year, has led to alliances with top independent production companies such as Andy Vajna's Cinergi Productions (which, at the time of this writing, is preparing a version of *The Scarlet Letter* starring Demi Moore) and Merchant/Ivory (whose first projects for Disney include *Jefferson in Paris,* a historical drama based on Thomas Jefferson's years as minister to France).

In 1992, Joe Roth, former chairman of Twentieth Century Fox, brought his Caravan Pictures under the Disney umbrella, and in 1993, Disney purchased Miramax, the company which had released such gritty off-beat hits as *The Crying Game* and *The Piano.* These moves signified the determination of both Eisner and Katzenberg to emphasize quality production. This did not mean, of course, that low-budget comedies and other commercial films would be abandoned, but it did mean that there would be a continuing policy of presenting prestigious films.

Among the more interesting movies to be released by Buena Vista in 1994 were *Quiz Show,* Robert Redford's well-crafted look at the television game show scandals of the 1950s, and *Ed Wood,* Tim Burton's affectionate portrait of the man who produced and directed some of the worst-crafted movies in the history of the American cinema. Much more of a commercial success was *The Santa Clause,* a clever Christmas comedy featuring the talents of Tim Allen.

By the time these films were released, Jeffrey Katzenberg was gone, though not before fulfilling his mandate of making Disney a major live-action studio. In the wake of Katzenberg's departure, Joe Roth was appointed chairman of Walt Disney Motion Pictures (see chapter 11).

Just as The Walt Disney Company has expanded its movie base since 1985, so has it greatly expanded its television base. It had entered the cable world in 1983 with The Disney Channel®, an outlet for family programming that was largely the brainchild of Jim Jimirro, who had been pressing for the company to become involved in cable and satellite distribution for several years. To a significant extent, The Disney Channel has been able to recycle existing Disney library material, as well as generating much new programming, and it has established itself as a major force in the cable industry.

Since 1984, there has also been a strenuous attempt, largely under the guidance of Richard Frank, to involve the Studio in supplying both new prime-time and daytime shows to the television networks and for syndication. In 1986, *The Disney Sunday Movie* made its debut on ABC with

Michael Eisner as host. This series featured reruns of Disney theatrical releases along with made-for-TV movies. Scheduled against a perennial audience favorite, *60 Minutes*, the show's ratings were disappointing, and in 1988 it was shifted, as *The Magical World of Disney*, to NBC, where it continued to perform lethargically.

More satisfactory has been Disney's attempt to enter the situation-comedy market, generally in the form of co-production deals with established television producers such as Witt-Thomas-Harris. Among the Disney successes in this area have been *The Golden Girls, Blossom, Dinosaurs* – the latter a favorite with children – and the enormously popular *Home Improvement,* starring Tim Allen, which quickly established itself at the top of the weekly Neilson ratings.

Most interesting of all has been Disney's enthusiastic entry into the field of television animation, which began almost as soon as the new management took control of the company. For decades, Disney had shied away from television animation, the argument being that animation for the small screen was economical only if standards were lowered to a level that was incompatible with Disney's reputation. It was true that Disney had pioneered some of the limited animation techniques that other companies were now exploiting on television – techniques that involved fewer drawings (hence, lower costs) per foot of film – but as a matter of policy Disney was not interested in anything that did not fit the description of what it proudly called "full animation," the standard it employed in its features and theatrical shorts.

In the early 1980s, however – lean years for Disney – there was some reassessment of this point of view. The main champion of the potential of television animation at the Studio was Gary Krisel, who had spent the previous several years reviving the fortunes of the Disney record company and the merchandising division. When The Disney Channel went on the air, Krisel was distressed to see that Disney programming was removed from the public airwaves. It was his argument that there should be some way of reaching out to the millions of kids who had no access to Disney's cable shows. Krisel persuaded Ron Miller that the Studio should at least reinvestigate the possibilities of television animation.

As far as technical quality was concerned, Krisel was convinced that Disney could protect its reputation by aiming for a standard that, while it might not be satisfactory for a theatrical release, would work very well on the small screen – a standard that was significantly higher than the norm for television animation. For his part, Ron Miller made the stipulation that any experiment in television animation must be made *without* benefit of any of the classic Disney characters.

To set the experiment in motion, Krisel began to assemble a small team, beginning with Michael Webster, a producer with extensive experience of working with animators in the Far East, especially Japan. The initial idea was to produce animated specials and then look into the possibility of developing a series after gaining some experience.

All this was still at the talking stage when Michael Eisner and Frank Wells took charge of the company. Krisel and his team were invited to

Ducktales has been one of the success stories
of Disney's television animation division

Eisner's Bel Air home, and there Eisner expressed his enthusiasm for the idea of the company becoming involved in animated television shows and said that he'd like to see four series on the air as soon as possible. Krisel pointed out that they weren't set up to handle four series right away and suggested that they try for two. Eisner asked what ideas they had, and Krisel mentioned the possibility of building a show around the Wuzzles – characters created by Hasbro Toys, each of which was a combination of two animals. Eisner liked that idea and suggested as a second possibility the idea of developing a series featuring Gummi Bears, his reason being that his then seven-year-old son was obsessed with the translucent, rubbery, candy creatures.

"We weren't entirely enraptured with the idea," said Krisel. "We were supposed to take some candy and make a show out of it? That seemed a little outlandish. Everybody was rebelling at the idea, but then I saw some funny drawings that had been done of the candy and I began to think that what we needed to do was come up with the myth behind these bears."

And so Krisel's team invented a noble sextet of bears who lived, many years ago, in the kingdom of Dunwyn, protecting Princess Calla and their other human friends from the forces of evil. Meetings were set with CBS, NBC, and ABC. CBS committed to the Wuzzles and NBC took the Gummi Bears. By the time Krisel met with ABC there was nothing left to sell. When they made their debut in 1985, the two shows competed against each other in their Saturday morning slot, and, while *The Wuzzles* won the ratings war for the first few weeks (and continued to enjoy moderate success), it was *The Gummi Bears* that turned out to be the first big hit for Disney's television animation division.

Success brings credibility, and the TV animation team was now given permission to tackle established Disney characters. The first fruits of this policy was *The New Adventures of Winnie the Pooh*, made for The Disney Channel then rebroadcast on ABC. These Pooh stories were worthy successors to the theatrical featurettes, and continue to enjoy popularity. An even bigger hit was *DuckTales* – a daily syndicated series that had its roots in the comic books of Carl Barks, who had created his own Disney mythology built around Scrooge McDuck, the irrepressible Huey, Dewey, and Louie, and a dazzling cast of supporting players. *DuckTales* did not blatantly cannibalize the comic books but rather managed to rethink the concept in television terms. The series has been enormously popular and has led to a spin-off theatrical feature (see chapter 10).

Another Disney-rooted series was *TaleSpin*, set in the town of Cape Suzette and featuring three characters from *The Jungle Book* – Baloo the bear, King Louie the ape, and Shere Khan the tiger – who were given, however, somewhat different roles.

"We treated them as actors," explains development head Greg Weisman. "We said, 'Here are three guys who were great in one big movie. Let's cast them in a whole different show.' So Baloo became a cargo pilot, Louie became a barman, and Khan became a kind of magnate who owns all this stuff, and we gave the whole thing a thirties-adventure-movie kind of atmosphere."

Another lively series with a period feel was *Darkwing Duck*, the eponymous hero of which was conceived as a larger-than-life character who recalls, tongue in cheek, classic comic strip and pulp heroes like Will Eisner's *The Spirit* and Walter B. Gibson's *The Shadow*.

The theatrical success of *The Little Mermaid* created a demand for a television series based on the character of Ariel, a series that has enjoyed a considerable following among girls. The continuing popularity of the television arm's work with established Disney characters finally led to permission for its artists to take on one of the "big three" from the classic theatrical shorts – namely Goofy, who was promptly cast in a series titled *Goof Troop*.

Originally conceived as a science-fiction comedy, *Goof Troop* evolved into a touching animated situation comedy which deals with the relationship between single parent Goofy and his son, Max. So successful has the interplay between these characters proven to be that it has been made the basis for a theatrical feature (see chapter 12).

In the last decade, the television animation division has launched more shows than can adequately be described here. Many of them have derived from past Disney successes while others have been comedies, or comedy dramas, rooted in a tradition that Disney helped establish. In 1994, however, Gary Krisel's team launched a new series titled *Gargoyles* which moved into wholly new territory.

"*Gargoyles* is our first venture into pure drama," says Greg Weisman. "There have been gargoyles in many cultures. The Chinese had dragon-style gargoyles. The Aztecs had them. They are on totem poles. But our gargoyles belong to a clan that had its origin a thousand years ago in Scotland. They are the guardians of a castle, but most of them were destroyed and the few that remain are wrongfully blamed for betraying the occupants of the castle. They are cursed to sleep in the form of stone figures until the castle rises above the clouds. That finally happens when a rich guy buys the castle and moves it to the top of a skyscraper in Manhattan. That's when the gargoyles come back to life. . . ."

Gargoyles shows that Disney television animation is ready to move in new and independent directions. Another important development was the 1993 release of *The Return of Jafar*, a feature-length video spin-off of *Aladdin*. Intended as a promotional vehicle for a television series based on the *Aladdin* characters, *The Return of Jafar* performed so well on its own (selling more than twelve million units to date, thus becoming one of the top ten videos ever) that it suggests intriguing possibilities for the artists who have established the viability of the television animation team.

"I can imagine the day," says Gary Krisel, "when, instead of producing shows for the networks or syndication or even for cable, our main business will be making shows that are intended primarily for home video consumption. It would be a logical development, and it might well become the most efficient way of delivering our product to our consumers."

IV The Magic Kingdoms

15   Beyond Film

Walt Disney was a man with a knack for doing the right thing at the right time – a person with an almost uncanny instinct for gauging what the public wanted and the courage to act on his intuitions. It is essential to realize, though, that his intuitions were backed up by hard work and thorough preparation. Never was this more evident than in the most important of his postwar endeavors.

Disneyland Park grew from a seed that had been germinating in Disney's mind for fifteen or twenty years, since the time he had taken his young daughters to local amusement parks and wondered why there could not be a place that was as entertaining for adults as it was for children. There is some evidence to suggest that he was thinking about specific rides as early as the late thirties, but economic realities made it impossible for him to pursue such ideas at the time.

Shortly after World War II, Disney's doctor suggested that he find a hobby to counter the stress of running the Studio. Disney – who had been a news butcher on the Santa Fe Railroad (see chapter 1) – had always loved trains and was aware that two of his top animators, Ollie Johnston and Ward Kimball, were serious railroad buffs. He admired Johnston's backyard railroad and decided to build one for himself in his own garden. Next he began thinking about running a full-size narrow-gauge railway around the Studio, using engines that had been built for the 1915 Pan American Exposition in San Francisco. He soon decided

DISNEYLAND

SCHEMATIC AERIAL VIEW
APPROX. 45 ACRES
WITHIN RAILROAD TRACKS
DESIGNED BY WED ENTERPRISES.

Opposite left: Walt Disney's passionate interest in railroads had an important influence on his plans for Disneyland

Opposite right: Disney stands beside the trolley tracks on Disneyland's Main Street

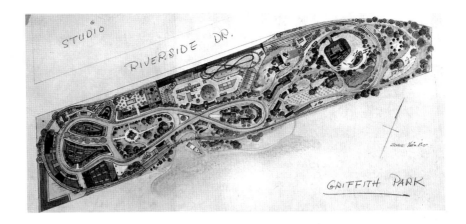

Before he committed himself to the Disneyland that has become so familiar, Walt Disney briefly considered the possibility of building an amusement park directly across the street from the Burbank home of the Studio. This plan gives some idea of what that park might have looked like

This imaginary aerial view of the proposed park, drawn by Herb Ryman, was used as a sales tool when Walt Disney was presenting the idea of Disneyland to potential investors. A 1958 map of Disneyland, overleaf, shows how the final plan evolved

that there wasn't enough room to install a railroad at the Studio, but he began to think about that innovative kind of amusement park again: a railroad circling the perimeter would make a wonderful feature of such a park.

In 1952, Disney set up an organization called WED (his initials) to begin planning the park in earnest. At first WED consisted of a few designers – men like Claude Coats and John Hench, mostly co-opted from the animation department – who understood how Disney worked and who were well equipped to interpret his ideas. (They would be called Imagineers, and later the company was renamed WDI, for Walt Disney Imagineering.)

Plans and models were made for an as yet unchosen site. There were thoughts of building in Burbank, directly across the street from the Studio, but that idea was abandoned and the Stanford Research Institute was called in to recommend a suitable location for the Park within the greater Los Angeles area. Soon Disney owned 160 acres of orange groves in Anaheim, to the south of Los Angeles. The land was relatively inexpensive, yet it was adjacent to the planned route of the Santa Ana Freeway, which soon would link Orange County with metropolitan Los Angeles. The mild climate would permit year-round operation of the Park.

With conventional Coney Island–type parks failing in many parts of the country, an amusement park hardly seemed like a sound investment. Disney sought out the advice of experts, all of whom told him he had invented a new way of losing money. Some officers of Disney's own company – his brother Roy included – were also skeptical about the venture, but Walt went ahead with his plans, financing development from his own pocket and with funds from companies that agreed to pay advances on Disneyland concessions.

Major progress came in 1954 when the American Broadcasting Company–Paramount Theaters group agreed to purchase slightly more than one-third of the shares of a company called Disneyland, Inc., in return for Disney's providing ABC with a prime-time television series, *Disneyland* (see chapter 13). The remaining shares were divided between Walt Disney Productions, Walt Disney himself, and Western Printing and Lithographing, which had a longtime association with the Studio. Before long, Walt Disney Productions was able to buy out the holdings of both Western and ABC–Paramount.

The improved financial situation of Disneyland, Inc., offered banks more than adequate security, and funds were advanced, setting the stage for construction to begin. Meanwhile, Disney planned the television series in such a way as to afford Disneyland maximum publicity.

His overall concept for the Park had its own kind of logic, which has proved enormously effective over the years. The plan called for a vintage railroad defining the perimeter of the Park, with its main station right at the entrance. Once past the station, the visitor would have to pass down Main Street – an idealized reproduction of a small Midwestern town of the sort Disney himself had known as a boy. Main Street was calculated to correspond with one of the archetypes of the American imagination, establishing an ambience that would put visitors in an appropriate frame of mind. Its scale would be slightly less than life-size, enhancing the sense of friendliness and intimacy. Transportation would be available – vintage trams and horse-drawn trolleys – but people on foot would be drawn down Main Street by the imposing edifice at its far end – Sleeping Beauty Castle – the likes of which had never been seen in any Mississippi Valley community. In fact, all of Disneyland was conceived in terms of visual magnets that would draw people through the Park and keep the crowds moving. Sleeping Beauty Castle was the greatest of these magnets, and all paths would converge on the traffic circle immediately in front of it.

A visitor who followed a clockwise route from this central feature would find himself, first of all, in Adventureland, next in Frontierland, then in Fantasyland, and finally in Tomorrowland. Each of these areas would have a specific atmosphere, appropriate to its name. Disney characters and references to Disney movies and television shows would be found throughout, but in a sense the Park was conceived in such a way as to seem like a tribute to the Hollywood movie tradition as a whole. Many of the familiar genres were there, from Westerns to science fiction and from costume dramas to exotic safari sagas. If there was an emphasis on material derived from animation, that was understandable. The bottom line was that visiting Disneyland would be like spending a day *inside*

Walt Disney welcomes visitors to the park

a cluster of Hollywood films, each one spilling magically into the next. Entering the Park would permit people to visit places where only the camera had taken them before.

Some of the individual features of Disneyland had been foreshadowed at Coney Island, and especially at fairs like St. Louis's Louisiana Purchase Exposition and Chicago's Century of Progress Exposition. What made Disneyland very different was the fact that it was organized in a way, and built on a scale, that was user-friendly decades before that term was coined.

Disney's plan was sound. It had a sense of structure and continuity that was new to this kind of enterprise, it exploited genres of popular culture that had already demonstrated their staying power, and it capitalized fully on the established Disney image. Every element had been thoughtfully considered and imaginatively developed.

Disneyland was opened on July 17, 1955. Television crews were on hand to record the opening ceremonies while thirty thousand guests thronged Main Street and explored the farthest reaches of the complex. Millions more witnessed the event on their home screens. No entertainment facility had ever received this kind of publicity, and Disneyland became a national phenomenon overnight.

Walt Disney had built the Versailles of the twentieth century – but it was a Versailles designed for the pleasure of the people rather than the amusement of the nobility.

At the time of its inauguration, it was not, of course, quite the dense complex we find today. As yet, no monorail had been installed, no New Orleans Square linked Adventureland to Frontierland. A grove of trees stood where the Matterhorn would one day rise. Disney had created an unusual and agreeable environment suitable for further expansion but already providing novel entertainments for both children and adults. The Park could be enjoyed by those who were anxious to participate as well as by those who chose to stroll and observe. It was a place for families, a place to visit – and revisit – for the whole day, an environment that seemed inexhaustible. Hours could be spent just browsing in the stores along Main Street (this at a time, it should be remembered, when the galleria-type shopping mall did not yet exist).

Apart from the originality of its plan, what made Disneyland radically different from other earlier amusement parks was the fact that it resembled the back lot of a movie studio. The skills that go into building movie sets are the same skills that have gone into Main Street and Frontierland. The differences are that Disneyland's "sets" are built to withstand extended use and that, while a movie street may consist of facades that open onto storage areas or empty spaces, Disneyland's thoroughfares are punctuated by doors that give access to shops and restaurants along with rides and entertainments.

Filmmakers are trained to think sequentially: One situation must lead to another to create a narrative flow. These same narrative skills were employed in planning the layout of the Park. As the visitor is drawn from one place to another, calculated scenic changes give the impression of a

This aerial view of The Magic Kingdom at Walt Disney World in Florida shows a Main Street parade in progress. Overleaf: Cinderella Castle at Walt Disney World (left) and Sleeping Beauty Castle in Disneyland, with Anaheim's version of the Matterhorn in the background (right)

Modes of transportation, from horse-drawn trolleys to rockets, play an important role in establishing the atmosphere of the theme parks. Above: the Walt Disney World edition of Tomorrowland with Space Mountain silhouetted against the sky; left: the *Mark Twain* cruises sedately through Frontierland at Disneyland; opposite top left: the Disneyland railroad; opposite top right: transportation in Town Square at Disneyland; opposite bottom: the Walt Disney World monorail glides through Epcot

definite and satisfying sequence of events. The difference is that a movie narrative moves in a straight line, from beginning to end, whereas a visitor to the Park is free to choose among many options, as in an interactive video game. He can, in effect, write his own story, although its basic elements have been carefully preplanned by the designers.

A plaque in Disneyland's Town Square reads as follows:

> TO ALL WHO COME TO THIS HAPPY PLACE:
> WELCOME.
> DISNEYLAND IS YOUR LAND. HERE AGE
> RELIVES FOND MEMORIES OF THE PAST . . .
> AND HERE YOUTH MAY SAVOR THE CHALLENGE
> AND PROMISE OF THE FUTURE.
> DISNEYLAND IS DEDICATED
> TO THE IDEALS, THE DREAMS, AND THE HARD
> FACTS THAT HAVE CREATED AMERICA . . .
> WITH THE HOPE THAT IT WILL BE A SOURCE OF
> JOY AND INSPIRATION TO ALL THE WORLD
> JULY 17, 1955

When those words were written, even Walt Disney cannot have imagined quite how thoroughly his park would capture the imagination of the world. For a while, at least, Disneyland must have seemed like an end in itself. Before very long, however, Disney was beginning to think about how ideas implicit in his first theme park could be expanded elsewhere. The 1964 New York World's Fair provided opportunities to experiment, and then he turned his attention to Florida.

Walt Disney and Card Walker visit the site of Walt Disney World

In part, Disney's intention was to build a theme park that would be a magnet for the East Coast as Disneyland had become a magnet for the West Coast. Beyond that, he wanted to avoid some of the problems that had plagued the first theme park. When it opened, Disneyland had been an island of fantasy set in an ocean of orange trees. That soon changed as urban sprawl arrived to surround the park with motels, gas stations, and fast-food joints. Walt Disney watched these haphazard developments with displeasure and vowed that in Florida he would build a Magic Kingdom that was completely insulated from the outside world.

To this end, he set out to acquire a large tract of land that could accommodate not just a Disneyland-type theme park but also other attractions – including EPCOT (then thought of as an experimental community) – served by Disney-operated hotels and other visitor services. Every effort would be made to preserve as much as possible of the existing topography, to control pollution, and to maintain an ecological balance.

The success of Disneyland made financing for Walt Disney World Resort (as the project was named) relatively easy. Locating the right property was the next order of business. A Disney publication tells the story in the following words:

"Sheathed in necessary obscurity, Disney representatives set out early in 1964 to obtain control of a large area straddling the line separating Orange and Osceola counties in central Florida. Located between the cities of Orlando and Kissimmee, the site is at the crossing point of several heavily travelled highways.

"By October, 1965, they had put together 27,443 acres – almost 43 square miles – at a cost of just over $5,000,000. This size would permit for plenty of future expansion and would assure control of its perimeter. For comparison: Walt Disney World covers about the same land area as the city of San Francisco; it is about twice the size of the island of Manhattan."

On November 15, 1965, accompanied by Florida Governor Haydon Burns, Walt and Roy Disney spoke to the press and officially launched the Walt Disney World project.

Surveying his property from the air, Walt Disney decided that the shore of Bay Lake – the largest natural body of water – was the spot to begin Phase One of the development. Just months after the first earth-moving equipment arrived at the site, however, Disney was in the hospital and dying. During this final illness, he could think of nothing but the Florida project and spent his remaining reserves of energy describing every detail of his vision to his family.

John Hench, a senior vice president of WDI and dean of the Imagineering team, describes Roy Disney's report of one of his last visits to his brother. "Walt was hallucinating, but it was as if he could see this map of the property on the ceiling, and he was pointing to it with one hand and describing it, explaining why we'd have to build an east-west road running through, and so on. It was as if the whole thing was there in full detail. He was obsessed."

"And Walt was right," Hench adds. "We did have to build that east-west road to make the whole thing work."

"The problem was," says Marty Sklar, president of WDI, "that, when Walt died, many people thought that we couldn't carry the thing through without him, especially since Florida was looked on as an extension of the New York market, where Disney had never performed as well as in the rest of the country. People within WED, like Dick Irvine and John Hench, had to persuade management that some version of Walt's vision was still possible."

Normally a fiscal conservative, Roy Disney was the easiest member of the management team to convince.

"He had seen how important it was to Walt," says Sklar, "and as a result he really dedicated the rest of his life to beginning Walt's dream. It wasn't EPCOT, which is what Walt had really cared about most, but it *was* Walt Disney World, and that provided the foundation for everything else that has been done down there since. EPCOT was always the underlying aim – the building codes were written with that in mind – but the key thing was to get something going and building the Magic Kingdom first was the wise thing to do, I believe. It gave people something they could identify with the Disney name. It didn't frighten anybody. Roy got wholeheartedly behind that.

" 'Personally I had my doubts,' Roy told Hench, 'but I knew I had to do it for Walt – because if I hadn't he would have given me hell when I died.' "

As scheduled, Walt Disney World was opened by Roy Disney in October of 1971. A few weeks later, just five days before Christmas, Roy Disney – who had been looking forward to retirement – was dead, his life shortened, some speculated, by his exertions in realizing his brother's last dream.

16 Magic Kingdoms

Expansion in Florida, and later into Japan and Europe, has enabled Disney's Imagineers to explore many aspects of the theme park concept, from the creative marriages of entertainment and science found at Epcot to the cultural variations on basic Disney themes introduced at Tokyo Disneyland and Disneyland Paris (originally known as Euro Disney). Those themes still find their archetypal expression in the two original Magic Kingdoms, in Anaheim and near Orlando. From the beginning, they contained the seeds of much that would come later (Tomorrowland, for example, anticipated EPCOT Center). Over the almost three decades since Walt Disney's death, many additions and alterations have been made to the Magic Kingdoms, providing visitors with new experiences, from Space Mountain to Mickey's Toontown to the the multimedia Alien Encounter, yet these primary parks are still essential expressions of the original vision.

For more than forty years, John Hench has been a key creative figure in the organization first known as WED, then WDI. Along with Claude Coats, Marc Davis, Herb Ryman, and a handful of other animation veterans, he was handpicked to work on Disneyland. While Davis periodically returned to the animation department, Hench stayed on and remains at WDI today – the individual who, next to Walt Disney himself, has probably had the greatest input into design decisions relating to the theme parks.

Hench has given extensive thought to the reasons for Walt Disney's success, both with regard to the parks and to his career in general:

"Part of it, I suppose, was Walt's exploitation of very old survival patterns. He had an instinct for this. I think that if anyone really wanted to take the time to examine it, he would see that these survival patterns are the basis of our aesthetics, our sense of pleasure. We've carried these things around for twenty million years, in our DNA chains or whatever it is. We are the successful survivors, so we must still carry those mechanisms with us. The things that please us are obviously the ones that boost our survival potential – and the ones that we don't like are those that threaten us."

Hench illustrates Disney's instinct for exploiting survival patterns by referring back to the early cartoons:

"Mickey was so-called Lollipop Art – because he was made from circles. I'm oversimplifying it, but circles have never hurt anybody – they are women's breasts and clouds and other soft forms. Felix the Cat, on the other hand, was full of angles and sharp points, and I really think this was the difference between the two. It explains the success of Mickey, who just won't quit. Walt was a highly intuitive person and he sensed these things, and, as a result of this, the Studio has probably developed more awareness than any other design group in this field.

"A lot of designers allow contradictions into their work because they're careless or because they don't really understand what they're doing. These contradictions will cancel out what they're trying to say. If someone wants to make an automobile that will look slick and powerful and he designs something that triggers a very old image of a dead whale on the beach, the customers won't buy it. Look at the Hudson. It was a perfectly good car, but nobody would believe it. I haven't really analyzed the Edsel, but again it gives you an example of [something designed by] a company which was perfectly skilled at engineering, and did a wonderful job of preselling the car – but nobody would touch it."

Hench, whose animation experience included stints as a background painter, a layout artist, an effects animator, and an art director, emphasizes the ways in which Walt Disney's unique cinematic background influenced the design concepts that give the Magic Kingdoms their special character:

"Walt had a high sensitivity, I think, for timing and the way things relate to each other – and this, of course, came from the film work. This is what film is all about, connecting ideas so they relate to one another. A motion picture is an act of communication. It consists of ideas – sometimes very complex ones – that you want other people to understand, and you want them to understand them the way you intended them to, without wandering off on their own. So you want to keep the structure clean and simple. Live-action filming has to count on a lot of accidents, but in a cartoon we could gradually eliminate the things that contradicted what we were trying to say. With the background we had, this was a very easy thing to apply to the third dimension."

As has been seen in earlier chapters, animation is the most controlled form of filmmaking imaginable, with everything preplanned and nothing

Previous pages: Mickey Mouse plays host in Mickey's Toontown left to the temperament of stars or the vagaries of light and weather. The Magic Kingdoms are controlled environments engineered to conform to the principles Disney had evolved while making his animated films. All the elements of an animated movie must be planned so as to complement each other, and this same criterion was adapted to the design of the theme parks.

"It's a concept of relating things in a noncompetitive way," Hench explains. "One of the worst things about, for instance, a World's Fair is that every facility is trying to outshout the others. People are subject to pressure from the Russian pavilion as opposed to the French, as against the Italian – and it does make for a curious kind of mental fatigue. Also, you have to pick up ideas and then drop them completely as you go on to another exhibit – it's like overrecording on a tape, I guess. Eventually you get very confused. Most people have this experience when they go to a World's Fair. They walk out absolutely exhausted and then can't remember very much of what they've seen – most of the attractions have cancelled each other out, as they were probably designed to do.

"Disneyland is a much more pleasant experience – and Walt Disney World, too – because at least there's an attempt to relate one idea to the next. You don't have to drop one before you pick up another – they carry through. This again comes from the motion-picture background. The division into related themes gives a sense of continuity."

The motion-picture influence is most obvious within the context of the individual attractions. Each version of the Haunted Mansion, for example, presents the visitor with a ride that unfolds in time in exactly the same way a movie does. A movie transports an audience from point A to point Z by means of a carefully structured sequence of visual devices – the camera following the action and the audience traveling with the camera. In other words, the camera is a moving vehicle which carries the audience through the narrative, following its assigned route. In the Haunted Mansion, as in other attractions of that type, a car that runs on rails is substituted for the camera. In the Disneyland edition of the ride, the visitor is first ushered into a gothic lobby where he finds himself in a crowd of people in a circumscribed space overhung by cobwebs and surrounded by sinister portraits. A disembodied voice issues a few words of warning, then the lights are extinguished and the show begins with a teaser – a device designed to establish the atmosphere and to draw the visitor into the unfolding scenario. The floor begins to drop and a body suddenly appears, hanging by the neck from the ceiling high above. The sinking floor immediately establishes a feeling of insecurity, but it has the added practical purpose of bringing visitors down to a basement level where they board the "doom buggies" that take them through the rest of the show. These vehicles carry the visitors through a series of spooky environments, each of which exposes them to a new kind of "supernatural" phenomenon. The "buggies" are wired for stereo sound and are built in such a way that the rider can see only what is directly in front of him. Each vehicle is on a swivel so that it can be turned, by electronic signals,

The Haunted Mansion at Walt Disney World
looms in the night. Like other attractions in
the theme parks, the interiors of the various
versions of the Haunted Mansion are developed
from continuity drawings like those, opposite,
which are used in much the same way that
storyboard drawings are used in the planning
of an animated film

AUDIO-ANIMATRONICS figures have evolved a great deal over the decades since they were first introduced. They range from the simple and stylized characters that adorn the several editions of It's a Small World (top) to the elaborate and lifelike mythical beast that inhabits the Dragon's Lair beneath the Château at Disneyland Paris (bottom)

to face just what the designers want it to face at any given moment.

In such traditional Magic Kingdom rides, the rider is not given the choice of where to look. That decision has already been made by the designers, who determined what will be seen just as a movie director determines what a movie patron will see. For one recent attraction, however – Roger Rabbit's Car Toon Spin in Mickey's Toontown at Disneyland Park– a variation on this approach has been successfully used.

Mickey's Toontown is a new section of Disneyland which derives in part from the film *Who Framed Roger Rabbit* but also provides a home for venerable Disney cartoon characters like Mickey, Minnie, Goofy, and Donald. Planned under the supervision of senior show manager Dave Burkhart and senior concept designer Joe Lanzisero, Toontown is a three-dimensional, walk-through cartoon world featuring, among its other attractions, many interactive gags. (A mailbox talks back to anyone who attempts to deposit a letter. A manhole cover protests when stepped on.)

The designers decided to make the Roger Rabbit ride itself as interactive as possible. For this attraction, visitors are seated in Lenny the Cab (a lookalike cousin of Benny, the cartoon taxi featured in the movie). Lenny then takes the rider through a toonscape peppered with suitably toonish adventures. What makes this ride different, however, is the fact that the occupants of the cab have some control over its movements. They can manipulate the steering wheel and alter the direction in which they are facing and therefore have some choice as to how each set piece of the ride is viewed.

"You can take this ride any number of times," says Lanzisero, "and never repeat exactly the same experience."

That limited control enhances this particular ride – providing novel perceptual pleasures while adding to the sense of careening through cartoon space. The route of the vehicle through the set pieces is as fixed as it is with any more traditional ride. It is only the viewpoint that can be manipulated, and, oddly enough, the degree of control the vehicle's occupant is provided with actually creates the illusion of being *out* of control, as though in a skidding car. In the end, the interactive element built into this highly enjoyable ride is really another form of illusion.

This cinematic sensibility is evident throughout the Magic Kingdoms, though – as noted in the previous chapter – it is necessarily deployed in a less deterministic way. The parks are planned to give visitors a pleasant experience (free of those World's Fair pressures described by Hench) no matter which route they happen to select.

To get a full sense of the cinematic character of the Magic Kingdoms, one need only sample their various transportation systems. Like the parks as a whole, these systems deal in everything from unadulterated nostalgia to space-age technology. Main Street is served by trolley cars and horse-drawn vehicles, yet a short walk will take the visitor to a streamlined Monorail. The engines and rolling stock of the railroad circling the Park conjure up the golden age of steam, but the PeopleMover that runs through Tomorrowland is a silent, electrically powered system that addresses the late-twentieth-century need for nonpolluting vehicles

An aerial view of Big Thunder Mountain at
Walt Disney World (top) and a building on
Big Thunder Mountain which shows how the
Disney Imagineers have transformed what is
essentially a simple roller coaster by adding a
level of scenic detail found in the movies

Roger Rabbit's Car Toon Spin offers visitors to Disneyland an opportunity for interactive fun (right). Goofy's Gas Station (below) offers a good idea of the cartoonlike architecture and props that give Mickey's Toontown its special character

(which Walt Disney was already thinking about in the fifties). Other forms of transport abound, meshed into a complex network made up of components that are designed to afford the visitor pleasure by taking him on a cinematic ride through or around the Park. Their routes are planned not as the shortest way between A and B, but rather so as to afford the rider the greatest possible degree of visual satisfaction. The Florida monorail offers its passengers impressive panoramas of the lakes and the surrounding countryside blended with glimpses of fairy-tale worlds that are conjured up as, for example, it glides out of the futuristic Contemporary Hotel, affording distant views of the turrets and spires of Cinderella Castle.

The theme parks exploit all kinds of technical novelties, the most celebrated of which (though they are no longer unique to Disney) are the *AUDIO-ANIMATRONICS*® figures that provide "animation in the round" for so many of the Magic Kingdom attractions.

Long before he began to build Disneyland, Walt Disney had been a collector of clockwork toys. In the mid-forties he began to experiment with mechanical puppets, filming a Buddy Ebsen dance routine, which was then reproduced in the form of a miniature figure built by Studio engineers. The Ebsen puppet worked, but the machinery involved was too clumsy and bulky to suggest any immediate application.

The building of Disneyland prompted a new round of experiments with mechanical figures. At first Imagineers worked with models that had simple cam and lever joints, but before long they began to try out more flexible systems employing pneumatic and hydraulic power transmission controlled by electrical inputs. This was efficient enough to supply the kind of crude movements needed for such things as the animals dotted around the jungle ride. Then someone came up with the idea of using sound,

Soon after World War II, Walt Disney tries out a dance routine with Buddy Ebsen. Ebsen's routine was filmed and served as the basis for Disney's first mechanical figure, the ancestor of all the *AUDIO-ANIMATRONICS* figures in the parks

Brought back to life by *AUDIO-ANIMATRONICS*, President Lincoln confronts his audience

recorded on magnetic tape, to activate the pneumatic and hydraulic valves. At that point, the potential of *AUDIO-ANIMATRONICS* began to be realized. Sound impulses triggered mechanisms, buried within lifelike plastic figures, that could control movements down to the flicker of an eyelid. The tape system also permitted these movements to be synchronized with prerecorded dialogue or music, as well as with lighting effects and whatever else might contribute to the atmosphere of the ride.

The first *AUDIO-ANIMATRONICS* figures were some exotic birds, which eventually formed the basis of the Disneyland Enchanted Tiki Room. It was at the 1964 New York World's Fair, however, that *AUDIO-ANIMATRONICS* had its first major outing. Disney contributed a number of the fair's major attractions, including the Ford Motor Company's "Magic Skyway," General Electric's "Carousel of Progress," and Pepsi-Cola's "It's a Small World" (all of which were later adapted for the theme parks). The most dramatic exhibit was "Great Moments with Mr. Lincoln," which Disney prepared for the Illinois pavilion.

Visitors were confronted with a startlingly lifelike facsimile of the nation's sixteenth president. Lincoln not only spoke but also emphasized his thoughts with naturalistic gestures. His eyes raked the audience as though challenging opponents to debate. He shifted his weight from one foot to the other and his expression changed with the sense of his words. The impact was extraordinary.

This success was not easily won. Indeed, only a few months before the opening of the pavilion it seemed that Lincoln might never be ready in time. The sheer energy locked up in the pneumatic and hydraulic systems of any AUDIO-ANIMATRONICS figure is considerable, and unless this energy can be precisely regulated the figure is apt to become violent. Before he was finally tamed, Mr. Lincoln smashed his chair and threw mechanical fits that threatened the safety of the men working on him.

Just in time for the fair, the power was harnessed, and soon equally sophisticated AUDIO-ANIMATRONICS figures were being featured at Disneyland and Walt Disney World, populating attractions such as Pirates of the Caribbean, the Mickey Mouse Revue, the Country Bear Jamboree, and the Hall of Presidents (which once again featured the words of Abraham Lincoln, who this time appeared surrounded by his peers).

Later, computer chips and other electronic innovations helped make the mechanical figures still more sophisticated, but always their effectiveness has been predicated on the Disney artists' years of experience with animation. They understand, for example, the importance of animating the eyes because, as in film animation, the attention of the audience is instinctively drawn to the eyes. If they are not convincingly naturalistic, the entire illusion will break down. The Imagineers also understand, from two-dimensional animation, that a sense of reality may often be best expressed by suppressing or limiting movement. A character may express surprise more effectively by raising an eyebrow than by throwing up his hands in shock. It is this kind of knowledge that has made AUDIO-ANIMATRONICS so valuable an asset to the parks. Without it, the engineering skill that goes into these figures would be wasted.

For all the technological innovations to be found in the Magic Kingdoms, the Disney organization's primary area of expertise is show business. The theme parks are a kind of total theater which exceeds the wildest dreams of dramatists and which provides entertainment for millions of visitors each year.

17 Themes and Variations

In its early days, Walt Disney World consisted of the Magic Kingdom, three hotels, various satellite resort areas (including campgrounds), a small model community (Lake Buena Vista), three golf courses, and a magnificent 7,500-acre wildlife preserve designed to save the last vestige of the Central Florida wilderness. (The sections of the property that have been developed were not part of this wilderness and do not impinge upon it since it was carefully isolated from the resort areas before building began.)

Already, in this skeletal form, Walt Disney World was a test bed for enlightened technology, innovative urban planning, and responsible environmental management. The advanced building code encouraged the use of state-of-the-art construction techniques so that, for example, some buildings on the property pioneered a new method of modular construction using lightweight steel frames. The Magic Kingdom itself was built on a giant platform which permitted a network of corridors, storage areas, and service systems beneath the surface of Main Street and the other principal areas of the Park. This infrastructure provided all kinds of advantages. Supplies and costumed employees could be delivered to any point in the Park without ever appearing on the streets. Garbage could be disposed of without benefit of conspicuous trucks.

Elsewhere in the Park, an advanced wastewater treatment plant was constructed, and experiments were conducted in treating wastewater by natural means that could generate methane gas as a by-product. Water

management in general was handled with great care, so as to maintain the ecological balance of the area, while the use of solar energy was also explored in one of the complex's office buildings.

In many ways, getting Walt Disney World up and running was rather like building a medium-size city from scratch:

"There was nothing there," says John Hench. "We had to install everything from a power plant to a laundry. You couldn't get phone calls in and out until equipment was put in. Even a simple thing like paint – there was nowhere to get it locally so you had to bring it in from somewhere else. And, of course, there was no trained work force available. When it came to staffing the Park and the hotels, we had to hire people wherever we could find them and train them ourselves."

All this effort and experimentation pointed toward EPCOT Center, the Experimental Prototype Community of Tomorrow that had been Walt Disney's main reason for wanting to develop the Florida property.

Disney envisioned EPCOT as an actual community; when he announced the project, in 1966, he described his aims in the following terms.

"I don't believe there's a challenge anywhere in the world that's more important to people everywhere than finding solutions to the problems of our cities. But where do we begin . . . how do we start to answer the great challenge?

"Well, we're convinced we must start with the public need. And that need is not just for curing the ills of the old cities. . . . EPCOT is . . . an experimental prototype community that will always be in a state of becoming. It will never cease to be a living blueprint of the future. . . .

"We don't presume to know all the answers. In fact we're counting

The focal point of EPCOT Center, comparable to the castles in the Magic Kingdoms, is Spaceship Earth (top), a geodesic sphere housing a theme show devoted to the history of communications.

When EPCOT Center was being planned, a flexible master model (above) enabled Disney's Imagineers to experiment with many arrangements of the various elements

on the cooperation of American industry to provide their best thinking during the planning of our . . . community. And most important of all, when EPCOT has become a reality, and we find the need for technologies that don't even exist today, it's our hope that EPCOT will stimulate American industry to develop new solutions that will meet the needs of people expressed right here in this experimental community."

The participation of industry was to be a big part of the scheme.

"It seems clear in retrospect," says Marty Sklar, "that Walt used the 1964 New York World's Fair as a stepping-stone toward EPCOT. Certainly we didn't need the extra work at the time, but it gave Walt access to the chief executives of GE and other companies he would want to deal with in the future."

The first designs for EPCOT show a domed city that has its roots both in the work of visionary planners like R. Buckminster Fuller and in pop culture versions of the future that might be found in a Buck Rogers comic strip.

"Had Walt Disney lived," Michael Eisner speculates, "I'm sure that EPCOT would have evolved, just like everything else he worked on. It would have changed. What he left behind . . . is just the first expression of an idea that he didn't have time to follow through on."

This is probably true. Still, there is something about the vision of an experimental community that is a perfect expression of the belief in progress that was so characteristic of Americans of Walt Disney's generation.

For Disney the distance from Main Street to EPCOT Center was not so very far.

On opening day, in the fall of 1971, people responded to the inauguration of Florida's Magic Kingdom by staying away in droves, and for several weeks Walt Disney World was half empty. Disney's critics had a field day, gloating that such a theme park could never succeed on the "more sophisticated" East Coast. By Christmas, however, customers began to pour into the park, and the critics were having to eat their words. Apparently, families had stayed away at first only because they had anticipated that the crowds would be overwhelming. Very quickly, business built up to the anticipated level, then easily surpassed it. Projections for the first year had called for WDW to greet six million customers, about the annual attendance level of Disneyland in those days. In fact, ten million people streamed through the gates of the Magic Kingdom during its first twelve months of existence.

"Once again," says Marty Sklar, "we had to put EPCOT on the back burner for a while because the Park became so successful so quickly that for the next four years we were running just to keep up with demand in the Magic Kingdom. For example, Walt Disney World had no thrill rides when we opened. We had no Space Mountain, a very sparse Tomorrowland, no Pirates of the Caribbean. Shows we had thought of for Disneyland had to be adapted for Florida. It was a full-time job just getting more capacity into the Park. It would have been difficult to think seriously about

EPCOT, in those early days, let alone to get any work done on it."

By the mid-seventies, EPCOT was under serious consideration again, with Walt Disney's protégé Card Walker, now president of Walt Disney Productions, as its champion. Walker realized that the original experimental community idea would be difficult to sell to the financial community. (To mention just one problem, how could such a community guarantee the democratic rights of its residents while functioning under the corporate control that would be necessary to justify its existence?) There is some evidence that Disney himself had recognized these difficulties before he died. In any case, Walker decided that the only way to realize a viable version of Disney's dream was to reconceptualize EPCOT as a theme park that would be "a showcase for prototype concepts," which would provide "an ongoing forum of the future" and would serve as "a communicator to the world . . . a permanent international people-to-people exchange."

In a sense, this new version of EPCOT would be something like a permanent World's Fair, with one group of pavilions presenting man's technological challenge (Future World) and another presenting the cultures of various nations (World Showcase). It would differ from a World's Fair, however, in that the pavilions would complement one another rather than compete for attention. To this end, it would be pleasingly organized around circular ponds and a large circular central lagoon that would help create a soothing environment for the visitor.

The multinational aspect of the concept was not new. One of the earliest ideas for Disneyland had been an international street (it was to branch off from Town Square), and EPCOT would present an opportunity to implement that concept on a much grander scale. Similarly, Future World had its roots in Tomorrowland. At the crossroads between Future World and World Showcase would be an exhibit called the American Adventure inspired by Herman Melville's observation that "America has been settled by the people of all nations. . . . We are not a nation so much as a world."

"Around 1975," says Sklar, "after we'd finally gotten Space Mountain open, and some other key rides, we were able to focus on what we were going to do with this EPCOT idea. Our first move was to hold a series of meetings in Florida. We had conferences about energy and about health and about communications. It was pretty extraordinary because we were able to bring in all these dozens of experts and there were very few of them who didn't believe that Disney had an important role to play as an agent of change, and as a communicator who could bring people together. That was how we defined our role. We knew how to communicate ideas, but we didn't claim to know what it was that should be communicated. We left that to the experts.

"I remember one meeting we had when we were doing the Living Seas pavilion. Bob Ballard – the guy who found the *Titanic* – told us, and his fellow experts, that everybody had been wrong about what was at the bottom of the ocean. 'We've found that there's life down there.' It changed everybody's thinking. We already had a story for the film we were doing in connection with the pavilion, but the advisory board told us, 'You can't do that.' So we had to start over again. And this was typical. We weren't looking to present propaganda. We wanted to have the best people in any given field tell us what we should be doing."

WED's best talents – young men like Randy Bright and Tony Baxter, along with veterans John Hench, Marc Davis, and Herb Ryman – were turned loose on EPCOT, which finally opened in October of 1982, eleven years after the opening of Walt Disney World. Visitors could eat shepherd's pie in an English pub or *foie de veau* in a French bistro, then move on to the AT&T pavilion, where Walter Cronkite narrated a show based on the concept of spaceship earth.

As had been the case with the Magic Kingdom, early attendance figures were disappointing, and some visitors found certain of the exhibits overly didactic, but ticket sales built steadily. Over a period of time, EPCOT Center, as it became known, developed into a formidable foil for the Magic Kingdom – a totally novel kind of theme park in which the magic had more to do with scientific and cultural curiosity than with fairy tales and nostalgia.

Over the years, it has expanded – with spectacular new shows, such as the Living Seas, featuring "sea cabs" and an underwater restaurant – and, most importantly, the Imagineers back in California, along with their panels of experts, have kept close tabs on developments in the various fields of endeavor represented at EPCOT Center with the intention of updating films and exhibits. By 1994, almost everything in EPCOT Center was scheduled for renewal.

"The Energy Pavilion is a case in point," says Sklar. "There have been major developments in the energy field since that was built, and we are now in the process of rethinking it completely to reflect new discoveries and possibilities."

EPCOT Center was a new kind of theme park, but it was by no means the final development at Walt Disney World. Early in 1985, Michael Eisner raised the idea of an arts pavilion for EPCOT Center. This quickly evolved into a concept for a motion-picture arts pavilion, which fit together nicely with the notion of a movie ride that had been suggested by parks chief Dick Nunis.

Eisner and Frank Wells (whose earliest responsibilities at Disney included making the already profitable parks still more profitable) began to think that this concept had too much potential to be contained by a single pavilion shoehorned into EPCOT Center. Why not develop a whole new theme park that was also a working motion-picture studio, where visitors could enjoy movie- and television-related rides and exhibits? They could also have the opportunity of watching a film being made on an actual sound stage and see animators at work on a forthcoming Disney feature.

To maximize the appeal of such a facility, it was considered desirable to supplement automatic access to the Disney backlog of films by acquiring rights to another library of film classics. The library that proved to be

The World Showcase section of Epcot utilizes expertise derived from filmmaking to evoke different countries and cities, such as Japan (above), Venice (opposite top), and Paris. In the case of Paris, the Eiffel Tower is built as a large miniature projecting above the mansard roofs, just as it might be for a movie set. The illusion is quite striking, especially at dusk when the surrogate tower becomes a silhouette against the Florida sky

The World Showcase pavilions at Epcot are notable for their wealth of decorative detail. Above: a traditional gateway welcomes visitors to China. Below: the statue of St. George and the Dragon in Germany is a copy of a famous original in Munich's Marienplaz

Scenes from Epcot: A diver feeds a dolphin in The Living Seas pavilion, and a robot valet performs his duty in the Horizons exhibit

available was MGM/UA's – a cornucopia of films, including such all-time favorites as *The Wizard of Oz*. Disney negotiated permission to use these movies, and characters from these movies, in the new park. It also licensed the right to employ the MGM name and trademark in connection with the park. (Later, Disney gained limited access to other libraries, further enhancing the company's ability to capitalize on Hollywood's past.)

In April of 1985, it was officially announced that Disney would build a new $300 million Hollywood theme park on the Florida property. Eventually, this park would include not only a working studio but also reconstructions of Grauman's Chinese Theater and the Sunset Strip, as well as a variety of show biz-oriented entertainments such as innovative special-effects movies conceived and directed by master entertainers George Lucas and Jim Henson. Back in the spring of 1985, however, the Disney-MGM Studio was just a grand idea.

Bob Weis – a senior vice president for creative affairs – was one of those who was called in on the early brainstorming sessions. With a college background in architecture and theater, Weis had gravitated naturally to the Imagineering team and in the early eighties had spent almost two

A reproduction of Grauman's Chinese Theater, leading to The Great Movie Ride, is one of the attractions of the Disney-MGM Studios at Walt Disney World

years in Japan during the construction of Tokyo Disneyland (see chapter 18). In the spring of 1985, he had been back in Glendale for some time, working on a master plan for the expansion of the Tokyo park and on EPCOT Center projects.

"After Michael and Frank broached the idea of an arts and entertainment pavilion," he remembers, "it snowballed very quickly from a pavilion to being a self-contained entity. Jeffrey Katzenberg had been brought over to Disney to beef up motion-picture production. He wanted to do many more films a year, and that meant that there was a need for more sound stages. It became one of those ideas that had a life of its own, so that very soon we were working on a whole new park – a Hollywood studio tour."

Weis became the chief designer for the studio tour, and he and his associates found themselves dealing with some unprecedented problems.

"There was the basic matter of what a movie studio should look like, because the public has definite expectations. Forget what the new ones look like. They're much the same as any factory complex. What the visitor is expecting is the kind of studio that was built back in the golden age of Hollywood – something that looks like the Disney lot in Burbank – so we had fun going back to Kem Weber's original drawings for the old Animation Building and his master plan for the studio. We even went back to the furniture he designed for the studio and asked ourselves 'How can we reproduce all this with contemporary materials and stay within a reasonable budget? How do we make this place look like it has this intangible quality that says it's a movie studio?' That was a very exciting process."

Then there was the matter of providing visitors with the opportunity to watch animators at work without making the situation impossibly uncomfortable for the artists themselves.

This New York street is part of the Disney–MGM Studios' back lot

The Disney parks have formed a close relationship with George Lucas, which has
led to the development of attractions based
on his movies such as the Indiana Jones Stunt
Spectacular, at the Disney-MGM Studios
in Florida (above), with live actors, and the
Indiana Jones Adventure at Disneyland Park.

Concept art for the Indiana Jones Adventure

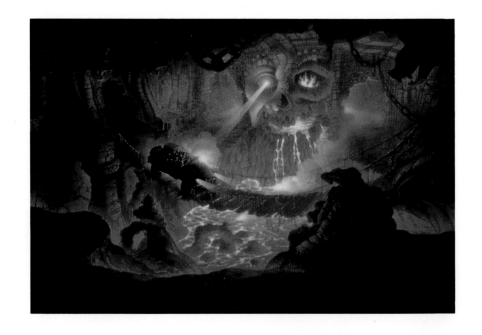

Opened in 1994, the Tower of Terror – located on Sunset Boulevard in the Disney–MGM Studios – has become one of the most popular attractions at Walt Disney World. Its sedate Edwardian architecture and decor belies its raison d'être, a *Twilight Zone* adventure that culminates in a hair-raising ride in a runaway elevator

Concept art for the Tower of Terror

"We had to meet with animators," Weis reports, "and try to understand how they work. What kind of personality quirks do they have? How can you make them feel comfortable when you're about to violate the sanctity of their working environment by bringing guests through to stare over their shoulders?"

The Disney–MGM Studios complex has the advantage of providing a perfect setting for anything connected with the entertainment industry. The Teenage Mutant Ninja Turtles belong there, and so do the Muppets. Recently added attractions include the Tower of Terror – a major thrill ride that draws on memories of Rod Serling's *Twilight Zone* – and a spectacular Indiana Jones show that continues the Disney organization's fruitful association with George Lucas, which dates back to the mid-eighties (see chapter 18). Under the guidance of Eric Jacobson, who succeeded Weis when the latter moved on to new projects, the Florida studio continues to grow and to attract increasing numbers of visitors while functioning as an efficient production facility.

Gradually, more and more of Walt Disney's original vision – as re-thought by Michael Eisner and his Team Disney – is entering the Walt Disney World site. Soon the Park will become home to the Disney Institute, an educational and cultural experiment that will provide vacationers with a unique experience.

"The Disney Institute," Eisner explains, "will be located in what is now known as the Disney Village Resort. The ambience will be that of a dynamic arts community. . . . Guests will choose from scores of programs that reflect their own interests and are personally relevant to their lives, from the arts to fitness and health. These programs will be hands-on and interactive. Guests can help run a radio station, learn circus acts, take cooking classes – even produce their own animated short. And we will also promote a sense of community with maximum emphasis on interaction between guests and instructors."

Still in the early planning stage for the Walt Disney World complex is Celebration, which has been described as "a think tank in the form of a living community."

If this sounds rather like Walt Disney's first concept for EPCOT, perhaps we should not be too surprised.

"Walt's original ideas are still very much alive," says Sklar. "We never really forgot about them. It was just a question of saving them for the right moment."

18 Renewal

It could be argued that Walt Disney was the archetypal American of his generation – an Everyman of genius – and, while he cherished the values and institutions of Middle America, he also seemed to feel, in a very straightforward way, that America's ethnic plurality permitted him to tap into other cultures and environments from around the world. In his movies he explored British historical legend, European folklore, and the wildlife of Africa, Asia, and Alaska. He did not build his proposed International Street in Disneyland, but Africa was present (in the form of the Jungle Cruise), as was the colorful architecture of the Caribbean, half-timbered cottages out of the Bavarian forests, and even a simulation of one of Europe's natural marvels – the Matterhorn.

EPCOT Center carried the international theme still further. Nor was this a one-way romance. Visitors from overseas loved Disneyland and Walt Disney World. In a typical year, one out of every five visitors to the Florida park is from outside the United States. It was only a matter of time before the question of building a Disney theme park abroad would be placed on the agenda.

The first move came from Japan.

Dreamland – an unlicensed imitation of Disneyland – had been built there in the early sixties, but failed to live up to expectations largely because the entrepreneurs behind it had overlooked the rather obvious fact that a Disney-type park would be less than complete without Disney characters and Disney expertise.

In 1978, a group of executives representing Japan's Keisei Electric Railway Company approached Disney management with an invitation to build an authentic version of the Magic Kingdom on a 201-acre property it owned on the outskirts of Tokyo. Real estate is enormously valuable in Japan. Normally, such a site would have been developed as housing or commercial space. In this case, government regulations forbade that usage, insisting that this tract of landfill on Tokyo Bay be reserved for recreational purposes. Keisei had financial problems at the time and wanted to maximize its profits from the site. It was suggested that building a version of Disneyland – the ultimate recreational facility – on the property would satisfy everyone's requirements.

Disney management was both intrigued by the proposal and worried that the scheme might be flawed. For one thing, Tokyo's climate was very different from that of Anaheim and Orlando. Would people attend the Park in significant numbers during the cold winter season? And what about cultural differences? Surely some of the Magic Kingdom's attractions would have to be replaced with Japanese-oriented shows?

"Don't worry about the climate," Japanese executives reassured them. "If the park is built right, people will come. And don't worry about adapting to Japanese tastes. The reason people will come is precisely because it is so American."

There was also the matter of investment. Disney was pouring much of its resources into building EPCOT Center and did not want to assume additional debt to invest in a Japanese park. But the Japanese entrepreneurs had an answer to this, too. The park would be built, owned, and operated by a new Japanese company named Oriental Land (jointly owned by Keisei and Mitsui Real Estate), which would provide financing. Disney would design the Park and have an ongoing right and

In Tokyo Disneyland, Main Street has been replaced by a covered arcade known as World Bazaar which offers shelter from inclement weather

Most of the rides in Tokyo Disneyland – such as Big Thunder Mountain – would seem to be familiar to anyone who had visited Disneyland in Anaheim or The Magic Kingdom in Orlando

A corner of Adventureland at Tokyo Disneyland

responsibility to advise in its operation, in return for which the company would receive 10 percent of park admissions and 5 percent of revenues from concessions.

This was the arrangement that was agreed to. In retrospect, given the enormous success of Tokyo Disneyland, it might be argued that Disney should have found a way to invest its own capital in the project at the outset. That said, however, the deal proved profitable for everyone concerned, and Tokyo Disneyland demonstrated that the Magic Kingdom concept could indeed be exported to other parts of the globe.

Anyone who has visited Anaheim's Disneyland or the Magic Kingdom in Orlando would find much in Tokyo Disneyland that is very familiar. There is a fairy-tale castle at the hub – Cinderella's, in this case – fronting onto a circular plaza where turn-of-the-century vehicles glide gracefully by. There is a Fantasyland, an Adventureland, and a Tomorrowland; and although Frontierland has been transformed into Westernland, it retains many features of the American parks, such as Big Thunder Mountain, the Country Bear Theater, and the Mark Twain River Boat. Adventureland has a Jungle Cruise, a Swiss Family Treehouse, and its own edition of Pirates of the Caribbean. Tomorrowland has Space Mountain and

The Western River Railroad at Tokyo Disneyland takes its passengers past exotic sights such as this Native American encampment

George Lucas's Star Tours show. The Haunted Mansion has strayed into Fantasyland, where it makes an appropriate neighbor for Cinderella's Golden Carousel and It's a Small World.

But there are some significant differences, too. No railroad circles the park (though a smaller Western River Railroad threads its way around Adventureland and Westernland). Most surprisingly, perhaps, Main Street has been replaced by a cruciform, glass-covered arcade known as World Bazaar. In practice, World Bazaar offers many of Main Street's familiar attractions, boutiques, and cafés, such as the Main Street Cinema and the Disney Emporium, while also affording protection from inclement weather.

As the Japanese investors had predicted, bad weather does little to keep customers away from the Park. One member of the Imagineering team recalls a day when the forecast reported the possibility of the edge of a typhoon brushing the Tokyo area:

"There was talk of closing the Park, for safety reasons, but so many visitors showed up that it would have been more dangerous to try to keep them out. Attendance that day was over fifteen thousand!"

In the first ten years of its existence, total attendance at the Tokyo park was greater than the total population of Japan.

The notion of building a Disney theme park in Europe had been discussed as early as the seventies, but there had been no follow-through at the time because more weight had been given to the myriad problems – site, climate, possible culture clashes, financing – than to the long-term potential of such a project. The success of the Tokyo park began to change the prevailing attitude. Preliminary discussions with the governments of France and Spain were inaugurated in the early eighties, as various sites were investigated by a team led by Dick Nunis, but it was not until after the new management team took over the reins in 1984 that concrete moves were made to realize a European park.

Frontierland in Disneyland Paris: Cottonwood Creek (left) and the Phantom Manor, as the European edition of the Haunted Mansion is called

Spain and Portugal had both campaigned for the Park – the search team had studied other parts of Europe, too – but it was France that was eventually selected as the home for EuroDisney, a name that eventually would be changed to Disneyland Paris in deference to the proximity of the site, Marne-la-Vallée, to the French capital. Michael Eisner had been open to other possibilities, but he was an unabashed champion of the eventual choice, his rationale being that Paris is the hub of Europe.

By the time Eisner signed an agreement with Laurent Fabius, prime minister of France, in December of 1985, Imagineers had been at work on concepts for the Park for some time. One of these Imagineers, Tony Baxter – a senior vice president for creative development – points out that the proximity to Paris brought with it some special considerations.

"This was a new kind of challenge," says Baxter, who grew up in Disneyland's backyard and scooped ice cream on Main Street before becoming an Imagineer. "We had to go into an environment where art and artistry and culture have traditions going back thousands of years. It wasn't like Anaheim or Florida, where there was nothing to judge us against. In France we were going up against fine shopping, historical architecture, and a landscape that defines the words 'charming' and 'pastoral.' We had to go into that environment and redefine Disneyland. What we built had to be recognizable as Disney product, but we had to adjust to a different set of values."

Some decisions, says Baxter, were relatively easy.

"Rethinking the Old West, for example. Walt had visualized it as an idyllic, pastoral Mississippi River landscape, where two boys – Tom and Huck – could run away to an island. It was the perfect escape for consumers who had been sitting in a traffic jam on the Santa Ana Freeway. But Europeans are looking for something completely different. They take serenity and pastoral beauty for granted. When they think of the Old West, they think of the *wild* West. An exciting, energetic place. We realized that our EuroDisney Frontierland would have to reflect that. What we would have to give them was the raucous, roaring atmosphere of the

Main Street Motors (opposite top) is typical of the businesses along Main Street at Disneyland Paris in that it emphasizes Americana to the nth degree. In other parts of Disneyland Paris, however, tribute is paid to European popular culture. In Discoveryland, for example, the submarine *Nautilus* (opposite bottom) pays tribute to the French science-fiction pioneer Jules Verne

Located on the perimeter of Disneyland Paris is Festival Disney, an area that features American-style entertainment, from jazz to country-and-western music

The Château at the hub of Disneyland Paris is the ultimate storybook castle

1849 Gold Rush – something that had captured the imagination of the whole world – and we would have to cater to their fascination with Native American culture, and to their Hollywood-nurtured love of the rowdy world of the cowboy, including the rustler and the bad guy.

"We even did the Haunted Mansion in a sinister Western land-baron style, like some cattle mogul's palatial spread, and we changed the ride itself so that instead of ending in a gothic graveyard it ends in a California ghost town, with coyotes baying at the moon and ghost riders in the sky.

"That was easy. Far more difficult was deciding what to do with the castle. How do you compete with all those real castles along the Loire? We had to reinvent the castle, and our solution was to make it more like an illustration in a book of fairy tales – an illustration by someone like Arthur Rackham. So it's built on a crag, and part of the second floor is supported by stone trees. The colors are fairy-tale colors and the architecture is deliberately distorted. There's a dragon living in a cavern underneath the castle and Merlin's workshop is in the middle of it all. And we've added a hedge maze, like the one at Hampton Court Palace in England, which is an interactive experience of the most primitive kind. People were predicting that there would be no lines for that, but it's turned out to be a thirty-minute wait."

Unlike the Japanese, Europeans *were* expecting to find reflections of their own world in the Park, and the contract with the French government called for appropriate tributes to French civilization in particular and European culture in general.

"One way we tried to do this," says Baxter, "was to replace Tomorrow-land with something we called Discoveryland, which is based around the idea of Jules Verne's Discovery Bay. Verne's vision of the future had inspired Walt, yet it remains very European, very French, and it gave us the opportunity to come up with something that would let us pay tribute to other visionaries, from Leonardo da Vinci to H. G. Wells to George Lucas."

To a large extent, Discoveryland is about the history of the future, which has the advantage of not going out of date as quickly as the future itself, as represented in the various Tomorrowlands. Even so, it does have the Lucas-inspired Star Tours ride and other concessions to contemporary futurism.

Unlike its Tokyo cousin, Disneyland Paris has a conventional open Main Street, but it is a Main Street that is even more American, if possible, than those in the original Disneyland and Florida's Magic Kingdom.

"Europeans," Baxter theorizes, "are interested in what's behind the storefronts. The facades are not enough. Instead of having Coke Corner, which is just a place where you go for a Coke and a hot dog – something Americans take for granted – we gave European visitors Casey's Corner, which is a kind of vintage soda fountain environment in which visitors are enveloped in American atmosphere and imagery – baseball memorabilia all over the place and baseball songs playing over the speakers."

Disneyland Paris would also feature a huge entertainment center known as Festival Disney. With buildings designed by postmodernist architect Frank Gehry, this area would be home to a wild West show and to streets representing American destinations such as New York, Los Angeles, and Key West, their neon signs luring the visitor into American-style steakhouses, a nightclub, and even a country-and-western bar.

Ownership and management of the entire complex would be primarily European, but this time Disney held onto 49 percent of the stock. Ground was broken in 1990 and the Park was opened in 1992. Almost immediately there were rumors that it was doing poorly, and soon Disney management acknowledged that it was losing money.

One serious problem was that the consortium that built the park sank a great deal of capital into five huge hotels grouped around a lake on the edge of the property. The consortium had not reckoned sufficiently with the fact that Paris, with its vast selection of hotels – from cheap pensions to the finest deluxe establishments – was barely an hour away from the Park by train. Many Park-bound visitors preferred to spend their nights in the city, and the Disneyland Paris hotels remained underbooked to the point where they were operating at a substantial loss. Recession and European habits – like bringing a picnic lunch instead of eating at one of the park's restaurants – also cut into profits.

The theme park itself, however, was a resounding success, attracting more than ten million visitors in its first year. Reports that losses from the resort (as opposed to the theme park) might cause the entire complex to close proved premature when a plan to refinance the enterprise was announced in the spring of 1994. In part, this involved the purchase of 74.6 million shares of EuroDisney s.c.a by Prince Alwaleed of Saudi

Arabia, chairman of the United Saudi Commercial Bank, already a major stockholder in the operating company. The Walt Disney Company's financial interest in the enterprise was thereby reduced from 49 percent to 40 percent.

"Europeans love Disneyland Paris," says Michael Eisner. "Some French intellectuals objected to our presence at first, but that's calmed down now and President [François] Mitterrand's recent visit to the Park had considerable symbolic importance. The theme park itself already does wonderful business and I'm convinced the whole complex will be profitable in the near future. To mention just one thing, with the Channel Tunnel open the British are now able to travel from London to Paris in three and a half hours by high-speed train. That alone will make a big difference."

Asked whether he would still pick Paris as his site for the Park if he were starting over today, he says that he has not changed his mind about that.

"As I said when we first launched the idea, Paris is the hub of Europe. . . . It's at the center of three hundred million people living on a landmass the size of the USA east of the Mississippi. And the climate has not been a problem. Not everything has to be done in the sun. Northern Europeans are used to doing things in cold weather. They don't just sit at home. Our attendance figures prove that."

Disney's dedication to the Paris park is apparent in the fact that several new rides have been opened in anticipation of the need for increased capacity, and other attractions, including a version of Space Mountain, are already committed as well. This is only part of a program of updating and expansion that applies to all the parks.

Visitors to the Magic Kingdom at Walt Disney World enjoy the planned scares of Alien Encounter

"The audience changes," says Tony Baxter, "and we have to change with it. That doesn't mean that everything has to be replaced. The Jungle Cruise has stayed the same for decades. It's technologically crude, but it still works because of the rapport the guides build with the visitors. But other things must change because the last thing we want is for Disneyland, or any of the parks, to be like a museum, full of things that have rich associations for people who grew up in the fifties but meaningless to kids who were born in the eighties.

"Even the pace of a ride has to change. When we put together a version of It's a Small World for Europe, we brought the continents closer together to make room for America, which doesn't exist in the other parks. In doing so, we cut the ride from eleven minutes to eight minutes, and the interesting thing is that it seems right at that length. No one feels they're being shortchanged because people expect information to be delivered more quickly these days. That's why commercials run ten seconds now instead of ninety seconds, and our animated features are faster paced than they were in the days of *Snow White*. You have to be aware of these changes in sensibility whether you're making a movie like *Aladdin* or designing an attraction for the parks."

The recent success of special-effects movies – from the *Star Wars* trilogy to *Jurassic Park* – has certainly influenced the way in which Imagineers think about the design of certain rides. *Jurassic Park* is not only set largely in a theme park but with its shock effects, it is actually very much like an extended theme park ride, the thrills more important than the narrative. The George Lucas *Star Wars* ride now in the Disney theme parks derives directly from the films on which it is based. Instead of placing the rider in an actual moving vehicle, as in earlier Disney attractions, the *Star Wars* ride uses almost purely cinematic means – optical effects and sophisticated sound technology – to create the illusion of travel through deep space and the excitement of intergalactic warfare. The seats the riders are strapped into are rigged to jolt and vibrate, but beyond that they go nowhere, though the ride seems to cover thousands of miles. This kind of special-effects ride, dependent upon sensual illusionism, is likely to be encountered more and more often in future attractions.

The very existence of a *Star Wars* ride points out another important change in the philosophy of the Disney theme parks. Introducing fresh imagery began to be a problem in the seventies when the Studio was not supplying film hits that could be exploited by the Imagineers. By the early eighties, it became obvious that there were advantages to opening the parks to non-Disney imagery. The first major step in this direction came when a deal was struck with George Lucas that would lead to entertainments based on *Star Wars* and the *Indiana Jones* movies, as well as to original concepts for the parks.

Marty Sklar credits Ron Miller as being the person who first approached Lucas to test his interest in working with the Imagineers, though it was not until after the Eisner team took control that a deal was finally signed. John Hench recalls that Lucas visited WED and confessed

Disney chairman Michael Eisner (left) with Steven Spielberg (center) and George Lucas at the opening of Mickey's Toontown in Anaheim

that he'd been a childhood devotee of Disneyland.

"Apparently," says Sklar, "George's parents would come down here for vacations, and they'd stay at the Disneyland Hotel because they knew that George would spend his whole time at the park and they would be free to go anywhere they wanted to."

"He told us," Hench remembers, "that it had always been his ambition to work for Walt Disney, but Walt died before he got out of high school. Then it became his ambition to make a Disney film. When *Star Wars* was released he felt he'd finally done it. 'You guys may have forgotten how to do it,' he said, 'but I did it.' "

With Lucas aboard it was logical to look for other non-Disney attractions that fit with the spirit of the parks, and consequences of this have been limited license agreements permitting Muppet characters and the Teenage Mutant Ninja Turtles to be used in shows at the Disney–MGM Studios. Access to MGM material, and film properties from other studios, enabled Disney to create film and Audio-Animatronics attractions like the Great Movie Ride.

Much special film material – such as the Muppet and Michael Jackson 3D movies – is produced for the parks, and this is the responsibility of a specially formed unit called Theme Park Productions. Headed by Tom Fitzgerald, this unit works with celebrity directors like Francis Ford Coppola and the late Jim Henson, uses the Studio's production facilities, is able to call upon the feature animation department for assistance, and can also turn to Lucas's Industrial Light and Magic special-effects team when necessary.

The most important thing the parks provide, however, is a sense of place.

"For me," says Tony Baxter, "half of the success of the great animated features, like *Snow White* and *Pinocchio,* was that they took you to interesting places you couldn't visit in real life, like Pleasure Island and the Seven Dwarfs' mine. It's the same with a historical movie like *Davy Crockett,* or a special-effects movie like *Star Wars,* and what we do in the parks is to make it possible for everybody to actually experience those places. We are not able to involve you in the story, except by illusion, but we can give you the sense of really having been there. One reason we have to constantly update things is to keep that sense of having experienced a special place as fresh as possible."

When he transcended the old notion of the amusement park to create Disneyland, Walt Disney created the first of a series of "special places" – each different from the rest, each blending entertainment and imagination in different ways, each adding up to an experience that is greater than the sum of its parts, each leaving the visitor with the sense that he has experienced a world that is not quite like anything else on the face of the planet.

The present management is committed to expanding the number of these special places. At the time of writing, it seems almost certain that a new park will be built in Japan, adjacent to Tokyo Disneyland and themed to the idea of exploring the seven seas. There are plans, too, for a second Anaheim park, possibly to be known as WESTCOT, but these are contingent on a variety of practical considerations. More controversial has been the much-publicized scheme to build an American history theme park in Virginia, an idea that polarized opinion on both a local and a national scale. The site originally chosen was thought by many to be a threat to actual historical sites – Civil War battlefields – in the vicinity and to the rural character of the locale. In the fall of 1994, it was unexpectedly announced that Disney was abandoning its efforts to develop that particular property and would seek another, less controversial site for the history park.

While WESTCOT and the history park remain conjectural, there is still a good deal of property capable of development in the Orlando complex, and a Disney team has been combing the Far East and Australasia, from Singapore to Sydney (and not excluding the People's Republic of China), with a view to developing one or more parks in a part of the world that Disney management sees as ripe for its kind of entertainment on the eve of the twenty-first century.

"An important part of our plan," says Michael Eisner, "is to find people in places like India and China who understand the grit and humor of those cultures. We don't want to make the mistake of just imposing our own ideas. We had better find those people for the sake of the health of the whole company, the films as well as the parks."

In the end, the films and the parks are expressions of a single basic philosophy, which can be traced back to the imagination of Walt Disney.

"The Disney name," says Eisner, "conjures up not only an intellectual response but also an emotional response. It carries with it a certain expectation of quality, and it's been our responsibility, for the past decade, to deliver on the promise that is implicit in the Walt Disney name because of his achievements. But we can't just rest on his laurels. We have to move forward."

It is almost seventy years since Mickey Mouse first captured the imagination of the world and brought the Disney name to the fore. It is forty years since Disneyland launched the then novel idea of the theme park, which has proven so fruitful for Disney and for others around the world. And there has not been a point in all those decades when the Disney organization has not been moving forward on some front, whether pioneering the animated feature film or building a theme park as radical as EPCOT Center.

As the lights of the Magic Kingdom come on, Mickey walks through the Florida dusk toward Cinderella Castle

In the mid-nineties, The Walt Disney Company is stronger than it has ever been and is moving forward with unprecedented energy on many fronts. The present management has succeeded in sustaining Walt Disney's legacy while providing the organization with a level of financial security that was never enjoyed during the founder's lifetime.

There were a number of times when Walt Disney quite literally had to mortgage his home in order to realize his next project. And there were few times when he could comfortably finance more than one major project at a time, so that – for all his imaginative flair – there was generally some part of the company that was being underutilized.

That has changed. Perhaps the greatest achievement of Michael

Eisner and the late Frank Wells has been to build a company in which no project – whether it be an animated feature, a big-budget live-action movie, a television series, or a new theme park – will be aborted or placed on the back burner for simple lack of proper funding.

To have done this while encouraging the level of creativity that has produced films like *Beauty and the Beast* and *Pocahontas,* and theme parks like Disney–MGM Studios and Disneyland Paris, makes that achievement still more remarkable.

Clearly, Eisner is correct in saying that the Studio's management must look to the future. At the same time though, there is no ignoring the continuance of the legacy that Walt Disney established during his lifetime. Evidence of that legacy is available to anyone visiting the theme parks, and it is apparent to anyone watching *The Little Mermaid* or *The Lion King*. The artists who work on the new animated classics have every intention of moving forward and breaking new ground, but to spend any time with them – or with the Imagineers at WDI – is to discover that they live and breathe the Disney tradition. It has become coded into their synapses, and they could not shed it if they wanted to. Whatever they do in the foreseeable future, however innovative, will be touched by Walt Disney's vision.

That vision was rooted in the extraordinary freedom of visual and narrative invention that is inherent in animation. Walt Disney was not the first to produce animated films, but he was the most inventive and visionary filmmaker the medium has seen. Mickey, Donald, Goofy, and the Silly Symphonies signaled the arrival of a major talent, but it was the notion of making a feature-length animated movie that was his boldest idea. A man who could make a success of that might be capable of almost anything.

To place this achievement in perspective, we need only consider the fact that since *Snow White and the Seven Dwarfs* was released, in 1937, no other producer has succeeded in making an animated feature that comes close to it in quality, nor to any of at least a dozen of the Disney animated features that have followed.

A question often asked in Hollywood circles is "What is the Disney secret?" The answer is "The persistence of the Disney legacy." It was founded by Walt Disney himself, supported by his brother Roy and Ub Iwerks, and nourished by the generation that included artists like Bill Tytla, Grim Natwick, Fred Moore, Art Babbitt, and Norm Ferguson; it was carried on by the nine old men, and they handed it on to the present generation.

It is a legacy that represents more than seven decades of accumulated knowledge – a legacy that is unique in the history of popular culture.

Index

Acknowledgments

Preparing this revised and updated version of *The Art of Walt Disney* was an enjoyable assignment thanks in large part to the encouragement and enthusiastic assistance of the officers and employees of The Walt Disney Company. In particular I would like to offer special thanks to Michael Eisner and Roy E. Disney who were generous with their time and provided me with crucial insights into the company's operations and ambitions.

Present and former Studio executives who provided me with wide-ranging assistance include Jeffrey Katzenberg, Peter Schneider, Tom Schumacher, Gary Krisel, and John Dreyer. Howard Green was always available to answer my questions, and beyond that he offered an insider's perspective on the recent history of the company that was perceptive, objective, and invaluable.

I was fortunate enough to be able to spend a great deal of time with members of the feature animation department, conducting interviews, sitting in on meetings, attending screenings, etc., and I would like to extend my gratitude to everyone in the department who made me feel so at home there, with special thanks to Don Hahn, John Musker, Ron Clements, Jim Pentecost, Don Ernst, Roy Conli, Rob Minkoff, Roger Allers, Gary Trousdale, Kirk Wise, Mike Gabriel, Eric Goldberg, and Hendel Butoy. My gratitude as well to Gretchen Albrecht, Cathy Alexander, Ruben Aquino, Hans Bacher, Doug Ball, James Baxter, Janet Bruce, Hortensia Casagran, Brenda Chapman, Karen Comella, Patti Conklin, Andreas Deja, Alice Dewey, Randy Fullmer, Andy Gaskill, David Goetz, Dee Haramia, Scott Johnston, Glen Keane, Vera Lanpher, Zoe Leader, Tony Meagher, Irene Mecchi, Jonathan Roberts, Robyn Roberts, James Russell, Dan St. Pierre, Chris Sanders, Scott Santoro, Stacy Slossy, and Ann Tucker. From the television animation division, I received valuable assistance from Greg Weisman and Patrick Reagan.

It's difficult to imagine how a book such as this could have been assembled without the generous assistance I received from the splendid team Kay Salz has assembled at the Disney Animation Research Library. My warm thanks to Kay herself, to Susie Lee, Doug Engalla, Larry Ishino, and Ariel Levin. Thanks also to Steven M. Rogers and Ed Squair of the photo library who found many images without which the book would have been incomplete.

Among the gifted team at Walt Disney Imagineering I would like to offer my gratitude to Marty Sklar, John Hench, Mickey Steinberg, Tony Baxter, Bob Weis, and Joe Lanzisero. Where visual materials pertaining to the parks were concerned, I received much assistance from Jill Centeno of WDI Visual Art Services.

Marty Sklar and John Hench are two of only three people whom I interviewed for both the 1973 edition and the present edition. I would like to reiterate my thanks to the people – some no longer with us – who helped me two decades ago. Among these I must single out Walt Disney's daughter Diane Disney Miller, Ron Miller, Card Walker, Vince Jefferds, and Jim Stewart. Others who offered much valuable information at that time include veterans of the Disney talent pool such as James Algar, Ken Anderson, Art Babbitt, George Bruns, Les Clark, Jack Cutting, Marc Davis, Al Dempster, Floyd Gottfredson, Don Graham, Don Griffith, Joe Hale, Dick Huemer, Ollie Johnston, Milt Kahl, Ward Kimball, Eric Larson, Jim Macdonald, Lester Novros, Woolie Reitherman, Frank Thomas, Grace Turner, and the greatly underrated Bill Walsh.

Other Disney personnel from that period who should be thanked are Leroy Anderson, Jack Brady, Jan Hedge, Mary Holoboff, Bob King, John Landon, Don MacLaughlin, Jim Mathews, Bob Moore, Frank Reilly, Sue Schwendeman, Dave Spencer, Carol Svendsen, and Bob White.

The third link between both editions, and a crucial figure to all Disney scholarship during the past quarter century, is the indefatigable Dave Smith, architect of the Walt Disney Archives, which is a model of what a film archive should be. My debt to Dave is incalculable and I thank him and the other members of the highly efficient team he has built, including Robert Tieman, Rebecca Cline, Collette Espino, and Adina Lerner.

Another link to the 1973 edition is my wife Linda who researched that edition with me. It was she who found many of the wonderful images that appear in the first eight chapters.

Much of the new animation art in this edition was photographed by Michael Stern. The assembly of visual material – along with many other important tasks, from setting up interviews to obtaining permissions – was handled by the Disney Publishing Group and in particular by Virginia King and Heidi Miller, who were always diligent, patient, and a pleasure to work with. Also from Disney Publishing, I would like to thank Hunter Heller, who performed many useful services, and to single out Russell Schroeder, who gave the manuscript and proofs thoughtful readings at several different stages, offered valuable suggestions, and pointed out errors that might otherwise have slipped by.

Finally, very special thanks to my editor at Abrams, Eric Himmel, who was always supportive and brought sound judgment to the entire project.

Chris Finch

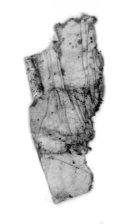